The Changing Face of Problematic Internet Use

This book is part of the Peter Lang Media and Communication list.
Every volume is peer reviewed and meets
the highest quality standards for content and production.

PETER LANG
New York • Bern • Berlin
Brussels • Vienna • Oxford • Warsaw

Scott E. Caplan

The Changing Face of Problematic Internet Use

An Interpersonal Approach

PETER LANG
New York • Bern • Berlin
Brussels • Vienna • Oxford • Warsaw

Library of Congress Cataloging-in-Publication Data
Names: Caplan, Scott E., author.
Title: The changing face of problematic internet use:
an interpersonal approach / Scott E. Caplan.
Description: New York: Peter Lang, 2018.
Includes bibliographical references and index.
Identifiers: LCCN 2017053419 | ISBN 978-1-4331-5099-9 (hardback: alk. paper)
ISBN 978-1-4331-3050-2 (paperback: alk. paper) | ISBN 978-1-4331-5100-2 (ebook pdf)
ISBN 978-1-4331-5101-9 (epub) | ISBN 978-1-4331-5102-6 (mobi)
Subjects: LCSH: Internet—Social aspects. | Cyberspace—Social aspects.
Compulsive behavior.
Classification: LCC QA76.9.C66 C365 2018 | DDC 303.48/33—dc23
LC record available at https://lccn.loc.gov/2017053419
DOI 10.3726/b12612

Bibliographic information published by **Die Deutsche Nationalbibliothek**.
Die Deutsche Nationalbibliothek lists this publication in the "Deutsche
Nationalbibliografie"; detailed bibliographic data are available
on the Internet at http://dnb.d-nb.de/.

© 2018 Peter Lang Publishing, Inc., New York
29 Broadway, 18th floor, New York, NY 10006
www.peterlang.com

All rights reserved.
Reprint or reproduction, even partially, in all forms such as microfilm,
xerography, microfiche, microcard, and offset strictly prohibited.

Contents

Foreword by Brian H. Spitzberg   vii

1. The Changing Face of Problematic Internet Use   1
2. Online Habits, Compulsion, and Addiction   21
3. Online Relational Transgressions   61
4. Cyberbullying and Online Interpersonal Aggression   103
5. Cyberstalking, Unwanted Pursuit, and Relational Intrusion   151
6. Copresent Device Use: Using Mobile Devices During In-Person Interaction   183
7. Moving Forward: An Agenda for Future Research   225

Author Index   237
Subject Index   243

Foreword

At a short distance from the inflection point between one millennium and the next, our species is struggling with any number of salient challenges and opportunities regarding its future. Among these challenges is the role that technologies play in our everyday interactions. Guttenberg compressed the time and space of knowledge diffusion and communication at distance, but the Internet has accomplished this at an altogether exponential scale. Several studies demonstrate that we live in a small world, ranging from 4 to 7 degrees of separation from everyone else on the planet. Further, several studies have found evidence for the Dunbar conjecture that we only have the cognitive capacity to optimally manage 80 to 180 actual relationships before our ability to negotiate relations in our social network begins to deteriorate. Little in our 5M years of hominid evolution has prepared us for the velocity, span, access, and capabilities that modern communication technologies now provide. It is little wonder then, that the pace of evolution in our technologies of communication are rapidly outstripping our ability to co-evolve with them.

There are obviously both respectable respective utopian and dystopian perspectives that can conceptualize these changes. For years now, I have been approaching such dialectics from what we refer to as a dark side perspective that incorporates both the benign and the baleful. Specifically, any phenomenon can be conceptually and empirically aligned along two dimensions: a functional dimension and a normative dimension. The functional dimension refers to the degree to which a phenomenon objectively facilitates or diminishes the ability of an organism, group, or system to sustain itself and pursue its functions and objectives. The normative dimension refers to the degree to which a person, group, society or culture subjectively perceives or evaluates a phenomenon as immoral evil, inappropriate, harmful or otherwise dysfunctional, on the one hand; or on the other hand as moral, good, appropriate, helpful, or otherwise functional. When these dimensions are crossed, they map four conceptual territories.

Functional and normatively good phenomena represent the bright side. In regard to technologies, this is the realm of dreamers and utopians, and probably most inventors and hi-tech businesses. Technologies will fulfill our needs, solve our problems, enrich us, relax us, and enhance us. Diametrically contrasted to the bright side is the space defined by dysfunctional phenomena that are widely viewed as harmful. In regard to technologies, a variety of candidates are increasingly becoming tarnished both by their science and the public tolerance for their effects; think nuclear power, fossil fuels, mass industrialized agriculture, big pharma, and ubiquitous technological privacy invasion. The most interesting domains of the dark side perspective, however, are the ambivalent quadrants: The things we think are good but have deleterious dysfunctional effects, and the things we think are bad that are often actually good for us. For example, physical attractiveness is widely valued subjectively, but often carries with it problems of objectification, excess celebrity, and self-handicapping. Alternatively, jealousy is widely viewed as unpleasant and destructive, yet can serve to bring some relationships closer and motivate self-enhancement to entice a partner back to the comfort of the relationship.

Scott Caplan has taken such nuances into account in his excellent examination of the complex terrain of our most common communication technologies, with emphasis on those technologies enabled by and dependent upon the increasingly omnipresent Internet. His umbrella term is problematic use, although he draws the connections among the dark side, socio-digital challenges, and digital stressors. Collectively, he is locating his interests closer to the dysfunctional and immoral ends of the spectra of the dark side. As interesting as the more paradoxical spaces of the dark side are, it makes sense to pursue the more dysfunctional/immoral quadrant. There is theory and research to support the notion that "bad tends to outweigh good," in the sense that negative experiences are more damaging than positive experiences are healing. As such, it is certainly timely to begin developing a census of the problematic uses and effects of the Internet. In doing so, Caplan has thoughtfully identified most of the more tangible contexts of problematic Internet use in interactional and relational contexts. The lens he uses is distinct from most of the other approaches that might or have been taken to date. Instead of focusing on the technology itself, or on the philosophical or purely psychological impacts of such technologies, he takes a distinctly interpersonal approach.

An interpersonal approach moves away from the mechanistic and hypodermic conceptions of technological effects, and instead centers on the more systemic relational processes and effects of communication technologies. Looking through this lens, Chapter One lays out the key concepts and concisely presages some of the most relevant theoretical models of problematic Internet use. The examination of Internet addiction in Chapter Two allows the highlighting of the interpersonal problems arising from an individual's addictive habits. Chapter Three examines transgressions from a more sophisticated perspective than popular magazine lists of netiquette rules. Research on infidelity, deceptions, incivilities, micro-aggressions, and relational breaches illustrate the degree to which technologies offer many affordances for relationship infringement. Chapter Four veers into the darker realms of the Internet and its communicative technological enablers. The study of cyberbullying is expanding rapidly, as the world begins to wake up to the realization that we have first aid kits for physical bruises, scrapes, scratches and cuts, but we have no obvious therapeutic bandages or salve for a savaged self-esteem. Here Caplan is keen to recognize some of the paradoxes entwined in the cyberbullying research—victims are often perpetrators, and bullies are often esteemed by others yet lacking in self-esteem. As the pale of technological shadows cast ever darker spaces for interpersonal relations, Chapter Five examines cyberstalking and unwanted pursuit. Stalking itself is a relatively new crime, in that it was only explicitly criminalized in the 1990s in most Western societies, but cyber-technologies gave stalkers an entirely new and powerful set of tools through which they could intrude upon and harass others. The liminal spaces between flirtation and fear, between courtship and coercion, become central to recognizing the ways in which technologies both enable and disable our tendencies to form and re-form our relations with others.

By Chapter Six, Caplan moves to a less intense but nevertheless important and more familiar space of everyday conversation. In the realm of not there-thereness, avatars, fomo, phubbing, telepressure, and co-present absence, we are discovering that technologies designed to enhance the quantity or accessibility of our communication in cyberspace often function to diminish the quality of our communication with those we face in our proximal realspace. It seems somehow poetic then, to traverse the arc of problematic Internet use from the mundane notion of the couch potato spending endless hours in digital space, to the dark apex of transgression, abuse, aggression, intrusion, and harassment, only to end up in the domain of the mundane—everyday interaction.

Such is the journey an interpersonal approach to problematic Internet use presents—and none too soon. Given the pace of technological evolution, a second edition may be overdue in a relatively brief horizon of speculation, but taking heed right "here and now" is necessary as a moment of perspective-taking—where is here, and what detours, traps and threats are we are likely to encounter as we perambulate this strange, continually new, space? This book is a much-needed yield sign, suggesting the need to take in the intersection we have been brought to, and where we want to go, rather than where we allow ourselves to be taken.

Brian H. Spitzberg, Senate Distinguished Professor
School of Communication, San Diego State University

Chapter One

The Changing Face of Problematic Internet Use

What does problematic Internet use mean today? When researchers first began studying the topic in the early 2000s, problematic Internet use referred to online behavior that created offline problems. In 2001, Beard and Wolf defined problematic Internet use as "use of the Internet that creates psychological, social, school, and/or work difficulties in a person's life" (p. 378). In my work, I defined problematic Internet use as "maladaptive cognitions and behaviors involving Internet use that result in negative academic, professional, and social consequences" (Caplan, 2003, p. 626). Although these definitions were useful in guiding early research, the term problematic Internet use can no longer be limited to compulsive or habitual use. As the online technology, and its role in our lives, has evolved, so have the problems people experience from computer-mediated communication.

The Internet use that early research described bore little resemblance to how we use or think about online social interaction today. In the late 1990s and early 2000s, when scholars first proposed and defined problematic Internet use, less than half of U.S. adults were online (Pew Research Center, 2017). A majority of online social interaction was limited to text-based messaging. In the early 2000s, no one was "always" online in the sense most of us are today. People thought of the Internet, metaphorically, as a place, or spatial location, separate from the rest of their lives (Markham, 2003). Popular terms such as "cyberspace," "world wide web," and "information super-highway" reflect this spatial metaphor of the Internet (Olson, 2005). The spatial metaphor is also evident in the names of early web browsers such as "Internet Explorer" and "Netscape Navigator." In the early years, people were either in cyberspace or were offline and in the real world.

One consequence of the geographic metaphor was early theory and research assumed that if a person was "online," they could not also be "offline." The difference between the two was stark and easily identifiable. Initial concerns about problematic Internet use assumed that being online diminished one's separate, offline life. The online versus offline dichotomy is reflected in early researchers' concerns with Internet use displacing or weakening in-person social ties.

Today, the lines between online and offline interaction are blurring. Most of our interpersonal relationships involve a complicated mix of device-mediated and in-person interactions. We use the greatest number of mediated channels with our closest relationship partners (Ledbetter, 2015). Throughout an ongoing interaction, people switch between modalities and the conversation moves back and forth between in-person and mediated channels (Caughlin & Sharabi, 2013; Ledbetter, 2015; Ramirez & Wang, 2008; Ramirez & Zhang, 2007).

Today, when I tell people that I study problematic Internet use, they often seem unsure of what I mean. However, if I mention specific examples, such as compulsive smartphone checking, digital distraction, social networking habits, compulsive gaming, cyberstalking, cyberbullying, and online infidelity, others react with instant recognition. The problems listed above illustrate the extent to which the meaning of problematic Internet use has changed and extended beyond concerns about overuse and social displacement. The changing face of problematic Internet use reflects a need for a more sophisticated vocabulary to talk about the variety dysfunctional and hurtful outcomes of online social interaction.

How might researchers study an ever-changing phenomenon like interpersonal technology use? This book argues that fundamental theories of *interpersonal and relational communication processes* can inform research on current and emerging types of problematic Internet use. Despite changing technologies, people's online interpersonal behavior is still guided by stable communicative principles. For example, most people seek praise and avoid embarrassment. Goffman (1959, 1967) argued that maintaining face and the aversion to face threat are fundamental goals in most interpersonal situations. Here, the desires to maintain face and avoid face threat are universal motivations that guide our social behavior regardless of whether we are speaking, texting, or using Twitter. Irrespective of the technology involved, the dynamics of face threats and facework remain unchanged; people get angry when their face is threatened and are pleased when others uphold their face. What is unique and interesting is how new interpersonal technologies create new opportunities for face management and face threats.

Similarly, whether a bully attacks a victim in person or online, or a combination of both, the fundamental aspects of bullying, as an interpersonal phenomenon, are relatively unchanging; all bullying involves a power difference and repeated aggression (Olweus, 1993). However, there are distinct changes that mediated communication brings to a bullying experience that reveal how online contexts may facilitate bullying and contribute to victims' suffering (Sticca & Perren, 2013).

Further, research on the dynamics of intimate relationships can explain how online social behavior may create problems in close personal relationships. Whether couples are arguing in person or with texting, communication research explains that relational partners must skillfully manage uncertainty (Baxter & Wilmot, 1984) and negotiate ongoing dialectical tensions (Baxter & Simon, 1993) to maintain a healthy relationship. Additionally, as technology evolves, close relational partners have begun to develop rules for online behavior. The fact that relationships have rules is a stable feature of personal relationships (Argyle & Henderson, 1985). Yet, the ways people use technology to break relationship rules continue to change. Here, theories of relational maintenance can help provide a framework for explaining how couples handle relational transgressions involving technology (Tokunaga, 2014).

Today, problematic Internet use may involve interpersonal aggression, unwanted pursuit, violating the rules of close relationships, and using communication devices in ways that diminish our in-person conversation partners. Scholars have studied these problems from many perspectives including, legalistic, sociological, and psychological research. This book emphasizes the utility of approaching these problems as *interpersonal problems*. Doing so allows researchers to connect their work to established theories of interpersonal and relational communication and avoids a myopic focus on specific technology that is likely to change over time (e.g., problematic MySpace use). The extensive literature on in-person interpersonal processes and relational principles can help guide research into the changing face of problematic Internet use.

What Is "Problematic"?

Conceptually, the topics covered in this book are examples of what some scholars approach as the "dark side" of online social interaction (Fox & Moreland, 2015; Spitzberg & Cupach, 2014) and others have conceptualized as "digital stressors" (Weinstein & Selman, 2014). Both approaches emphasize the importance of considering how interpersonal behavior can be destructive, immoral, and hurtful to others (Cupach & Spitzberg, 1998; Spitzberg & Cupach, 2007, 2014). From the dark side perspective, problematic behaviors are arrayed along two dimensions: moral-immoral and functional-dysfunctional. Cyberbullying, for example, would be an immoral, yet functional, way for a bully to get attention. On the other hand, regularly checking the phone during an intimate dinner is not immoral, but does reflect dysfunctional self-regulation or lack of interpersonal skill.

Weinstein and Selman's (2014) research on socio-digital stress among adolescents reveals that many of the most common digital stressors are interpersonal (e.g., humiliation, shaming, harassment, bullying, boundary management, device use during in-person interactions).

Further, Weinstein et al. (2016) explained that adolescents struggle with two general categories of "socio-digital challenges." First, hostility-oriented stressors include problems with online harassment, bullying, and aggression. Second, adolescents described problems navigating close relationships as sources of socio-digital stress. In its variety of forms, technology-mediated interpersonal behavior is problematic when it contributes to immoral, stressful, or dysfunctional outcomes.

Mundane to Severe Problems

Cyberbullying and cyberstalking reflect the extreme end along a continuum of problematic Internet use severity. At the other end of a continuum, people also experience a variety of relatively less severe, and more mundane types of problematic Internet use including, compulsive smartphone habits, online relational transgressions, or checking one's phone during an in-person conversation. Studying mundane problematic Internet use does not diminish the gravity of extreme cases of cyberstalking or devalue experiences of victims of online harassment. These examples reinforce the importance of considering the full spectrum of problematic online interperesonal behavior. Thus, the book examines a broad array of dysfunctional online social behavior ranging from the mundane to severe.

The variety of problems addressed in this book reflects almost twenty years of research on a phenomenon that continually changes. As technology has developed, the questions researchers began with in the late 1990s bear little resemblance to those that challenge current scholarship.

Changing Conceptualizations of Online Social Behavior

Concerns about problematic Internet use began with fears that people would be so drawn to it that they would neglect their offline social ties. Further concern involved the belief that online social interaction was a poor and inadequate substitute for in-person communication. As the technology evolved, new concerns arose around the ways people might exploit the characteristics of online interaction to their benefit. Most recently, concerns about interpersonal technology center around our "permanently online" and "permanently connected" society of smart devices and social networks. The paragraphs below overview the evolution of concerns about online interpersonal behavior.

Society often greets the arrival of new communication technology with fears about its harmful effects on people's well-being. The introduction of television brought questions about its addictive potential, its effects on children, and its impact on social relationships (e.g., Kubey, 1996; Kubey & Csikzentmihalyi, 1990; McIlwraith, Jacobvitz, Kubey, & Alexander, 1991; Preston, 1941; Smith, 1986; for reviews see Grohol, 1999; Tokunaga, 2015). Similar concerns began to emerge about people's dependencies on personal computers and console video games in the 1980s and 1990s (Egli & Meyers, 1984; Greenfield, 1984; Griffiths, 1992; Meyers, 1987). With the popularization of the Internet in the late 1990s, concerns arose about the harmful effects online activity (Kraut et al., 1998; Nie, Hillygus, & Erbing, 2002; Young, 1996).

Addictions and Displacement

The primary concern among early research on problematic Internet use was that people would be so captivated by, or habitually drawn to, online activity that they would neglect their offline relationships. The study of problematic Internet use began with concerns about interpersonal displacement. Kraut et al.'s (1998) "Internet paradox" paper was one of the first attempts to examine the psychological and social effects of online activity. Kraut and colleagues (1998) conducted one of the first formal tests of the consequences of Internet use on psychological health and social involvement and social ties. The study followed a sample of new Internet users (i.e., people who had never been online before) throughout their first year of being online and asked questions about their social relationships and well-being. Over that year, the researchers identified a "paradox" whereby people reported using the Internet mainly for interpersonal communication, but at the same time, reported being less socially engaged and less mentally healthy than before they went online. The paradox, as Kraut et al. (1998) explained, was that "the Internet is a social technology used for communication ... but it is associated with declines in social involvement and the psychological well-being" (p. 1029). Follow-up studies found the adverse effects, reported earlier (Kraut et al., 1998), had largely disappeared after people had been using the Internet for a year (e.g., Kraut et al., 2002). Despite the follow-up results, research continued to ask how online behavior might affect in-person social connections.

Researchers argued that Internet use threatened to displace in-person social activity. Here, Kraut et al. (1998) proposed that Internet use could have similar displacement effects as television and other entertainment media, such that spending time online might lead to withdrawal from in-person relationships, loneliness, and declines in mental health. Another early study by Nie et al. (2002) used time diaries to follow participants' Internet use and argued the results supported the displacement hypothesis. Researchers noted, "time online is largely an asocial activity that competes with, rather than complements, face to face social time" (Nie et al., 2002, p. 215). Displacement hypotheses also informed research on the "addictive" potential of Internet use (e.g., Young, 1996) with fears that people would neglect their in-person relationships as they lost the ability to control their Internet use.

One assumption underlying the displacement hypothesis was that online social interaction was "less personal" than face-to-face interaction. Here, Kraut et al. (1998) argued that "perhaps, by using the Internet, people are substituting poorer quality social relationships for better relationships, that is, substituting weak ties for strong ones" (p. 1029). Indeed, the assumption that Internet use displaced healthier, or more vital, in-person interaction guided much of the early research on Internet effects and compulsive Internet use. This view that online interaction was weaker, or less personal, than face-to-face behavior arose from early attempts to distinguish the communicative characteristics of computer-mediated and in-person interaction. Since the early 1990s online social behavior has become more interpersonal and more analogous to its offline counterparts.

Channel Differences and Interpersonal Deficits

To explain the interpersonal effects of computer-mediated communication, early research examined channel differences between mediated and face-to-face interaction. Given that primitive online technology permitted little more than text-based messaging, initial research on computer-mediated communication found dramatic differences compared to face-to-face interactions. Researchers noted that mediated communication involved a paucity of nonverbal cues and a diminished sense of social presence (Short, Williams, & Christie, 1976). Social presence refers to the degree to which a person is warm, personable, and shows signs of involvement. The cues-filtered out perspective suggested that some types of online communication were relatively more depersonalized than face-to-face activity because of the reduced nonverbal cues available online (Culnan & Markus, 1987). Here, scholars argued mediated communication lacked "media richness" or the ability to send nonverbal relational information. Consequently, early theorists suggested mediated communication might work well for task situations but less well for relational communication (Daft & Lengel, 1986; Dennis & Kinney, 1998).

Subsequent work on social information processing theory (Walther, 1993; Walther & Burgoon, 1992; Utz, 2000) suggested that online interpersonal relationship development was possible via computer-mediated communication, but required more time to develop than traditional face-to-face relationships.

Hyperpersonal Approach—Exploiting Channel Differences

As the research developed, scholars began to note potential benefits, or affordances, of the reduced social cues online. Data suggested people perceived greater anonymity online than face-to-face (Bargh, McKenna, & Fitzsimmons, 2002; McKenna & Bargh, 1999, 2000) and recognized the benefits of reduced nonverbal cues in computer-mediated interaction (for reviews see Walther, 2011; Walther & Parks, 2002). Walther's (1996) hyperpersonal theory suggested that communicative features of online interaction, such as minimal nonverbal cues, greater anonymity, enhanced ability to edit messages, and strategic control over self-presentation could be used to enhance interpersonal outcomes. Thus, the hyperpersonal perspective argued that the reduced cues in online communication could help people be more interpersonally effective than in face-to-face settings. Further, scholars argued that, compared to face-to-face interaction, hyperpersonal communication would result in people forming more idealized versions of their online partner and having more intimate exchanges (Tidwell & Walther; 2002; Walther, 1993, 1996; Walther & Burgoon 1992; also see Walther, 2006).

Researchers studying habitual Internet use argued that some people might be particularly drawn to the hyperpersonal features of online social interaction to compensate for offline deficits in social skill. In my research, I argued that people with lower social skills and social anxiety might be especially drawn to online social interaction as a way to compensate for their own perceived in-person interpersonal deficits. Further, I hypothesized that some people develop a preference for online social interaction because it makes them feel more effective and less face threatened than in-person interaction (Caplan, 2003, 2005).

Smartphones and Social Networking

By the early 2010s, the ubiquity of smartphones, messaging apps, and social networking had made the line between online and offline communication more difficult to see. As people began using networked devices in their every-day relationships, social networking made interactions less anonymous and more visual. In one article, Walther and Ramirez (2009) noted that the introduction of photographs and visual graphics to mediated communication posed serious theoretical challenges for theories based on the absence of visual cues. Recently, Baym argued the online/offline relationships distinction is outdated, suggesting, "These separate realms do not hold up under scrutiny" (Baym, 2015, p. 152).

Interpersonal researchers have begun to focus on how relational partners communcniate with different types of media and switch among them (Caughlin & Sharabi, 2017; Haythornthwaite, 2005; Ledbetter 2015; Walther, 2011). Media multiplexity theory proposes, "media use varies with the strength of the ties between communicators" (Haythornthwaite, 2005, p. 126). Results from recent studies support media multiplexity theory. For instance, consistent with media multiplexity theory, Sharabi and Caughlin (2017) found that partners in intimate relationships used the widest variety of modes of communication.

Research on modality switching illustrates that modern interpersonal relationships are a complex mix of online and mediated interactions (Ramirez & Zhang, 2007; Sharabi, 2015). Further, ongoing interpersonal interactions, such as relational conflicts, move across communication modes (Caughlin, Basinger, & Sharabi, 2017; Sharabi & Caughlin, 2015). For example, an early morning in-person argument can continue throughout the day as the couple uses different channels such as texting, email, and a later face-to-face interaction. Couples' abilities to manage communication across different modes are related to relationship strength. In one study, Caughlin and Sharabi (2013) found that romantic couples' integration of media use correlated with relational closeness and couples' difficulty transitioning among media was associated with lower closeness.

Perpetually Online and Constantly Connected

Smartphones and unlimited data plans reflect the current state of affairs that some describe as "permanently online—permanently connected" (Vorderer & Kohring, 2013), in which "many people have now developed the habit of being online and connected with others almost permanently (Vorderer, Krömer, & Schneider, 2016, p. 697). Turkle (2017) suggested adolescents find comfort in knowing their friends are online, regardless of whether they interact. For adolescents, Turkle (2017) argued, the comfort of knowing their closest friends and family are always online and reachable represents a source of security that an adolescent can carry to bed and keep plugged in on their night table.

The concepts of permanently online and connected raise questions about what problematic online behavior means today. For instance, what does Internet addiction or habitual use mean in a contemporary society where, "there seems to be hardly any social context whether in public or in private spaces, where individuals voluntarily go and stay offline and disconnected" (Vorderer et al., 2016, p. 695)? In other words, *being offline and disconnected is quickly becoming the new abnormal.* Particularly for young adults, maintaining constant contact and navigating the myriad of mediated communication channels has become a vital social skill.

After 20 years, the Internet has become increasingly more interpersonal, and so have the types of problems that its users experience. Today, in addition to concerns about addiction and compulsivity, researchers study online interpersonal relationship transgressions, online harassment and aggression (e.g., cyberbullying, cyberstalking), and interpersonal problems arising from using devices during in-person interactions. Each chapter of this book organizes, summarizes, and advances literature on these different types of problematic Internet use. The chapters also draw on theories and research from interpersonal and relational scholarship to bring theoretical organization and continuity to the literature. The next section briefly reviews each of the chapters.

Chapter Overviews

Chapter Two: Online Habits, Compulsion, and Addiction

Chapter Two addresses difficulties with controlling one's online behavior. The problem is commonly described as Internet addiction (e.g., Young, 1998; Young & Rogers, 1998), problematic Internet use, habitual use, or deficient self-regulation (e.g., Caplan, 2002; LaRose, 2015; LaRose, Lin, & Eastin, 2003). The chapter uses communication research on media habits and deficient self-regulation to help frame and organize a sprawling, inconsistent, and unorganized literature. The chapter also argues for future research to rally around a unified conceptual approach of habituation of interactive media use. Although technology will continue to change, conceptual models of self-regulation and habit formation are relatively stable across contexts and can help guide future research.

The chapter explores the interpersonal side of problematic online habits, demonstrating a connection between in-person relational difficulties and problematic online habits. Using a compensation metaphor, the chapter argues that people who lack in-person social skill will prefer the unique affordances of mediated interaction, which may help compensate for their deficits (Caplan, 2005). The chapter seeks to expand that idea by including additional relational and emotional predictors.

Framing the issue as an interpersonal problem helps explain strong links between interpersonal variables and online compulsivity. The chapter reviews research connecting compulsive Internet use with lower social skills and a preference for online social interaction (Caplan, 2003, 2005). More recently, other studies have identified additional interpersonal and relational deficits associated with online habit strength including, emotional intelligence, attachment security, and other indicators of unmet relational needs. Finally, the chapter examines the increasingly relevant issue of how online habits are influencing interpersonal relationships. In romantic relationships, one partner's online habit may create conflict and threaten intimacy.

Chapter Three: Online Relationship Transgressions

Chapter Three examines how romantic partners and friends negotiate relational rules around technology and the types of online relational transgressions they commonly experience. Since the late 1990s researchers have examined relationship problems arising from online affairs, compulsive online sexual behavior, and sexual activity with online partners (Cooper, 2002; Schneider, 2000; Schneider, Weiss, & Samenow, 2012). Today, romantic couples and friends must navigate a more complicated terrain of relational rules about online behavior. In both romantic relationships and friendships, online behaviors can spawn jealousy, betray trust, and cause embarrassment. Whereas some transgressions may be relatively mundane, others create conflict, hurt feelings, and may contribute to breakups.

Increasingly, close personal relationships involve rules and expectations about online behavior (Dardis & Gidycz, 2016; Fox & Moreland, 2015). One's need for relational rules to guide behavior indicates the seriousness of the potential threats arising from one partner's online social activity. Chapter Three demonstrates that interpersonal and relational communication theories can organize and guide the nascent literature on online relational transgressions. Understanding fundamental processes, such as facework, uncertainty reduction, expectancy violations, and dialectical tensions can inform future research into online relational transgressions. Here, the chapter helps illustrate the book's broader point that, although technologies and affordances change, the underlying processes that guide functional interpersonal and relational communication are well-established and stable.

Chapter Four: Cyberbullying and Online Interpersonal Agression

Concerns about cyberbullying emerged around the mid-2000s. Initially, researchers employed the literature on traditional bullying to help define cyberbullying (Patchin & Hinduja, 2006; Ybarra, 2004; Ybarra & Mitchell, 2004). Today, cyberbullying is one of the most researched topics in the study of online social behavior. Close to 1,000 scholarly works on cyberbullying were published between 2007 and 2017.[1] Cyberbullying receives attention in the popular press as well as among parents and educators. The chapter demonstrates that several popular beliefs about cyberbullying are "myths" that are not supported by data (Sabella, Patchin, & Hinduja, 2006). Further, despite the size of the literature, cyberbullying literature lacks organization and methodological consistency (Berne et al., 2013; Thomas, Connor, & Scott, 2014). The cyberbullying research is rich with descriptive data, but the literature needs detailed theory and consistent measurement. The chapter attempts to organize and conceptually clarify cyberbullying by using Goffman's (1959, 1967) dramaturgical model of social behavior. Chapter Four also explains why, compared to traditional bullying, the communicative features of cyberbullying might change the experience for both the bully and the victim.

Chapter Five: Cyberstalking, Unwanted Pursuit, and Relational Intrusion

Chapter Five considers cyberstalking, cyberobsessional pursuit, and obsessional online relationship intrusion. The literature on cyberstalking is less developed than other topics in the book. One of the biggest reasons being that, conceptually and empirically, cyberstalking is often confused and confounded with cyberbullying and other forms of online aggression. Chapter Five illustrates how researchers can conceptually distinguish cyberstalking from other forms of online harassment. Differences in motivations, behaviors, and the relationship between perpetrator and victim make cyberstalking an entirely different experience worthy of it is own line of inquiry.

The chapter employs interpersonal research on unwanted relational pursuit and obsessive relational intrusion in face-to-face settings as starting points for theory-based research on cyberstalking (e.g., Cupach & Spitzberg, 1998; Dardis & Gidycz, 2016; Spitzberg & Cupach, 200, 2014). Additionally, the chapter illustrates the importance of approaching cyberstalking as something that usually happens along with traditional stalking.

Chapter Six: Copresent Device Use: Using Mobile Devices During In-Person Interaction

Chapter Six explores one of the newest areas to emerge in the study of problematic online social behavior, copresent device use, or using mobile devices during in-person conversations (Turkle, 2015). Along with interest from media and popular press, social scientists have begun examining the phenomenon of copresent device use and the effects of copresent use on conversational outcomes (Vanden Abeele, Antheunis, & Schouten, 2016). The chapter also presents recent research on the problems copresent device use creates in romantic relationships (McDaniel & Coyne, 2016a, 2016b). Chapter Six employs theories of interpersonal interaction, nonverbal immediacy, and relational messages to organize and explain the effects of copresent device use. The chapter uses these and other lines of research to provide a theory-based narrative explaining how copresent device use can create problems in conversations, romantic relationships, and between children and parents.

Together, the following chapters tell the story of twenty years of research into online social behavior and its associated problems. Although the technologies continue to change rapidly, the basics of interpersonal and relational communication provide a firm grounding to organize and summarize previous work and conceptually frame future research.

Chapter Seven: Moving Forward—An Agenda for Future Research

Beyond presenting a summary of the book, the final chapter also offers an agenda for future research. The chapter poses three broad research questions for future research to pursue. Additionally, the chapter restates the book's broader thesis that interpersonal and relational communication research offers valuable conceptual tools for explaining problematic Internet use.

Note

1. Based on a 2017 search of the Scopus database for the words "cyberbullying," "cyberbully," or "cyberbullies" in keyword, title, or abstract.

References

Argyle, M., & Henderson, M. (1985). The rules of relationships. In S. Duck & D. Perlman (Eds.), *Understanding personal relationships: An interdisciplinary approach* (pp. 63–84). Thousand Oaks, CA: Sage.

Bargh, J. A., McKenna, K. Y. A., & Fitzsimons, G. M. (2002). Can you see the real me? Activation and expression of the "true self" on the Internet. *Journal of Social Issues, 58*(1), 33–48. doi:10.1111/1540-4560.00247

Baxter, L. A., & Simon, E. P. (1993). Relationship maintenance strategies and dialectical contradictions in personal relationships. *Journal of Social & Personal Relationships, 10*(2), 225–242. doi:10.1177/026540759301000204

Baxter, L. A., & Wilmot, W. W. (1984). "Secret tests": Social strategies for acquiring information about the state of the relationship. *Human Communication Research, 11*(2), 171–201. doi:10.1111/j.1468-2958.1984.tb00044.x

Baym, N. K. (2015). *Personal connections in the digital age* (2nd ed.). Malden, MA: John Wiley & Sons.

Beard, K. W., & Wolf, E. M. (2001). Modification in the proposed diagnostic criteria for Internet addiction. *CyberPsychology & Behavior, 4*(3), 377–383.

Berne, S., Frisén, A., Schultze-Krumbholz, A., Scheithauer, H., Naruskov, K., Luik, P., … Zukauskiene, R. (2013). Cyberbullying assessment instruments: A systematic review. *Aggression and Violent Behavior, 18*(2), 320–334. doi:10.1016/j.avb.2012.11.022

Caplan, S. E. (2002). Problematic Internet use and psychosocial well-being: Development of a theory-based cognitive-behavioral measurement instrument. *Computers in Human Behavior, 18*(5), 553–575. doi:10.1016/S0747-5632(02)00004-3

Caplan, S. E. (2003). Preference for online social interaction: A theory of problematic Internet use and psychosocial well-being. *Communication Research, 30*(6), 625–648. doi:10.1177/0093650203257842

Caplan, S. E. (2005). A social skill account of problematic Internet use. *Journal of Communication, 55*(4), 721–736. doi:10.1093/joc/55.4.721

Caughlin, J. P., & Sharabi, L. L. (2013). A communicative interdependence perspective of close relationships: The connections between mediated and unmediated interactions matter. *Journal of Communication, 63*(5), 873–893. doi:10.1111/jcom.12046

Caughlin, J. P., Basinger, E. D., & Sharabi, L. L. (2017). The connections between communication technologies and relational conflict: A multiple goals and communication interdependence perspective. In J. A. Samp (Ed.), *Communicating interpersonal conflict in close relationships: Contexts, challenges, and opportunities* (pp. 57–72). New York: Routledge.

Cavezza, C., & McEwan, T. E. (2014). Cyberstalking versus off-line stalking in a forensic sample. *Psychology, Crime & Law, 20*(10), 955–970. doi:10.1080/1068316X.2014.893334

Cooper, A. (2002). *Sex and the Internet: A guidebook for clinicians*. New York: Routledge.

Culnan, M. J., & Markus, M. L. (1987). Information technologies. In F. M. Jablin, L. L. Putnam, K. H. Roberts, & L. W. Porter (Eds.), *Handbook of organizational communication: An interdisciplinary perspective* (pp. 420–443). Thousand Oaks, CA: Sage.

Cupach, W. R., & Spitzberg, B. H. (1998). Obsessive relational intrusion and stalking. In B. H. Spitzberg & W. R. Cupach (Eds.), *The dark side of close relationships* (pp. 233–263). Mahwah, NJ: Lawrence Erlbaum.

Daft, R. L., & Lengel, R. H. (1986). Organizational information requirements, media richness, and structural design. *Management Science, 32*(5), 554–571. doi:10.1287/mnsc.32.5.554

Dardis, C. M., & Gidycz, C. A. (2016). The frequency and perceived impact of engaging in in-person and cyber unwanted pursuit after relationship break-up among college men and women. *Sex Roles, 76*(1–2), 56–72. doi:10.1007/s11199-016-0667-1

Dennis, A. R., & Kinney, S. T. (1998). Testing media richness theory in the new media: the effects of cues, feedback, and task equivocality. *Information Systems Research, 9*(3), 256–274. doi:10.1287/isre.9.3.256

Docan-Morgan, T., & Docan, C. A. (2007). Internet infidelity: Double standards and the differing views of women and men. *Communication Quarterly, 55*(3), 317–342. doi:10.1080/01463370701492519

Egli, E., & Meyers, L. (1984). The role of video game playing in adolescent life: Is there reason to be concerned? *Bulletin of the Psychonomic Society, 22*(4), 309–312. doi:10.3758/BF03333828

Fox, J., & Moreland, J. J. (2015). The dark side of social networking sites: An exploration of the relational and psychological stressors associated with Facebook use and affordances. *Computers in Human Behavior, 45,* 168–176. doi:10.1016/j.chb.2014.11.083

Goffman, E. (1959). *The presentation of self in everyday life.* New York: Doubleday Anchor Books.

Goffman, E. (1967). *Interaction ritual: Essays on face-to-face behavior.* New York: Doubleday Anchor Books.

Greenfield, P. M. (1984). *Mind and media: The effects of television, video games, and computer.* Cambridge, MA: Harvard University Press.

Griffiths, M. D. (1991). Amusement machine playing in childhood and adolescence: A comparative analysis of video games and fruit machines. *Journal of Adolescence, 14*(1), 53–73.

Grohol, J. M. (1999). Too much time online: Internet addiction or healthy social interactions? *CyberPsychology & Behavior, 2*(5), 395–401. doi:10.1089/cpb.1999.2.395

Haythornthwaite, C. (2005). Social networks and Internet connectivity effects. *Information, Communication & Society, 8*(2), 125–147. doi:10.1080/13691180500146185

Kraut, R., Patterson, M., Lundmark, V., Kiesler, S., Mukopadhyay, T., & Scherlis, W. (1998). Internet paradox: A social technology that reduces social involvement and psychological well-being? *American Psychologist, 53*(9), 1017–1031 doi:10.1037/0003-066X.53.9.1017

Kubey, R. W. (1996). Television dependence, diagnosis, and prevention. In T. MacBeth (Ed.), *Tuning into young viewers: Social science perspectives on television* (pp. 221–260). Thousand Oaks, CA: Sage.

Kubey, R. W., & Csikszentmihalyi, M. (1990). Television as escape: Subjective experience before an evening of heavy viewing. *Communication Reports, 3*(2), 92–100.

LaRose, R. (2015). The psychology of interactive media habits. In S. S. Sundar (Ed.), *The handbook of the psychology of communication technology* (pp. 365–383). Malden, MA: John Wiley & Sons.

LaRose, R., Lin, C. A., & Eastin, M. S. (2003). Unregulated Internet usage: Addiction, habit, or deficient self-regulation? *Media Psychology, 5*(3), 225–253. doi:10.1207/S1532785XMEP0503_01

Ledbetter, A. M. (2015). Media multiplexity theory: Technology use and interpersonal tie strength. In D. O. Braithwaite & P. Schrodt (Eds.), *Engaging theories in interpersonal communication: Multiple perspectives* (2nd ed., pp. 363–376). Thousand Oaks, CA: Sage.

Markham, A. N. (2003). Metaphors reflecting and shaping the reality of the Internet: Tool, place, way of being. A paper presented at *Association of Internet Researchers Conference,* Toronto, Canada.

McDaniel, B. T., & Coyne, S. M. (2016a). "Technoference": The interference of technology in couple relationships and implications for women's personal and relational well-being. *Psychology of Popular Media Culture, 5*(1), 85–98. doi:10.1037/ppm0000065

McDaniel, B. T., & Coyne, S. M. (2016b). Technology interference in the parenting of young children: Implications for mothers' perceptions of coparenting. *The Social Science Journal, 53*(4), 435–443.

McIlwraith, R., Jacobvitz, R. S., Kubey, R., & Alexander, A. (1991). Television addiction: Theories and data behind the ubiquitous metaphor. *American Behavioral Scientist, 35*(2), 104–121.

McKenna, K. Y. A., & Bargh, J. A. (1999). Causes and consequences of social interaction on the Internet: A conceptual framework. *Media Psychology, 1*(3), 249–269.

McKenna, K. Y. A., & Bargh, J. A. (2000). Plan 9 from cyberspace: The implications of the Internet for personality and social psychology. *Personality & Social Psychology Review, 4*(1), 57–75. doi:10.1207/S15327957PSPR0401_6

Morahan-Martin, J. (1999). The relationship between loneliness and Internet use and abuse. *CyberPsychology & Behavior, 2*(5), 431–439. doi:10.1089/cpb.1999.2.431

Morahan-Martin, J. (2008). Internet abuse: Emerging trends and lingering questions. In A. Barak (Ed.), *Psychological aspects of cyberspace: Theory, research, and applications* (pp. 32–69). Cambridge: Cambridge University Press.

Myers, D. (1987). Anonymity is part of the magic: Individual manipulation of computer-mediated communication contexts. *Qualitative Sociology, 10*(3), 251–266.

Nie, N. H., Hillygus, D. S., & Erbring, L. (2002). Internet use, interpersonal relations, and sociability: A time diary study. In B. Wellman & C. Haythornthwaite (Eds.), *The Internet in everyday life* (pp. 213–243). Malden, MA: Blackwell.

Olson, K. K. (2005). Cyberspace as place and the limits of metaphor. *Convergence, 11*(1), 10–18.

Olweus, D. (1993). *Bullying at school: What we know and what we can do*. Malden, MA: Blackwell.

Patchin, J. W., & Hinduja, S. (2006). Bullies move beyond the schoolyard: A preliminary look at cyberbullying. *Youth Violence & Juvenile Justice, 4*(2), 148–169. https://doi.org/10.1177/1541204006286288

Pew Research Center (2017). Internet/Broadband Fact Sheet. https://www.pewinternet.org/fact-sheet/internet-broadband/

Preston, M. I. (1941). Children's reactions to movie horrors and radio crime. *The Journal of Pediatrics, 19*(2), 147–168.

Przybylski, A. K., & Weinstein, N. (2012). Can you connect with me now? How the presence of mobile communication technology influences face-to-face conversation quality. *Journal of Social & Personal Relationships, 30*(3), 237–246. doi:10.1177/0265407512453827

Ramirez, A., & Wang, Z. (2008). When online meets offline: An expectancy violations theory perspective on modality switching. *Journal of Communication, 58*(1), 20–39. doi: 10.1111/j.1460-2466.2007.00372.x

Ramirez, A., & Zhang, S. (2007). When online meets offline: The effect of modality switching on relational communication. *Communication Monographs, 74*(3), 287–310. doi:10.1080/03637750701543493

Sabella, R. A., Patchin, J. W., & Hinduja, S. (2013). Cyberbullying myths and realities. *Computers in Human Behavior, 29*(6), 2703–2711. doi:10.1016/j.chb.2013.06.040

Schneider, J. P. (2000). Effects of cybersex addiction on the family: Results of a survey. *Sexual Addiction & Compulsivity, 7*(1–2), 31–58. doi:10.1080/10720160008400206

Schneider, J. P., Weiss, R., & Samenow, C. P. (2012). Is it really cheating? Understanding the emotional reactions and clinical treatment of spouses and partners affected by cybersex infidelity. *Sexual Addiction & Compulsivity, 19*(1–2), 123–139. doi:10.1080/10720162.2012.658344

Sharabi, L. L. (2015). *Modality switching in online dating: Identifying the communicative factors that make the transition from an online to an offline relationship more or less successful.* (Unpublished doctoral dissertation). University of Illinois at Urbana - Champaign. Retrieved from https://hdl.handle.net/2142/87959

Sharabi, L. L., & Caughlin, J. P. (2017). Usage patterns of social media across stages of romantic relationships. In N. M. Punyanunt-Carter & J. S. Wrench (Eds.), *The impact of social media in modern romantic relationships* (pp. 15–30). Lanham: Lexington Books.

Short, J., Williams, E., & Christie, B. (1976). *The social psychology of telecommunication.* London: Wiley.

Spitzberg, B. H., & Cupach, W. R. (2007). Disentangling the dark side of interpersonal communication. In B. H. Spitzberg & W. R. Cupach (Eds.), *The dark side of interpersonal communication* (2nd ed., pp. 3–30). New York: Routledge.

Spitzberg, B. H., & Cupach, W. R. (2014). *The dark side of relationship pursuit: From attraction to obsession and stalking* (2nd ed.). Mahwah, NJ: Lawrence Erlbaum Associates.

Sticca, F., & Perren, S. (2013). Is cyberbullying worse than traditional bullying? Examining the differential roles of medium, publicity, and anonymity for the perceived severity of bullying. *Journal of Youth & Adolescence, 42*(5), 739–750. doi:10.1007/s10964-012-9867-3

Thomas, H. J., Connor, J. P., & Scott, J. G. (2014). Integrating traditional bullying and cyberbullying: Challenges of definition and measurement in adolescents—A review. *Educational Psychology Review, 27*(1), 135–152. doi:10.1007/s10648-014-9261-7

Tidwell, L. C., & Walther, J. B. (2002). Computer-mediated communication effects on disclosure, impressions, and interpersonal evaluations: Getting to know one another a bit at a time. *Human Communication Research, 28*(3), 317–348. doi:10.1111/j.1468-2958.2002.tb00811.x

Tokunaga, R. S. (2014). Relational transgressions on social networking sites: Individual, interpersonal, and contextual explanations for dyadic strain and communication rules change. *Computers in Human Behavior, 39*, 287–295. doi:10.1016/j.chb.2014.07.024

Tokunaga, R. S. (2015). Perspectives on Internet addiction, problematic Internet use, and deficient self-regulation. *Annals of the International Communication Association, 39*(1), 131–161.

Turkle, S. (2011). *Alone together: Why we expect more from technology and less from each other.* New York: Basic Books.

Vanden Abeele, M., Antheunis, M. L., & Schouten, A. P. (2016). The effect of mobile messaging during a conversation on impression formation and interaction quality. *Computers in Human Behavior, 62*, 562–569.

Vorderer, P., & Kohring, M. (2013). Permanently online: A challenge for media and communication research. *International Journal of Communication, 7*(1), 188–196. doi:1932-8086/2013FEA0002

Vorderer, P., Krömer, N., & Schneider, F. M. (2016). Permanently online—Permanently connected: Explorations into university students' use of social media and mobile smart devices. *Computers in Human Behavior, 63,* 694–703. doi:10.1016/j.chb.2016.05.085

Walther, J. B. (1993). Impression development in computer-mediated interaction. *Western Journal of Communication, 57*(4), 381–398. doi:10.1080/10570319309374463

Walther, J. B. (1996). Computer-mediated communication: Impersonal, interpersonal, and hyperpersonal interaction. *Communication Research, 23*(1), 3–43. doi:10.1177/009365096023001001

Walther, J. B. (2006). Nonverbal dynamics in computer-mediated communication. In V. Manusov & M. L. Patterson (Eds.), *Handbook of nonverbal communication* (pp. 461–480). Thousand Oaks, CA: Sage.

Walther, J. B. (2011). Theories of computer-mediated communication and interpersonal relations. In M. L. Knapp & J. A. Daly (Eds.), *The handbook of interpersonal communication* (4th ed., pp. 443–479). Thousand Oaks, CA: Sage.

Walther, J. B., & Burgoon, J. K. (1992), Relational communication in computer-mediated interaction. *Human Communication Research, 19*(1), 50–88. doi:10.1111/j.1468-2958.1992.tb00295.x

Walther, J. B., & Parks, M. R. (2002). Cues filtered out, cues filtered in. In M. L. Knapp & J. A. Daly (Eds.), *Handbook of interpersonal communication* (3rd ed., pp. 529–563). Thousand Oaks, CA: Sage.

Walther, J. B., & Ramirez, A. (2009). New technologies and new directions in online relating. In S. W. Smith & S. R. Wilson (Eds.), *New directions in interpersonal communication research* (pp. 264–284). Thousand Oaks, CA: Sage.

Weinstein, E. C., & Selman, R. L. (2014). Digital stress: Adolescents' personal accounts. *New Media & Society, 18*(3), 391–409. doi:10.1177/1461444814543989

Weinstein, E. C., Selman, R. L., Thomas, S., Kim, J. E., White, A. E., & Dinakar, K. (2016). How to cope with digital stress: The recommendations adolescents offer their peers online. *Journal of Adolescent Research, 31*(4), 415–441. doi:10.1177/0743558415587326

Ybarra, M. L. (2004). Linkages between depressive symptomatology and Internet harassment among young regular Internet users. *CyberPsychology & Behavior, 7*(2), 247–257. doi:10.1089/109493104323024500

Ybarra, M. L., & Mitchell, K. J. (2004). Youth engaging in online harassment: Associations with caregiver-child relationships, Internet use, and personal characteristics. *Journal of Adolescence, 27,* 319–326. doi:10.1016/j.adolescence.2004.03.007

Young, K. S. (1998). Internet addiction: The emergence of a new clinical disorder. *CyberPsychology & Behavior, 1*(3), 237–244. doi:10.1089/cpb.1998.1.237

Young, K. S., & Rogers, R. C. (1998). The relationship between depression and Internet addiction. *CyberPsychology & Behavior, 1*(1), 25–28. doi:10.1089/cpb.1998.1.25

Chapter Two

Online Habits, Compulsion, and Addiction

Since the late 1990s, researchers studying problematic Internet habits, compulsive use, and online addictions have published over 2,000 scholarly works. In 2015 and 2016, over 300 manuscripts were published per year.[1] Despite the amount of research attention devoted to the subject, the scholarly literature on problematic Internet use and Internet addiction is confusing and difficult to summarize. The problem stems largely from almost two decades of researchers using inconsistent definitions of problematic Internet use and diverse methods to measure it. To advance our understanding of why people have trouble controlling online activities, researchers need to begin unifying around a common set of conceptual definitions and uniform measures (Tokunaga, 2014). Until that happens, making sense of the literature is difficult because it lacks an organizing framework shared among a community of researchers.

This chapter adopts the term "problematic online habits" to refer to the phenomenon previously described as "Internet addiction" and "problematic Internet use" (PIU) to minimize confusion and better summarize the literature. Here the term "online" describes various devices and applications people use to mediate interpersonal communication.

Although the word "online" may not be a perfect conceptual term to use here, it is somewhat more current and suggestive of newer technology than the term "Internet."[2] As the first main section will illustrate, the concept of habituation can help organize and integrate variations in terminology (LaRose, 2015, Tokunaga, 2015).

Tokunaga (2015) argues that the "study of Internet habits is squarely a communication problem" (p. 146). Further developing Tokunaga's argument, this chapter demonstrates that problematic online habits are, to a significant extent, *interpersonal* communication problems. For example, two of the most widely studied online habits, social networking and gaming, involve online social interaction (Griffiths, Király, Pontes, & Demetrovics, 2014; Griffiths, Kuss, & Demetrovics, 2014; Ryan, Chester, Reece, & Xenos, 2014). Second, online habit strength is associated with offline interpersonal problems such social skill deficits (Caplan, 2005; Tokunaga & Rains, 2016). Third, when problematic online habits become severe, they contribute to problems in offline personal relationships (Kerkhof, Finkenauer, & Muusses, 2011; Muusses, Finkenauer, Kerkhof, & Righetti, 2015; Lianekhammy & Van de Venne, 2015; Northrup & Shumway, 2014).

Conceptual Approaches

This section summarizes and organizes the research on "Internet addiction" or "problematic Internet use," and argues that "problematic online habit" is a more useful concept for organizing previous work and guiding future research and theory. Early in its development, research on compulsive Internet use split into two different paradigms or approaches, the "Internet addiction" paradigm and the cognitive models of problematic Internet use (for a meta-analysis see Tokunaga & Raines, 2010). Despite being the most widely used approach, the addiction approach has serious limitations (detailed below). As an alternative, cognitive theories centered on deficient self-regulation have proven more useful for building conceptual models (Caplan, 2002; Davis, 2001; LaRose, Lin & Eastin, 2003; Tokunaga & Raines, 2010). From this perspective, people's online behaviors become habituated, resulting in less conscious control and awareness and a diminished ability to self-regulate online behavior (LaRose, 2015). Moreover, the concept of habit strength allows researchers to examine a *range of dysfunction* from relatively harmless habits to extreme cases that might resemble addiction. Using the idea of online habituation can help us further extend this research in a conceptually consistent way.

The Addiction Paradigm

Early research in the mid-1990s began to consider whether people could become addicted to the Internet. Griffiths' work was among the earliest to raise the question of whether Internet addiction might be a clinical disorder (Griffiths, 1995, 1996). Around the same time, Young (1996, 1998; Young, & Rogers, 1998) proposed that an adapted version of the criteria for pathological gambling (defined by the DSM-IV) could be used to identify Internet users as either dependents or non-dependents. Young proposed using the American Psychological Association's diagnostic criteria for pathological gambling behavior as a template for the criteria for diagnosing Internet addiction. Conceptualizing compulsive use as an addiction implies that it shares symptoms of other behavioral addictions such as salience, mood alteration, tolerance, withdraw, relapse, and conflict/adverse consequences. The addiction perspective assumes that so-called online addictions contribute to negative social and psychological outcomes. Research supports the proposed links between diminished psychological and social well-being and various measures of online addictions (Weinstein, Feder, Rosenberg, & Dannon, 2014).

Over the years, the addiction framework has developed concurrently with trends in interpersonal technology. As new technologies emerged, scholars using this approach have examined specific types of online addictions such as Internet gaming disorder (Kuss, 2013; Pontes & Griffiths, 2014), social-networking addiction (Kuss & Griffiths, 2011a, 2011b; Ryan et al., 2014), and smartphone addiction (Elhai, Dvorak, Levin, & Hall, 2017). The empirical data reported in online addiction studies demonstrate that some *difficulty controlling online behavior* correlates with a variety of social and psychological problems (for reviews see Andreassen et al., 2016; Griffiths et al., 2014; Young, 2017). However, whether difficulty controlling online behavior is an *addiction* is highly controversial debate (e.g., Starcevic & Aboujaoude, 2016; Widyanto & Griffiths, 2006, 2007).

The online addiction approach has been widely criticized by both researchers and mental health practitioners (Starcevic & Aboujaoude, 2016; Tokunaga, 2015). Several reviews highlight the conceptual and methodological problems with the addiction approach (e.g., Kardefelt-Winther, 2014a, 2014b, 2014c; Starcevic & Aboujaoude, 2017; Widyanto & Griffiths, 2006, 2007). As Tokunaga's (2015) review describes, the addiction paradigm's major limitations are its "lack of standardized diagnostic criteria, conceptual inconsistencies, underdeveloped theory, and an absence of underlying theory in the body of research on Internet addiction" (p. 139).

From the beginning, early critiques of the concept of Internet addiction, and the disease metaphor it employs, argued that it pathologized otherwise normal online behaviors such as sending messages, playing games, and interacting with people (Beard & Wolf, 2001; Grohol, 1999; Shaffer, Hall, & Vander Bilt, 2000). In the decades since those initial arguments, scholars have identified other limitations of the addiction approach, summarized below.

One critique of the addiction approach is that, compared to other addictions, the negative consequences of Internet addiction seem relatively mild. Addictions are serious conditions that to merit clinical attention. Addictive behaviors result in serious functional impairment over time (Billieux, Maurage, Lopez-Fernandez, Kuss, & Griffiths, 2015; Carbonell & Panova 2017). According to Tokunaga's review, "Empirical support for 'negative outcomes' in the population of normal Internet users indicates that those who lose awareness, attention, intention, or control over their Internet use experience modest ill effects on their offline social involvement" (2015, p. 151). For a majority of people, difficulty controlling Internet use results in *relatively mild* or *moderate* functional difficulties that are far less severe than the serious life problems associated with other behavioral addictions (Caplan, 2003; LaRose et al., 2003). Notably, Tokunaga (2015) observed that using the term addiction "trivializes 'real' or medically recognized addictions, such as substance dependence" (p. 139).

Another significant drawback of the addiction approach is that is largely atheoretical (Caplan, 2002; Weinstein & Lejoyeux, 2010). For example, Van Rooij and Karderfelt-Winter (2017) argued, "there are serious issues" with the Internet gaming disorder literature because "the field lacks basic theory" (p. 128). Lee, Ho, and Lwin's (2017) recent review concluded that social networking addiction studies are overly descriptive and lack conceptual models. The same authors make a comparable argument about the growing popularity of neurophysiological approaches to online addictions, which often lack explanatory power (for reviews see Cerniglia et al., 2017; Griffiths, Pontes, & Kuss, 2015; Kuss & Griffiths, 2012; Park, Han, & Roh, 2017). The recent neurological studies have also been descriptive and insufficiently theory-driven. Here, Lee et al., (2017) argued, "even though it shows how the neural and physiological activity correlates with addictive tendencies, there are no distinct communication paradigms that undergird such research" (p. 314).

Without sufficiently detailed theory, it is impossible to operationalize and measure key variables. Critics have challenged the validity of online addiction measures (see Laconi, Rodgers, & Chabrol, 2014). Most research in this tradition involves self-report surveys that ask participants if they experience symptoms of Internet addiction. Moreover, the scales used to study online addictions have not been validated by clinicians.

Additionally, the methods rely on self-administered surveys rather than objective clinical assessment. The problem here is that "only clinical (interview-based) studies are suitable to claim that a certain behavior is truly pathological" (Maraz, Király & Demetrovics, 2015, p. 153). Across studies using the same scale, researchers may choose different cut-off points or different criteria for labeling someone as addicted. There is no guiding theory or standard about why having four symptoms or more on a checklist indicates addiction while someone with three symptoms is considered as asymptomatic (non-addicts).

Another limitation of the addiction studies is that data are collected from samples of relatively healthy people instead of diagnosed patients (Van Rooij & Karderfelt-Winter, 2017). LaRose (2015) argues that most addiction studies have not included people with "pathology that met the criteria for causing serious life consequences" (p. 366). Maraz et al.

(2003) noted, "From a statistical point of view, an instrument that has not been tested against a clinically valid (diagnosed) group is unsuitable to assess the disorder" (p. 153).

In 2013, the American Psychiatric Association (APA) chose not to include pathological Internet use and Internet gaming disorder in the Diagnostic and Statistical Manual V (Tokunaga, 2015, Petry & O' Brien, 2013). Despite the vigorous debate, the APA decided to include Internet Gaming Disorder in an appendix identifying it as condition warranting more clinical research.

As the discussion above demonstrates, researchers have raised concerns about the validity of the concept of online addiction and measures used to observe it. The next section presents cognitive models that researchers proposed as alternatives to the addiction paradigm.

Cognitive Approaches: Problematic Online Habits

As an alternative to the addiction paradigm, researchers proposed cognitive models to explain problematic Internet use. Both the cognitive-behavioral model (Caplan, 2002, 2010; Davis, 2001) and the social cognitive approach (LaRose et al., 2003) viewed the problem as a pattern of difficulty controlling thoughts and behaviors involving the Internet. Rather than using an addiction metaphor, these models conceptualized problematic Internet use as *cognitive and behavioral processes*. Theoretically, cognitive approaches to problematic Internet use emphasize the importance of explaining how and why thought and behavior interact to create problematic habits that can range in strength from harmless to debilitating.

Two models, the socialcognitive model of media habits and the cognitive-behavioral model of problematic Internet use, have proven useful for both building theory and guiding research on nonclinical populations of everyday Internet users. Together, these cognitive approaches can help organize and summarize previous literature and help guide future work. After briefly explaining the two cognitive models, following sections will integrate them into a model of problematic online habits.

Social Cognitive / Habits Model. The addiction literature primarily focuses on the most extreme cases and assumes that non-addicts are a homogenous group. Alternatively, the social cognitive model assumes that severity of online habit strength varies along a range from mundane to extreme (LaRose, 2010, 2015; LaRose et al., 2003; LaRose & Eastin, 2004; LaRose, Lin, Eastin, & Gregg, 2001). Drawing on Bandura's (1991) earlier social cognitive model, online habit research offers valuable new insights into the overlap of the Internet addiction, problematic Internet Use (PIU), and deficient-regulation (DSR) perspectives. LaRose and colleagues used social cognitive theory's concept of deficient self-regulation and a theory of media habits to propose a model that explains *both* the conscious and unconscious processes that are driving habituated online behavior.

Here, LaRose and colleagues have argued across a number of papers that, "the indicators of so-called 'media addictions' may be reinterpreted as markers of deficient self-regulation and the process of addiction as the struggle to maintain effective self-regulation over problematic media behavior" (LaRose et al., 2003, p. 233; see also LaRose, 2015). In other words, as a cognitive process, habituation is a "joint operation of controlled and automatic thinking" and as habits get stronger, "conscious control, predicated on consideration of the expected outcomes (or gratification expectations) of media behavior decreases" (LaRose et al., 2003, p. 234).

An important contribution of the social cognitive model is its conceptual detail, including its ability to explain the role unconscious cognitive processes may play in problematic online habits. LaRose (2010) argues that "the notion of media habits has been used to refine social cognitive explanations for losses of conscious self-control over Internet use," and further suggests that "media habits are automatic and do not involve conscious intentions" (p. 143).

The social cognitive model also explains the process whereby online habits develop. The theory proposes that habits arise from a reward-learning process where behaviors are associated with rewarding outcomes (LaRose, Eastin, & Gregg, 2001). For example, online habits are fueled by positive outcome expectations of online behavior, including improved self-esteem, enhanced social relationships, and mood regulation (LaRose & Eastin, 2004; LaRose et al., 2003; Song, LaRose, Eastin, & Lin, 2004). In other words, a process of reward-learning results in people associating online activity with improved moods and that expectation drives habituation. Later, environmental cues may instigate the routinized behavior.

The social cognitive model also provides a detailed explanation of the cyclical nature of deficient self-regulation and negative outcomes, where habits self-perpetuate through feedback processes. As habits strengthen, they begin to operate below the level of conscious awareness, which is why habits can become difficult to control. LaRose and Eastin (2004) described the process as a "downward spiral" into problematic usage (p. 263). Tokunaga (2015) explained, "habits involve a tight cyclical loop of cues, routines, and rewards" (p. 145). In sum, the social cognitive model offers a detailed conceptual account of how people may begin to lose conscious control of online behaviors as habitual use strengthens.

For researchers interested in explaining and predicting problematic online habits, one important goal is to develop a conceptual account explaining factors that reinforce or weaken problematic online habits. The social cognitive approach describes a reward-learning process that explicates how habits form. The cognitive-behavioral model, presented next, provides a detailed conceptual narrative articulating why some people are more likely to find online social interaction particularly rewarding and, thus, habit-forming.

The Cognitive-Behavioral Model. The cognitive-behavioral model of problematic Internet use (Caplan, 2002; Davis, 2001) developed around the same time as the social cognitive approach and shares many of the same assumptions. The cognitive-behavioral model argues that difficulty controlling Internet use is the result of a pattern of maladaptive thoughts and behavior that arise from pre-existing psychosocial problems, called distal predictors (Caplan, 2002, 2003; Davis, 2001; Davis et al., 2002). Specifically, the model argues that emotional and social problems, such as depression or social anxiety, are distal predictors that predispose some people to develop online habits that may become problematic (Davis, 2001). For example, distal problems with loneliness or social anxiety may lead people to develop patterns of using the Internet for mood alteration (i.e., habits) and develop a preference for online social interaction that contributes to habituation (Caplan, 2003, 2005).

At the time of its introduction in the early 2000s, the cognitive-behavioral model made a necessary distinction between *specific* and *generalized* forms of problematic Internet use. Early Internet use only offered a handful of content-specific functions that might be habit forming such as online gambling, stock trading, and sexual material. Davis (2001) argued that such stimuli-specific problems were not unique to the Internet and would likely be manifested in some alternative way if the individual were unable to access the Internet. On the other hand, Davis described *generalized problematic Internet use* as a general overuse of the Internet to procrastinate and avoid responsibilities. In my work, I argued that generalized problematic Internet use occurred among people who were "drawn to the experience of being online, in, and of itself" (Caplan, 2002, p. 556). In other words, I was suggesting generalized problematic Internet use was rewarding because of the "unique social context available on the Internet" (Caplan, 2002, p. 557). At the time, communication researchers focused on distinguishing the characteristics of computer-mediated interaction from in-person conversations. Many of the affordances associated with early online communication resulted in greater anonymity, greater control over self-presentation, and less potential risk compared to in-person interaction (Walther, 1996). I argued that certain people were particularly drawn to the features of online social interaction because of these affordances (Caplan, 2003, 2005). Fifteen years ago, the idea of generalized PIU described the problems associated with the unique online activities that did not have offline counterparts.

Today, the concept of generalized PIU is less useful (Pawlikowski, Nader, Burger, Stieger, & Brand, 2014) and it is becoming increasingly important to recognize different online habits (Laconi, Tricard, & Chabrol, 2015; Montag et al., 2015; Tokunaga & Rains, 2010). For example, the communicative affordances of texting are different from those on Instagram or Snapchat. Further, it is challenging to separate online context from its content. In fact, some of the fastest-growing areas of research on problematic Internet use pertain to different online activities that do not have analogous offline counterparts, such as massively multiplayer gaming (Billieux, Thorens et al. 2015; Griffiths, Pontes, & Demetrovics, 2014; Pontes & Griffiths, 2015), texting (Billieux, 2012; Chiu, 2014; Sultan, 2014), social networking (Grifths, Kuss, & Demetrovics, 2014; Kuss & Griffiths, 2011a, 2011b; LaRose, Kim, & Peng, 2011). Given the wide variety of mediated channels people use (Ramirez & Zhang, 2007), there are no longer many *general* characteristics of online interaction. People use many different applications, platforms, and technologies, each with unique and specific types of communicative affordances and features. Snapchat allows users to share video, images, and text that disappear after a short time. Instagram allows people to create an ever-changing online profile that people follow. These are two small examples of unique affordances associated with different forms of mediated interaction. Thus, rather than a generalized online context, people today employ a variety of mediated channels that change the interpersonal process in unique ways.

Research has identified several maladaptive cognitive predictors of problematic habit strength (Caplan, 2003, 2005). Studies demonstrate that preference for online social interaction (a cognition in the sense that it is a preference or value) is associated with stronger and more problematic online habits (e.g., Caplan, 2003, 2005, 2010; Casale, Tella, & Fioravanti, 2013; Fioravanti, Dèttore, & Casale, 2012; Ye & Lin, 2015).[3] Similarly, other research has demonstrated that metacognitions, such as appreciating the ability to escape online and appreciating the enhanced communicative control online both predicted online habit strength (Casale, Caplan, & Fioravanti, 2016). Research on maladaptive cognitions reveals that self-related metacognitive beliefs are associated with online habit strength (Spada, Langston, Nikčević, & Moneta, 2008).

Studies support the cognitive-behavioral model's claim that maladaptive cognitions mediate the link between well-being and habit strength (Caplan, 2005; Casale, Lecchi, & Fiorvaranti, 2015; Casale et al., 2016; Tokunaga & Rains, 2010). For example, one study revealed that the association between social anxiety and online habit strength was mediated by a preference for online social interaction (Caplan, 2007). The study also found people with higher anxiety reported a greater preference for online social interaction, stronger habits, and more negative outcomes.

The cognitive approaches reviewed above suggest difficulty controlling online behavior is most usefully conceptualized as a problematic online habit. From the cognitive perspectives, habits become problematic when they strengthen to the point of creating problems in one's personal and professional life.

Organizing and Summarizing 20 Years of Research: Three Common Threads

The habit framework provides a useful way of organizing the disparate lines of research to glean some common patterns that we can confidently say have empirical support. Three common threads run through the last two decades of empirical research on problematic online habits (Tokunaga & Rains, 2010, 2016). First, research demonstrates that problematic outcomes arise from the compulsive or habitual aspect of online behavior, rather than due to excessive activity or overuse (e.g., Caplan & High, 2006). Put differently, the amount of time online is not the problem; rather, the negative outcomes are results of diminished conscious control of online behavior (LaRose, 2010). It is the habit strength, not the amount of time engaged, that seems to create problems.

Across the literature, a second consistent finding is that problematic online habits are motivated by the desire for mood alteration. Despite the many differences between approaches to studying problematic Internet use, most emphasize using the Internet to alleviate dysphoric moods, loneliness, and depression. The social cognitive theory provides a detailed explanation of *why* deficient self-regulation is commonly associated with motivations to alter mood. From the habit perspective, the improved mood is an expected reward outcome that drives the habituation process. As people increasingly rely on going online to alter their mood, the habit strengthens (Caplan, 2002; LaRose et al., 2003; Song et al., 2004). Consequently, stress and other psychosocial problems lead to increased habit formation as users increasingly rely on the Internet to alleviate dysphoric feelings. Habitual usage develops from a dependence on interactive media to cheer up, alleviate boredom, feel less anxious, or less lonely (LaRose et al. 2003). Moreover, as stress or negative moods increase, habits strengthen, resulting in less behavior control (LaRose, 2010).

A third theme throughout the literature is that problematic online habits are related to online social behavior and offline interpersonal problems (Caplan & High, 2011; Chou et al., 2017; Tokunaga & Rains, 2016). People who have difficulty controlling their Internet use are also likely to be attracted to its interpersonal affordances. Moreover, online habit strength is associated with indicators of diminished interpersonal or relational skill (Caplan, 2005; Ryan et al., 2014).

Problematic Online Habits as an Interpersonal Communication Issue

Problematic online habits can be viewed as an interpersonal communication problem. This section presents three lines of research that explore how interpersonal communication relates to problematic online habits. The first section examines the links between online social activity and problematic habit strength. Next, research has identified a variety of interpersonal and relational problems that predict problematic online habit strength. Finally, researchers have begun examining how one's online habits create problems and conflict in their personal relationships. Together these three areas of research highlight the central associations between online habits and interpersonal communication.

Problematic Habits and Online Interpersonal Behaviors

One of the most consistent and robust findings in early studies of problematic online habits was that people who reported negative outcomes associated with their Internet use were also especially drawn to the interpersonal functions of the Internet, including meeting new people, developing online relations, chatting, and seeking emotional support from others online (Caplan, 2002, 2003, 2005; Davis, Flett & Besser,

2002; Chak & Leung, 2004; McKenna & Bargh, 2000; Morahan-Martin, 1999; Young, 1996, 1998; Young & Rogers, 1998).

Before Internet use was common in most homes, Young (1996) noted that Internet dependent users spent most of their time online using chat rooms or messaging applications. Around the same time, Scherer (1997) made a similar observation; compared to "non-dependent" students, "Internet-dependent" college students were especially attracted to the unique social experiences available online. The Internet-dependent students were 26% more likely to go online to meet new people.

In another early study, Wallace (1999) observed "synchronous [i.e., chat and instant messaging] spaces are not the only compelling Internet environments, but they do seem to be chief culprits in excessive Internet use" (p. 182). Kubey, Lavin, and Barrows (2001) demonstrated that Internet-dependent students used synchronous chat applications significantly more frequently than non-dependent students. Studies by Morahan-Martin and Schumacher (2000, 2003) revealed that people who exhibited problematic Internet use were more likely to go online to meet new people, chat with others, seek online emotional support, participate in online forums, and play interactive games. Thus, as one review noted, "the unique social interactions made possible by the Internet are central to the development of problematic habits" (Morahan-Martin, 2008, p. 335).

Implicit in many of the studies reviewed above is the idea that there is something about the online social context, the interpersonal affordances of mediated communication, that appeals to some people and, perhaps, may be a key precursor to problematic habit development (Caplan, 2005; Morahan-Martin, 2008). The point here is not that social uses are the most problematic or only problematic forms of Internet use. Rather, research consistently indicates that problematic habits are especially prominent among interpersonal Internet use (for reviews see Caplan & High, 2011; Morahan-Martin, 2008; Tokunaga & Raines, 2010).

More recently, studies of modern interpersonal technologies such as social networking, online gaming, and texting reveal a similar pattern. Despite the changing platforms and affordances, online social behavior is still associated with habit strength. There are growing lines of research on gaming, social networking, and smartphone habits.

Contemporary online games frequently entail some type of interpersonal interaction with other players that one may know offline or only online. This is especially true in games that require the development of guilds, groups, or teams (e.g., massively multiplayer online role-playing games; MMORPGs). King and Delfabbro (2016) uncovered a significant correlation between preference for MMORPG games and problematic gaming. The study also indicated that problematic gaming was associated with the proportion of gaming time spent with strangers. One consistent pattern in the problematic gaming research is that social motivations are associated with compulsive gaming (Van Rooij, Schoenmakers, Van de Eijnden, & Van de Mheen, 2010). Problematic online gaming is especially prominent in role-playing games (Lemmens, & Hendriks, 2016).

Research on social networking reveals similar patterns of habits strong enough to create functional difficulties (for reviews see Andreassen et al., 2016; LaRose et al., 2011; Kuss & Griffiths, 2016). A recent Pew report revealed that social networking is one of the most popular online activities because of its social affordances (Greenwood, Perrin, & Duggan, 2016). Researchers have established a significant literature on problematic social networking habits (for reviews see Carbonell & Panova, 2017; Griffiths et al., 2014; Kuss & Griffiths, 2011b; LaRose et al., 2011; Ryan et al., 2014). Studies of smartphone habits indicate that using the phone for social networking was a stronger predictor of habit strength than using the device for gaming (Jeong, Kim, Yum, & Hwang, 2016).

Thus far, the literature reviewed above supports claims associating online interpersonal behaviors and problematic online habits. Why are online social activities especially related to problematic habits? The next section attempts to answer the question with an interpersonal and relational deficit hypothesis.

Interpersonal and Relational Deficits and Problematic Online Habits

The section below presents an *interpersonal and relational resource deficit framework* to explain problematic online habits (Caplan, 2005; Tokunaga & Rains, 2016). The research presented here demonstrates that problematic online habit strength is often correlated with lower social skills and other relational resource deficits. The interpersonal and relational deficit hypothesis suggests that people use online applications to compensate for offline social difficulties and relational problems (Caplan, 2005; Tokunaga & Rains, 2016) and, over time, the online activity can become habituated. Whereas early research focused primarily on how social skill deficits contributed to problematic habits (e.g., Caplan, 2005), more recent research has identified a broader range of interpersonal and relational resource deficits that correlate with online habit strength (Tokunaga & Rains, 2016). Here, Tokunaga (2015) describes "communication deficits and interpersonal failures as the kernel out of which [problematic] habits grow" and, consequently, "communication researchers are thus well-positioned to make significant contributions to the literature on this phenomenon" (p. 146).

Using Riggio and Zimmerman's (1991) model of social skill, one of my earlier studies proposed a social skills deficit hypothesis predicting that people lacking self-presentational confidence would be particularly drawn to online social interaction (Caplan, 2005). Results from the initial study supported the proposed association between lower skill and habit strength; the effect was mediated by a preference for online social interaction (Caplan, 2005). The model implies a compensation process whereby people attempt to use mediated communication to offset "real world" interpersonal shortcomings by capitalizing on the interpersonal affordances of mediated communication (e.g., decreased nonverbal cues, increased editing time) in ways that help them feel more confident and effective (Caplan, 2003, 2005; Walther, 1996). Here, the research drew from Walther's hyperpersonal model, which emphasized the potential attractiveness of reduced nonverbal cues and suggested that people could exploit the reduced cues to be more effective at self-presentation (Walther, 1996). In other words, the skill deficit hypothesis suggests that people with interpersonal problems may be drawn to unique communicative affordances available in online social interactions and develop strong habits to compensate for their offline skill deficits (Caplan, 2005).

More recently, studies have revealed that low social skills are just one example of a wider set of interpersonal and relational resources deficits associated with problematic online habit strength (Tokunaga & Rains, 2016). One recent meta-analysis of 22 studies noted that social anxiety is associated with feeling more comfortable online, online gaming habit strength, and general severity of problematic online habits, but it is not associated with time spent online (Prizant-Passal, Shechner, & Aderka, 2016). Recent studies have employed the deficit hypothesis to examine relationships between social skill deficits and online social networking habits. In a review of 24 studies, Ryan et al. (2014) observed that the social skill deficits hypothesis successfully predicted Facebook habits.

Research exploring links between social skills and online gaming habits has produced inconsistent results. Consistent with the skill deficit hypothesis, a study on MMOG (Massively Multiplayer Online Games) players found that gaming habit strength was related to lower social skills and a cognitive preference for online social (Liu & Peng, 2009). Another study examining online video game involvement and social competence reported mixed results (Kowert & Oldmeadow, 2013). While some aspects of social skill were correlated with gaming involvement, others were not, or were correlated in the opposite direction than expected. However, the study found, "more involved video game players perceive themselves as less verbally fluent, with difficulties in initiating and guiding conversation" (Kowert & Oldmeadow, 2013, p. 1876). Lemmens et al. (2011) reported a longitudinal study revealing that low social skill predicted subsequent online gaming habit strength.

In the years since the social skill deficit model was first proposed, the research has progressed to include a wider variety of interpersonal and relational resource deficits that may lead people to develop strong online habits. Tokunaga and Rains (2016) suggested that in addition to social skill deficits, other types of interpersonal vulnerabilities, such as "deficits in offline relationships and relationship-building resources" may also predict problematic online habits (p. 169). As the following paragraphs illustrate, social skill deficit is only one of a broader set of interpersonal and relational resource deficits that are associated with problematic online habit strength. The research presented next links online habit strength with lower emotional intelligence, attachment and relational insecurity, and fear of missing out.

Emotional Intelligence. Emotional intelligence refers to a constellation of skills involving emotions including reading others' emotional signals, awareness of one's own emotions, and an ability regulate or control one's emotions (Mayer & Salovey, 1997; Salovey & Mayer, 1990). Emotional intelligence is important for successful interpersonal interactions and relationships (see Lopes, Brackett, Nezlek, Schutz, Sellin, & Salovey, 2004). Specifically, low emotional intelligence makes it more difficult to empathize, to take others' perspectives, and to read others' nonverbal cues. One study found lower emotional intelligence among college students was correlated with less positive relations with peers and more negative interactions with parents (Lopes, Salovey & Straus, 2003).

Consistent with the resource deficit hypothesis, lower levels of emotional intelligence predict stronger online habits and greater preference for online social interaction (Chong, Chye, Huan & Ang, 2014). Others have linked lower emotional intelligence with problematic online gaming habits (Parker, Summerfeldt, Tayler, Kloosterman, & Keefer, 2013), social networking habits (Hormes, Kearns, & Timko, 2014) and smartphone habit strength (Van Deursen, Bolle, Hegner, & Kommers, 2015).

Researchers have also linked problems with emotion self-regulation (a core component of EI) to stronger online habits. In one study, Hormes et al. (2014) determined that Facebook habit strength was associated with poor emotional self-regulation skills. Similarly, Casale et al. (2016) demonstrated that difficulty controlling emotions was a positive predictor of problematic online habit strength. The authors proposed that "emotional dysregulation might drive symptoms of [problematic Internet use] to a greater extent than high negative emotionality" (Casale et al., 2016, p. 84). In other words, the problematic use develops from difficulty with emotional regulation, a key component of emotional intelligence. Lower emotional intelligence also predicts greater preference for online social interaction (Chong et al., 2014) and other metacognitions associated with the perceived communicative benefits of technology-mediated interaction (e.g., appreciation for reduced nonverbal cues and increased control) (Casale et al., 2013).

The important theoretical question here is, "Why is online social interaction particularly attractive to people with lower emotional intelligence?" The hyperpersonal account (Walther, 1996) would argue that online, people rely less on reading their partners' nonverbal emotional cues. For people with lower emotional perception skill, online contexts may require less cognitive effort and afford greater confidence than face-to-face conversations. Online, people may have to try harder to emphasize their own emotional cues, which might make it easier for lower emotional intelligence people to notice. The hypotheses above are the type of predictions that can help direct future theory-driven research into interpersonal predictors of problematic online habits.

Thus far, the discussion has focused primarily on the idea of problematic online habits developing as a byproduct of turning to online interaction to compensate for offline social and emotional skill deficits. However, in addition to low competencies, interpersonal resource deficits may draw people to online behavior to compensate for *relational insecurities* and *anxieties*.

Attachment & Relational Insecurity. Whereas emotional intelligence and social skill are competencies, interpersonal insecurity has more to do with anxiety around intimacy. This section argues that people may use online social interaction to compensate for relational insecurities and unmet attachment needs (e.g., belonging, attention, affection, appreciation, intimacy).

Attachment theory was originally developed to explain how infants bond with their caregivers, arguing that children need to establish a "safe base," or secure attachment with a caregiver who regularly and reliably meets the infants' needs for attention, affection, and nurturing (Anisworth, 1979; Bowlby, 1958). The theory suggests that early experiences with caregivers shape children's views and beliefs about interpersonal relationships that persist into adulthood. The immense literature on adult attachment highlights the importance of attachment security in facilitating healthy intimate relationships (Feeney, Noller, & Roberts, 2000; Kirkpatrick, & Hazan, 1994). Among adults, attachment security refers to being comfortable with variations in emotional intimacy, both in terms of closeness and distance (Bartholomew, 1990; Bartholomew & Shaver, 1998).

Whereas social anxiety is rooted in fear of negative evaluation by others, attachment insecurity reflects fear about emotional vulnerability, interpersonal intimacy, and closeness (Bartholomew, 1990; Brennan & Shaver, 1995; Hazan & Shaver, 1987). According to adult attachment research, anxious, or preoccupied, adults are more likely to crave closeness and pursue intimacy whereas avoidant adults often seek distance to reduce anxiety. Avoidant adults use distancing behaviors as a defense against fear of people getting too close, and preoccupied/anxious adults use pursuit as a defense against being abandoned or alone (Bartholomew, 1990; Brennan & Shaver, 1995; Hazan & Shaver, 1987).

Researchers argue that problematic social networking habits may develop when people rely too heavily on interpersonal technology to fulfill attachment needs. Oldmeadow, Quinn, and Kowert (2013) proposed, "Facebook could potentially serve needs for belonging, closeness, and security for those with high levels of attachment anxiety and/or avoidance. This, in turn, suggests that Facebook may provide a sense of closeness or belonging that satisfies attachment needs in individuals who are otherwise anxious or avoidant in close personal relationships" (p. 1142). Thus, people with greater needs for closeness or distance may initially turn to Facebook use to meet those needs and, over time, some may develop habitual use.

Similar to earlier arguments about preference for online social interaction, research on attachment and social networking suggests "social networking sites like Facebook may offer a form of social connecting that is particularly appealing to certain types of individuals whose needs for belonging and connection with others are not fully realized in offline social interactions" (Oldmeadow et al., 2013, p. 114). In one study, Kalaitzaki and Birtchnell (2014) revealed that poor parental bonding early in life had an indirect effect on adult Internet addiction that was mediated by difficulty relating to others offline. In other words, early attachment problems resulted in greater interpersonal and relational difficulties in young adulthood that contributed to problematic online habits. Other studies suggest that, for the most extreme cases of attachment disorders, online gaming may help people with disorganized attachment dissociate, an attempt to self-protect from memories of neglect during childhood (Schimmenti, Guglielmucci, Barbasio, & Granieri, 2012).

For insecurely attached people, online habits may develop from the reward outcomes associated with social technologies that help regulate their insecurity (Campbell & Marshall, 2011; Drouin, Miller, & Dibble, 2014; Monacis, de Palo, Griffiths, & Sinatra, 2017). An insecure and jealous girlfriend might experience brief reassurance from constantly checking her partner's accounts and finding no threat. There is also a rewarding outcome if the jealousy leads to discovery of infidelity—in this case, the reward is a reliable confirmation of suspicions. During times of jealousy and stress, online checking habits may create problems in the relationship, leading to greater jealousy and more habitual online behavior (Dunn, & Billet 2017; Muscanell, Guadango, Rice, & Murphy, 2013; Stewart, Dainton, & Goodboy, 2014).

In other cases, where attachment insecurity makes closeness uncomfortable, social networking offers interpersonal affordances that appeal to those who have a greater need for emotional distance. Online habits may offer a way to compensate for discomfort with closeness. Monacis et al. (2017) argued that people with dismissive/avoidant attachment "tend to satisfy their need of social belonging by using the online format, which affords such a dismissive approach to close relationship by maintaining a 'safe distance' from others" (np). One study suggested that insecure attachment led people to use social networking to "hold relationships at a psychological arm's distance" (Nitzburg & Farber, 2013, p. 1182). On the other hand, Schimmenti, Passanisi, Gervaisi, Manzella, and Famá (2013) found no support for the claim that avoidant attachment predicted social networking habits. Future research needs to study different types of attachment insecurity and their relationship to compensatory online habits. The idea that people who are uncomfortable with closeness might appreciate some of the intimacy-reducing affordances of interpersonal technologies is an important direction for research to pursue.

Fear of Missing Out. Recent studies indicate that fear of missing out (FOMO) is associated with problematic online habits (Przybylski, Murayama, DeHaan, & Gladwell, 2013; Wegman, Oberst, & Stodt,

2017). Przybylski et al. (2013) define FOMO as "a pervasive apprehension that others might be having rewarding experiences from which one is absent" and "is characterized by the desire to stay continually connected with what others are doing" (p. 1841). Using this definition, Przybylski et al. (2013) developed a measure of FOMO that included items such as "I fear my friends are having more rewarding experiences than me," "I get worried when I find out my friends are having fun without me," "it is important that I understand my friends' inside jokes," and "I get anxious when I don't know what my friends are up to" (p. 1847).

Although conceptually distinct, there are clear similarities between attachment insecurity and FOMO. Whereas attachment security primarily pertains to intimate relationships, FOMO involves one's broader peer network rather than one's closest relationships. Researchers have used the interpersonal and relational resource deficit approach to explain how FOMO might work in conjunction with attachment insecurity to promote problematic online habits (Blackwell, Leaman, Tramposch, Osborne, & Liss, 2017). For example, Przybylski et al. (2013) argued, "FOMO could serve as a mediator linking deficits in psychological needs to social media engagement" (p. 1842). In one study, the results revealed that FOMO mediated associations between well-being (anxiety and depression) and problematic social networking habit (Oberst, Wegmann, Stodt, Brand, & Chamarro, 2017). Similarly, Buglass, Binder, Betts and Underwood (2017) presented longitudinal data indicating "that decreased self-esteem might motivate a potentially detrimental cycle of FOMO-inspired online [social networking] use" (p. 248). These studies offer empirical support for a mediation hypothesis whereby FOMO mediates the link between a more distal insecurity and social networking habit strength.

Several studies have documented the empirical association between FOMO and various forms of problematic online habits (Beyens, Frison, & Eggermont, 2016; Blackwell et al., 2017; Kuss & Griffiths, 2017; Wegman, Oberst, Stodet, Brand, 2017). Consistent with the view that online habituation derives from a reward-learning process of feedback and reinforcement, other scholars suggest FOMO driven habits can "plunge the user into a spiral of behavior which is unlikely to offer them the sense of control or social belonging they increasingly crave" (Buglass et al., 2017, p. 254). Further indicating habit strength, participants with higher FOMO "were more likely to give in to the temptation of composing and checking text messages and emails while operating motor vehicles" (Przybylski et al., 2013, p. 1847).

Summary of Interpersonal and Relational Resource Deficits and Problematic Online Habits. This section presented an interpersonal and relational resource deficit perspective to organize and integrate research on predictors of online habit strength. From this perspective, one important reason that problematic habits are associated with online social activity is that people attempt to capitalize on the affordances of various interpersonal technologies to compensate for lower social skills and diminished relational resources. Thus, interpersonal and relational variables, especially those regarding competencies and mood management, can help explain individual differences in online habit strength. In sum, this section suggests that one important predictor of online habituation is deficits in core social and interactional abilities and further reinforces the argument that problematic online habits are, to a significant extent, interpersonal problems. The next section examines how problematic online habits affect offline relationships.

Interpersonal and Relational Consequences of Problematic Online Habits

Online habits become problematic when they create difficulties in one's close personal relationships. Initially, early research proposed that spending time too much time online would displace time that would otherwise have been spent with offline relational partners (e.g., Kraut et al., 1998). The displacement hypothesis argued that people were thought to be so busy online that they did not have sufficient time or resources to devote to important offline relationships. However, research results presented in this section reveal strong support for the idea that online habit strength, rather than displacement, is a better predictor of offline relationship problems. In a study designed to test the unique effects of displacement and habituation on relationships, Kerkhof et al. (2011) observed that it is "neither the frequency of the Internet use that is problematic for close relationships nor the combination of frequency and compulsive Internet use but uniquely the compulsive use of the Internet that is problematic for relationships" (p. 164).

The habituation model presented in this chapter suggests that, when people use online interaction to compensate for various interpersonal deficits and to regulate affect, they develop strong reward-outcome expectations (especially about the interpersonal affordances of online activity and mood alteration that further reinforce habituation). Thus, despite people using online activity to overcome interpersonal deficits, habitual online behavior later contributes to interpersonal problems offline. As previous sections noted, online habituation is conceptualized as a cyclical process, rather than a linear one (LaRose et al., 2011). In a meta-analysis of Internet habit research, Tokunaga (2017) identified "some support for the reciprocal, sometimes cyclical relationships found in the psychosocial problems–Internet habits relationships" (p. 14).Thus, it may not be until habits reach a certain strength than they begin to create offline relational problems. Those types of relational problems may further exacerbate online habit strength and lead to further personal difficulties.

The Poor Get Poorer Hypothesis. Researchers have presented evidence supporting a "poor get poorer" hypothesis whereby individuals with little offline social capital experience worse outcomes from the same online activities that those with greater social resources benefit from (Forest & Wood, 2012; Herman, M. Van Zalk, & N. Van Zalk, Kerr, & Stattin, 2014). Forest and Wood argued, "Individuals with low self-esteem recognize but do not reap the benefits of self-disclosure on Facebook" (2012, p. 295). Similarly, Clerkin, Smith, and Hames (2013) suggested "individuals who are most in need of the social benefits from Facebook may be ineffective in their communication strategies, and thereby sabotage their potential to benefit interpersonally" (p. 28).

To test the "poor get poorer" hypothesis, Clerkin et al. (2013) conducted a longitudinal study tracking changes in self-esteem and reassurance seeking on Facebook. Consistent with the poor get poorer hypothesis, the study observed "that Facebook reassurance seeking predicted lower levels of self-esteem, which in turn predicted increased feelings that one does not belong and that one is a burden" (Clerkin et al., 2013, p. 525). A longitudinal study of loneliness and Facebook motives indicated that using Facebook contributed to greater loneliness when people used it to compensate for social skill deficits. Yet, people who used Facebook to make new friends indicated they were less lonely over time (Teppers, Luyckx, Klimstra, & Goossens, 2104). A longitudinal study of adolescent gamers suggested loneliness was both a cause and a consequence of problematic gaming habits (Lemmens, Valkenburg, & Peter, 2011). Similarly, Buglass et al.'s (2017) longitudinal study found "prolonged use of social network services" contributed to damaging social comparisons and feelings of social exclusion," and participants' level of FOMO indirectly "served to maintain the potentially detrimental psychological effects of such perceptions of social ineptitude" (p. 254). Thus, social networking habits that originally developed to compensate for insecurity may end up leaving people feeling more excluded and worse about themselves. Such a process is consistent with the cyclical model of online habituation presented earlier.

Now that researchers have begun to recognize associations between online habit strength and relational problems, the next important questions for theory and research to address is how and why online habits contribute to offline interpersonal problems. There is little empirical research addressing these questions. However, as the next section explains, the extant research does suggest that online habits create relational conflict and weaken intimacy.

Effects on Romantic Relationships. In close relationships, one person's online habits can contribute to problems for the other partner. Understanding how online behavior impacts offline relationships is becoming increasingly necessary for studying close personal relationships. As Kerkhof et al. (2011) argued, "studying the antecedents and consequences of Internet use within the context of relationships can shed light on the micro dynamics of how new media affects well-being and allows us to explore its social effect" (p. 167).

Some of the earliest research on the relational effects of maladaptive Internet habits involved relational conflict and dissatisfaction resulting from one partner's strong online sexual habits (Meerkerk et al., 2006). Early work on "cybersex addiction" (Schneider, 2000) found that, upon learning about their partner's online sexual habits, the "respondents felt hurt, betrayal, rejection, abandonment, devastation, loneliness, shame, isolation, humiliation, jealousy, and anger, as well as loss of self-esteem" (p. 38). It is difficult to distinguish whether relational harm was due to the potentially transgressive nature of the content (i.e., sexual online activity) versus harm resulting from the strength of the habit, or deficient self-regulation. The research reviewed below indicates that that negative effects of online habits may involve more than just transgressive behavior, rather the habit strength itself can be a source of conflict that erodes of intimacy and relational closeness

Data from longitudinal studies indicate that online habit strength erodes relational intimacy by increasing distrust (Musses et al., 2015). In a longitudinal study of online habit strength in new marriages, researchers observed that online habit strength predicted lower subsequent levels of marital well-being (within-partner), and not vice-versa. In the study, people with strong online habits later "felt less intimate with their partner, less passionate about their partner, and more excluded by their partner" (Kerkhof et al., 2011, p 159). Additionally, the compulsive users reported engaging in less relational maintenance and greater concealment about the habit over time. In other words, data indicated that online habit strength eroded romantic intimacy. The researchers concluded that "compulsive Internet use, beyond the frequency of Internet use, contributed to explaining variance in the respective indicators of relationship quality" (Kerkhof et al., 2011, p. 159). Thus, the data presented here suggest online habit strength may weaken intimacy, eroding trust, breeding concealment, and creat emotional distance between partners.

At this point, researchers need to begin identifying mediating variables that can help explain how or why online habit strength may weaken intimacy in romantic relationships. One hypothesis that researchers have explored is that online habit strength contributes to relational conflict and weakens intimacy.

Data on social networking and relational health supports the claim that conflict mediates the process in which online habit strength results in relational damage (Clayton 2014, Clayton, Nagurney, & Smith, 2013). For example, in a study on Facebook use, researchers observed a "significant mediational effect for [social network]-related conflict, such that SNS use predicted negative relationship outcomes (i.e., infidelity and breakup/divorce) through SNS-related conflict (i.e., jealousy and conflict pertaining to users' SNS use)" (Clayton et al., 2014, p. 719).

Research on problematic gaming habits has revealed similar patterns of associations between strong gaming habits and relational problems. Qualitative researchers have explored the experiences of the non-gaming spouses, or "gamer widows" (Northrup & Shumway, 2014). One study (Northrup & Shumway, 2014) examined postings in an online support group for people whose partners had strong gaming habits (i.e., World of Warcraft Widows). The postings described negative effects that the spouse's online habits have *on the marriage and broader family functioning*. For instance, the "widows" described struggling with a lack of help from the gamer with managing the household and child-rearing.

In a separate study, interviews with gaming widows described similar concerns over marital roles and responsibility. Here, widows were concerned with trying to compensate for the unavailable gaming spouse (Lianekhammy & Van de Venne, 2015). Gaming widows also reported serious personal effects associated with their spouse's gaming habit including feelings of resentment, hopelessness, anger, and frustration. In online support forum postings, gamer widows' "negative emotions appear to stem from situations created by their husband's online game playing and their own inability to stop the presence of gaming from being so problematic in their relationships" (Lianekhammy & Van de Venne, 2015, p. 461).

Gamer-widows in these studies also shared some detail about how the gaming habit hurts the marital relationship by weakening emotional intimacy. Northrup and Shumway (2014) surveyed partners of "online video game addicts" and observed that the gamer partner's habit diminished the couple's emotional connection. In the online support forums, postings mentioned feeling invisible or entirely unnoticed when their partner was gaming (Lianekhammy & Van de Venne, 2015). This observation is consistent with the habits approach, suggesting that as habit strengths, people "zone out" or become less consciously aware of both themselves and other people (LaRose & Eastin, 2004). Several postings mentioned women who "felt their husbands valued gaming relationships over their marital relationships" (Lianekhammy & Van de Venne, 2015, p. 460). In Northrup and Shumway's (2014) study, one widow felt so emotionally distant she said, "I talk to people at work in more depth than I do with my own husband" (p. 275).

Other research suggests that online habits affect sleep and bedtime routines in ways that can interfere with relational intimacy. For example, one study found those with strong gaming habits frequently stayed up after their partner went to bed alone each night (Ahlstrom Lundberg, Zabriskie, Eggett, & Lindsay, 2012). Today's mobile technology also means people can bring their habit to bed with them, being physically present, but psychologically absent (a theme that this book explores in Chapter Six).

When engaging in conflict, Northrup and Shumway (2014) observed widows argued with gamer spouses about not only about the habit itself, but also about its broader effects on the marriage and family. In response, the gaming spouses responded with defensiveness and anger. Northrup and Shumway (2014) explained, "distance between the gamer widow and the addict develops as the game is an escape from the fighting for the addict" (p. 277).

Conclusion

This chapter set out to demonstrate that problematic online habits are, to a significant extent, interpersonal communication problems. Across the dozens of measures, different definitions, and various approaches, there are three consistent themes relevant to interpersonal communication that emerge from the literature. First, from the earliest studies, researchers have noted the association between problematic online habits and online social interaction. Second, interpersonal and relational resource deficits, such as lower social skills, less emotional intelligence, insecure attachment, and fear of missing out are associated with greater preferences for mediated communication and stronger problematic habits. Although habituation is a cyclical process, interpersonal vulnerabilities may predict or contribute to subsequent online habit strength. Finally, the chapter explained how online habits might contribute to, or worsen, problems in offline relationships by instigating conflict and eroding intimacy.

The chapter presented the online habits model as a promising theoretical narrative to organize and summarize the literature. The habits perspective accounts for both the rare, yet extreme, habits described as "addictions" or "disorders" and the more common, milder types of problems that people experience because of their online habits. After two decades, the debate about the value and validity of the addiction/disorder perspectives continues. To date, researchers have noted important limitations of the addiction approach. However, the behaviors of interest in these studies do reflect some extreme degree of habit strength.

As with many of the topics covered in the current book, researchers are hindered by conceptual chaos, problematic measures and methods, and a general lack of focus. The addiction perspective's problems raise serious questions about how to continue that line of inquiry. Critics have noted problems with lack of theory, lack of progress, and an abundance of different addictions with the same basic criteria. Starcevic and Aboujaoude (2017) question whether Internet addiction is a relevant concept anymore, calling it an "increasingly inadequate concept" (p. 1). Research has found stronger support for the view that most of the problematic online habits studied reflect a spectrum of *moderate difficulties* people experience when they have trouble regulating online activity.

There is a good reason to study more than just the most extreme circumstances. This chapter emphasized the value of understanding the moderate problems that many experience as the result of relatively mild online habits. The concept of moderate, or every-day, problematic habits is also likely to be an increasingly important topic for relational and interpersonal researchers who study conflict and relational maintenance in couples. The challenge for researchers is to begin to consider online habits' role in mundane relational problems. As the rest of this book will explain, problematic online habits are just one of a myriad of interpersonal problems involving mediated communication.

Notes

1. Based on a 2017 Scopus search of title, abstract, or keywords that included any of the following terms: Internet addiction, compulsive Internet use, pathological Internet use, problematic mobile phone, problematic gaming, problematic Facebook, problematic Internet use, smartphone addiction, Facebook addiction, social networking addiction, gaming addiction, gaming disorder, problematic online gaming, or Internet addicts.
2. The term online is also quickly vanishing. Today, many people are permanently online and permanently connected with smart devices (Vorderer, & Kohring, 2013; Vorderer, Kromer, & Schneider, 2016). There is no perfect solution for describing a changing phenomenon, but for now, this book uses "online" rather than Internet where relevant. More importantly, using the term problematic online habits helps organize the literature around the theoretical framework of media habits presented below (LaRose, Lin, & Eastin, 2003). From this perspective, online habits vary in strength along a continuum of deficient self-regulation ranging from relatively mild problems to extreme cases.
3. The original study (Caplan, 2003) used the terms compulsive behavior and obsessive thoughts, but these are referred to as habits here for clarity and consistency.

References

Ahlstrom, M., Lundberg, N. R., Zabriskie, R., Eggett, D., & Lindsay, G. B. (2012). Me, my spouse, and my avatar: The relationship between marital satisfaction and playing massively multiplayer online role-playing games (MMORPGs). *Journal of Leisure Research*, 44(1), 1–22.

Ainsworth, M. S. (1979). Infant–mother attachment. *American Psychologist*, 34(10), 932–937.

American Psychiatric Association (2013). Internet gaming disorder. https://www.psychiatry.org/File%20Library/Psychiatrists/Practice/DSM/APA_DSM-5-Internet-Gaming-Disorder.pdf

Andreassen, C. S., Billieux, J., Griffiths, M. D., Kuss, D. J., Demetrovics, Z., Mazzoni, E., & Pallesen, S. (2016). The relationship between addictive use of social media and video games and symptoms of psychiatric disorders: A large-scale cross-sectional study. *Psychology of Addictive Behaviors*, 30(2), 252–262. doi:10.1037/adb0000160

Bandura, A. (1991). Social cognitive theory of self-regulation. *Organizational Behavior & Human Decision Processes*, 50(2), 248–287. doi:10.1016/0749-5978(91)90022-L

Bartholomew, K. (1990). Avoidance of intimacy: An attachment perspective. *Journal of Social and Personal Relationships*, 7(2), 147–178. doi:10.1177/0265407590072001

Bartholomew, K., & Shaver, P. R. (1998). Methods of assessing adult attachment: Do they converge? In J. A. Simpson & W. S. Rholes (Eds.), *Attachment theory and close relationships* (pp. 25–45). New York: Guilford Press.

Beard, K. W., & Wolf, E. M. (2001). Modification in the proposed diagnostic criteria for Internet addiction. *CyberPsychology & Behavior, 4*(3), 377–383.

Beyens, I., Frison, E., & Eggermont, S. (2016). "I don't want to miss a thing": Adolescents' fear of missing out and its relationship to adolescents' social needs, Facebook use, and Facebook related stress. *Computers in Human Behavior, 64*, 1–8. doi:10.1016/j.chb.2016.05.083

Billieux, J. (2012). Problematic use of the mobile phone: A literature review and a pathways model. *Current Psychiatry Reviews, 8*(4), 299–307. doi:10.2174/157340012803520522

Billieux, J., Maurage, P., Lopez-Fernandez, O., Kuss, D. J., & Griffiths, M. D. (2015). Can disordered mobile phone use be considered a behavioral addiction? An update on current evidence and a comprehensive model for future research. *Current Addiction Reports, 2*(2), 156–162. doi:10.1007/s40429-015-0054-y

Billieux, J., Thorens, G., Khazaal, Y., Zullino, D., Achab, S., & Van der Linden, M. (2015). Problematic involvement in online games: A cluster analytic approach. *Computers in Human Behavior, 43*, 242–250. doi:10.1016/j.chb.2014.10.055

Blackwell, D., Leaman, C., Tramposch, R., Osborne, C., & Liss, M. (2017). Extraversion, neuroticism, attachment style, and fear of missing out as predictors of social media use and addiction. *Personality & Individual Differences, 116*, 69–72. doi:10.1016/j.paid.2017.04.039

Bowlby, J. (1958). The nature of the child's tie to his mother. *International Journal of Psychoanalysis, 39*, 350–373.

Brennan, K. A., & Shaver, P. R. (1995). Dimensions of adult attachment, affect regulation, and romantic relationship functioning. *Personality & Social Psychology Bulletin, 21*(3), 267–283. doi:10.1177/0146167295213008

Buglass, S. L., Binder, J. F., Betts, L. R., & Underwood, J. (2017). Motivators of online vulnerability: The impact of social network site use and FOMO. *Computers in Human Behavior, 66*, 248–255. doi:10.1016/j.chb.2016.09.055

Campbell, L., & Marshall, T. (2011). Anxious attachment and relationship processes: An interactionist perspective. *Journal of Personality, 79*(6), 1219–1250. doi:10.1111/j.1467-6494.2011.00723.x

Caplan, S. E. (2002). Problematic Internet use and psychosocial well-being: Development of a theory-based cognitive-behavioral measurement instrument. *Computers in Human Behavior, 18*(5), 553–575. doi:10.1016/S0747-5632(02)00004-3

Caplan, S. E. (2003). Preference for online social interaction: A theory of problematic Internet use and psychosocial well-being. *Communication Research, 30*(6), 625–648. doi:10.1177/0093650203257842

Caplan, S. E. (2005). A social skill account of problematic Internet use. *Journal of Communication, 55*(4), 721–736. doi:10.1093/joc/55.4.721

Caplan, S. E. (2007). Relations among loneliness, social anxiety, and problematic Internet use. *CyberPsychology & Behavior, 10*(2), 234–242. doi:10.1089/cpb.2006.9963

Caplan, S. E. (2010). Theory and measurement of generalized problematic Internet use: A two-step approach. *Computers in Human Behavior, 26*(5), 1089–1097. doi:10.1016/j.chb.2010.03.012

Caplan, S. E., & High, A. C. (2006). Beyond excessive use: The interaction between cognitive and behavioral symptoms of problematic Internet use. *Communication Research Reports, 23*(4), 265–271. doi:10.1080/08824090600962516

Caplan, S. E., & High, A. C. (2011). Online social interaction, psychosocial well-being, and problematic Internet use. In K. S. Young & C. N. de Abreu (Eds.), *Internet addiction: A handbook and guide to evaluation and treatment* (pp. 35–53). Hoboken, NJ: John Wiley & Sons.

Carbonell, X., & Panova, T. (2017). A critical consideration of social networking sites' addiction potential. *Addiction Research & Theory, 25*(1), 48–57. doi:10.1080/16066359.2016.1197915

Casale, S., Caplan, S. E., & Fioravanti, G. (2016). Positive metacognitions about Internet use: The mediating role in the relationship between emotional dysregulation and problematic use. *Addictive Behaviors, 59*, 84–88. doi:10.1016/j.addbeh.2016.03.014

Casale, S., Fioravanti, G., & Rugai, L. (2016). Grandiose and vulnerable narcissists: Who is at higher risk for social networking addiction? *Cyberpsychology, Behavior, and Social Networking, 19*(8), 510–515. doi:10.1089/cyber.2016.0189

Casale, S., Lecchi, S., & Fioravanti, G. (2015). The association between psychological well-being and problematic use of Internet communicative services among young people. *The Journal of Psychology, 149*(5), 480–497. doi:10.1080/00223980.2014.905432

Casale, S., Tella, L., & Fioravanti, G. (2013). Preference for online social interactions among young people: Direct and indirect effects of emotional intelligence. *Personality & Individual Differences, 54*(4), 524–529. doi:10.1016/j.paid.2012.10.023

Cerniglia, L., Zoratto, F., Cimino, S., Laviola, G., Ammaniti, M., & Adriani, W. (2017). Internet addiction in adolescence: Neurobiological, psychosocial, and clinical issues. *Neuroscience & Biobehavioral Reviews, 76*, 174–184. doi:10.1016/j.neubiorev.2016.12.024

Chak, K., & Leung, L. (2004). Shyness and locus of control as predictors of Internet addiction and Internet use. *CyberPsychology & Behavior, 7*(5), 559–570. doi:10.1089/cpb.2004.7.559

Chiu, S. I. (2014). The relationship between life stress and smartphone addiction on Taiwanese university student: A mediation model of learning self-efficacy and social self-efficacy. *Computers in Human Behavior, 34*, 49–57. doi:10.1016/j.chb.2014.01.024

Chong, W. H., Chye, S., Huan, V. S., & Ang, R. P. (2014). Generalized problematic Internet use and regulation of social emotional competence: The mediating role of maladaptive cognitions arising from academic expectation stress on adolescents. *Computers in Human Behavior, 38*, 151–158. doi:10.1016/j.chb.2014.05.023

Chou, W. J., Huang, M. F., Chang, Y. P., Chen, Y. M., Hu, H. F., & Yen, C. F. (2017). Social skills deficits and their association with Internet addiction and activities in adolescents with attention-deficit/hyperactivity disorder. *Journal of Behavioral Addictions*, 6(1), 1–9. doi:10.1556/2006.6.2017.005

Clayton, R. B. (2014). The third wheel: The impact of Twitter use on relationship infidelity and divorce. *Cyberpsychology, Behavior, and Social Networking*, 17(7), 425–430. doi:10.1089/cyber.2013.0570

Clayton, R. B., Nagurney, A., & Smith, J. R. (2013). Cheating, breakup, and divorce: Is Facebook use to blame? *Cyberpsychology, Behavior, and Social Networking*, 16(10), 717–720. doi:10.1089/cyber.2012.0424

Clerkin, E. M., Smith, A. R., & Hames, J. L. (2013). The interpersonal effects of Facebook reassurance seeking. *Journal of Affective Disorders*, 151(2), 525–530. doi:10.1016/j.jad.2013.06.038

Davis, R. A. (2001). A cognitive-behavioral model of pathological Internet use. *Computers in Human Behavior*, 17(2), 187–195. doi:10.1016/S0747-5632(00)00041-8

Davis, R. A., Flett, G. L., & Besser, A. (2002). Validation of a new scale for measuring problematic Internet use: Implications for pre-employment screening. *CyberPsychology & Behavior*, 5(4), 331–345. doi:10.1089/109493102760275581

Drouin, M., Miller, D. A., & Dibble, J. L. (2014). Ignore your partners' current Facebook friends; beware the ones they add! *Computers in Human Behavior*, 35, 483–488. doi:10.1016/j.chb.2014.02.032

Dunn, M. J., & Billett, G. (2017). Jealousy levels in response to infidelity-revealing Facebook messages depend on sex, type of message and message composer: Support for the evolutionary psychological perspective. *Evolutionary Psychological Science*, 1–7. doi:10.1007/s40806-017-0110-z

Elhai, J. D., Dvorak, R. D., Levine, J. C., & Hall, B. J. (2017). Problematic smartphone use: A conceptual overview and systematic review of relations with anxiety and depression psychopathology. *Journal of Affective Disorders*, 207, 251–259. doi:10.1016/j.jad.2016.08.030

Feeney, J. A., Noller, P., & Roberts, N. (2000). Attachment and close relationships. In C. Hendrick & S. S. Hendrick (Eds.), *Close relationships: A sourcebook* (pp. 185–201). Thousand Oaks, CA: Sage. doi:10.4135/9781452220437.n14

Fioravanti, G., Dèttore, D., & Casale, S. (2012). Adolescent Internet addiction: Testing the association between self-esteem, the perception of Internet attributes, and preference for online social interactions. *Cyberpsychology, Behavior, and Social Networking*, 15(6), 318–323. doi:10.1089/cyber.2011.0358

Forest, A. L. AL, & Wood, J. V. (2012). When social networking is not working: Individuals with low self-esteem recognize but do not reap the benefits of self-disclosure on Facebook. *Psychological Science*, 23(3), 295–302. doi:10.1177/0956797611429709

Griffiths, M. D. (1995), Technological addictions, *Clinical Psychology Forum*, 76, 14–19.

Griffiths, M. D. (1996). Internet addiction: An issue for clinical psychology? *Clinical Psychology Forum*, 97, 32–36.

Griffiths, M. D., King, D. L., & Demetrovics, Z. (2014). DSM-5 Internet gaming disorder needs a unified approach to assessment. *Neuropsychiatry, 4*(1), 1–4.

Griffiths, M. D., Király, O., Pontes, H. M., & Demetrovics, Z. (2014). An overview of problematic gaming. In E. Aboujaoude & V. Starcevic (Eds.), *Mental health in the digital age: Grave dangers, great promise* (pp. 27–45). New York, NY: Oxford University Press.

Griffiths, M. D., Kuss, D. J., & Demetrovics, Z. (2014). Social networking addiction: An overview of preliminary findings. In K. P. Rosenberg & L. C. Feder (Eds.), *Behavioral addictions: Criteria, evidence, and treatment* (pp. 119–141). San Diego, CA: Elsevier Academic Press.

Griffiths, M. D., Pontes, H., & Kuss, D. (2015). Clinical psychology of Internet addiction: A review of its conceptualization, prevalence, neuronal processes, and implications for treatment. *Neuroscience and Neuroeconomics, 4*, 11–23. doi:10.2147/NAN.S60982

Grohol, J. M. (1999). Too much time online: Internet addiction or healthy social interactions? *CyberPsychology & Behavior, 2*(5), 395–401. doi:10.1089/cpb.1999.2.395

Hazan, C., & Shaver, P. R. (1987). Romantic love conceptualized as an attachment process. *Journal of Personality and Social Psychology, 52*(3), 511–524. doi:10.1037/0022-3514.52.3.511

Van Zalk, M., Van Zalk, N., Kerr, M., & Stattin, H. (2014). Influences between online-exclusive, conjoint and offline-exclusive friendship networks: The moderating role of shyness. *European Journal of Personality, 28*, 134–146.

Hormes, J. M., Kearns, B., & Timko, C. A. (2014). Craving Facebook? Behavioral addiction to online social networking and its association with emotion regulation deficits. *Addiction, 109*(12), 2079–2088. https://doi.org/10.1111/add.12713

Jeong, S. H., Kim, H., Yum, J. Y., & Hwang, Y. (2016). What type of content are smartphone users addicted to? SNS vs. games. *Computers in Human Behavior, 54*, 10–17. doi:10.1016/j.chb.2015.07.035

Kalaitzaki, A. E., & Birtchnell, J. (2014). The impact of early parenting bonding on young adults' Internet addiction, through the mediation effects of negative relating to others and sadness. *Addictive Behaviors, 39*(3), 733–736. doi:10.1016/j.addbeh.2013.12.002

Kardefelt-Winther, D. (2014a). A conceptual and methodological critique of Internet addiction research: Towards a model of compensatory Internet use. *Computers in Human Behavior, 31*, 351–354. doi:10.1016/j.chb.2013.10.059

Kardefelt-Winther, D. (2014b). Problematizing excessive online gaming and its psychological predictors. *Computers in Human Behavior, 31*, 118–122. doi:10.1016/j.chb.2013.10.017

Kardefelt-Winther, D. (2014c). The moderating role of psychosocial well-being on the relationship between escapism and excessive online gaming. *Computers in Human Behavior, 38*, 68–74. doi:10.1016/j.chb.2014.05.020

Kerkhof, P., Finkenauer, C., & Muusses, L. D. (2011). Relational consequences of compulsive Internet use: A longitudinal study among newlyweds. *Human Communication Research, 37*(2), 147–173.

King, D. L., & Delfabbro, P. H. (2016). Defining tolerance in Internet gaming disorder: Isn't it time? *Addiction, 111*(11), 2064–2065. doi:10.1111/add.13448

Kirkpatrick, L. A., & Hazan, C. (1994). Attachment styles and close relationships: A four-year prospective study. *Personal Relationships, 1*(2), 123–142.

Kowert, R., & Oldmeadow, J. A. (2013). (A)Social reputation: Exploring the relationship between online video game involvement and social competence. *Computers in Human Behavior, 29*(4), 1872–1878. doi:10.1016/j.chb.2013.03.003

Kraut, R., Kiesler, S., Boneva, B., Cummings, J. N., Helgeson, V., & Crawford, A. M. (2002). Internet paradox revisited. *Journal of Social Issues, 58*(1), 49–74. doi:10.1111/1540-4560.00248

Kraut, R., Patterson, M., Lundmark, V., Kiesler, S., Mukophadhyay, T., & Scherlis, W. (1998). Internet paradox: A social technology that reduces social involvement and psychological well-being? *American Psychologist, 53*(9), 1017–1031. doi:10.1037/0003-066X.53.9.1017

Kubey, R. W., Lavin, M. J., & Barrows, J. R. (2001). Internet use and collegiate academic performance decrements: early findings. *Journal of Communication, 51*(2), 366–382. doi:10.1111/j.1460-2466.2001.tb02885.x

Kuss, D. J. (2013). Internet gaming addiction: Current perspectives. *Psychology Research and Behavior Management, 6*, 125–37. doi:10.2147/PRBM.S39476

Kuss, D. J., & Griffiths, M. D. (2011a). Excessive online social networking: Can adolescents become addicted to Facebook. *Education and Health, 29*(4), 68–71.

Kuss, D. J., & Griffiths, M. D. (2011b). Online social networking and addiction—A review of the psychological literature. *International Journal of Environmental Research and Public Health, 8*(9), 3528–3552.

Kuss, D. J., & Griffiths, M. D. (2012). Internet and gaming addiction: A systematic literature review of neuroimaging studies. *Brain Sciences, 2*(3), 347–374. doi:10.3390/brainsci2030347

Kuss, D. J., & Griffiths, M. D. (2017). Social networking sites and addiction: Ten lessons learned. *International Journal of Environmental Research and Public Health, 14*(3), 311. doi:10.3390/ijerph14030311

Laconi, S., Rodgers, R. F., & Chabrol, H. (2014). The measurement of Internet addiction: A critical review of existing scales and their psychometric properties. *Computers in Human Behavior, 41*, 190–202. doi:10.1016/j.chb.2014.09.026

Laconi, S., Tricard, N., & Chabrol, H. (2015). Differences between specific and generalized problematic Internet uses according to gender, age, time spent online and psychopathological symptoms. *Computers in Human Behavior, 48*, 236–244. doi:10.1016/j.chb.2015.02.006

LaRose, R. (2010). The problem of media habits. *Communication Theory, 20*(2), 194–222. doi:10.1111/j.1468-2885.2010.01360.x

LaRose, R. (2015). The psychology of interactive media habits. In S. S. Sundar (Ed.), *The handbook of the psychology of communication technology* (pp. 365–383). Malden, MA: John Wiley & Sons.

LaRose, R., & Eastin, M. S. (2004). A social cognitive theory of Internet uses and gratifications: Toward a new model of media attendance. *Journal of Broadcasting & Electronic Media, 48*(3), 358–377. doi:10.1207/s15506878jobem4803_2

LaRose, R., Eastin, M. S., & Gregg, J. (2001). Reformulating the Internet paradox: Social cognitive explanations of Internet use and depression. *Journal of Online Behavior, 1*(2). Retrieved from http://www.behavior.net/JOB/v1n1/paradox.html

LaRose, R., Kim, J., & Peng, W. (2011). Social networking: addictive, compulsive, problematic, or just another media habit. In Z. A. Papacharissi (Ed.), *A networked self: Identity, community, and culture on social network sites* (pp. 59–81). New York: Routledge

LaRose, R., Lin, C., & Eastin, M. S. (2003). Unregulated Internet usage: Addiction, habit, or deficient self-regulation? *Media Psychology, 5*(3), 225–253. doi: 10.1207/S1532785XMEP0503_01

Lee, E. W. J., Ho, S. S., & Lwin, M. O. (2017). Explicating problematic social network sites use: A review of concepts, theoretical frameworks, and future directions for communication theorizing. *New Media & Society, 19*(2), 308–326. doi:10.1177/1461444816671891

Lemmens, J. S., & Hendriks, S. J. F. (2016). Addictive online games: Examining the relationship between game genres and Internet gaming disorder. *Cyberpsychology, Behavior, and Social Networking, 19*(4), 270–276. doi:10.1089/cyber.2015.0415

Lemmens, J. S., Valkenburg, P. M., & Peter, J. (2011). Psychosocial causes and consequences of pathological gaming. *Computers in Human Behavior, 27*(1), 144–152. doi:10.1016/j.chb.2010.07.015

Lianekhammy, J. & Van de Venne, J. (2015). World of Warcraft widows: Spousal perspectives of online gaming and relationship outcomes. *The American Journal of Family Therapy, 43*(5), 454–466. doi:10.1080/01926187.2015.1080131

Liu, M., & Peng, W. (2009). Cognitive and psychological predictors of the negative outcomes associated with playing MMOGs (massively multiplayer online games). *Computers in Human Behavior, 25*(6), 1306–1311.

Lopes, P. N., Brackett, M. A., Nezlek, J. B., Schütz, A., Sellin, I., & Salovey, P. (2004). Emotional intelligence and social interaction. *Personality & Social Psychology Bulletin, 30*, 1018–1034.

Lopes, P. N., Salovey, P., & Straus, R. (2003). Emotional intelligence, personality, and the perceived quality of social relationships. *Personality and Individual Differences, 35*(3), 641–658. doi:10.1016/S0191-8869(02)00242-8

Maraz, A., Király, O., & Demetrovics, Z. (2015). Commentary on: Are we overpathologizing everyday life? A tenable blueprint for behavioral addiction research. *Journal of Behavioral Addictions, 4*(3), 151–154. doi:10.1556/2006.4.2015.026

Mayer, J. D., & Salovey, P. (1997). What is emotional intelligence? In P. Salovey & D. J. Sluyter (Eds.), *Emotional development and emotional intelligence: Educational implications* (pp. 3–31). New York: Basic Books.

McKenna, K. Y. A., & Bargh, J. A. (2000). Plan 9 from cyberspace: The implications of the Internet for personality and social psychology. *Personality and Social Psychology Review, 4*(1), 57–75. doi:10.1207/S15327957PSPR0401_6

Monacis, L., de Palo, V., Griffiths, M. D., & Sinatra, M. (2017). Exploring individual differences in online addictions: The role of identity and attachment. *International Journal of Mental Health and Addiction.* doi:10.1007/s11469-017-9768-5

Montag, C., Bey, K., Sha, P., Li, M., Chen, Y. F., Liu, W. Y., ... Reuter, M. (2015). Is it meaningful to distinguish between generalized and specific Internet addiction? Evidence from a cross-cultural study from Germany, Sweden, Taiwan, and China. *Asia-Pacific Psychiatry, 7*(1), 20–26. doi:10.1111/appy.12122

Morahan-Martin, J. (1999). The relationship between loneliness and Internet use and abuse. *CyberPsychology & Behavior, 2*(5), 431–439. doi:10.1089/cpb.1999.2.431

Morahan-Martin, J. (2008). Internet abuse: Emerging trends and lingering questions. In A. Barak (Ed.), *Psychological aspects of cyberspace: Theory, research, and applications* (pp. 32–69). Cambridge, UK: Cambridge University Press.

Morahan-Martin, J., & Schumacher, P. (2000). Incidence and correlates of pathological Internet use among college students. *Computers in Human Behavior, 16*(1), 13–29. doi:10.1016/S0747-5632(99)00049-7

Morahan-Martin, J., & Schumacher, P. (2003). Loneliness and social uses of the Internet. *Computers in Human Behavior, 19*(6), 659–671. doi:10.1016/S0747-5632(03)00040-2

Muscanell, N. L., Guadagno, R. E., Rice, L., & Murphy, S. (2013). Don't it make my brown eyes green? An analysis of Facebook use and romantic jealousy. *Cyberpsychology, Behavior, and Social Networking, 16*(4), 237–242. doi:10.1089/cyber.2012.0411

Muusses, L. D., Finkenauer, C., Kerkhof, P., & Righetti, F. (2015). Partner effects of compulsive Internet use: A self-control account. *Communication Research, 42*(3), 365–386. doi:10.1177/0093650212469545

Nitzburg, G. C., & Farber, B. A. (2013). Putting up emotional (Facebook) walls? Attachment status and emerging adults' experiences of social networking sites. *Journal of Clinical Psychology, 69*(11), 1183–1190. doi:10.1002/jclp.22045

Northrup, J. C., & Shumway, S. (2014). Gamer widow: A phenomenological study of spouses of online video game addicts. *The American Journal of Family Therapy, 42*(4), 269–281. doi:10.1080/01926187.2013.847705

Oberst, U., Wegmann, E., Stodt, B., Brand, M., & Chamarro, A. (2017). Negative consequences from heavy social networking in adolescents: The mediating role of fear of missing out. *Journal of Adolescence, 55*, 51–60. doi:10.1016/j.adolescence.2016.12.008

Oldmeadow, J. A., Quinn, S., & Kowert, R. (2013). Attachment style, social skills, and Facebook use amongst adults. *Computers in Human Behavior, 29*(3), 1142–1149. doi:10.1016/j.chb.2012.10.006

Park, B., Han, D. H., & Roh, S. (2017). Neurobiological findings related to Internet use disorders. *Psychiatry and Clinical Neurosciences, 71*(7), 467–478. doi:10.1111/pcn.12422

Parker, J. D. A., Summerfeldt, L. J., Taylor, R. N., Kloosterman, P. H., & Keefer, K. V. (2013). Problem gambling, gaming and Internet use in adolescents: Relationships with emotional intelligence in clinical and special needs samples. *Personality and Individual Differences, 55*(3), 288–293.

Pawlikowski, M., Nader, I. W., Burger, C., Stieger, S., & Brand, M. (2014). Pathological Internet use—It is a multidimensional and not a unidimensional construct. *Addiction Research & Theory, 22*(2), 166–175. doi:10.3109/16066359.2013.793313

Petry, N. M., & O'Brien, C. P. (2013). Internet gaming disorder and the DSM-5. *Addiction, 108*(7), 1186–1187. doi:10.1111/add.12162

Pontes, H. M., & Griffiths, M. D. (2014). Assessment of Internet gaming disorder in clinical research: Past and present perspectives. *Clinical Research and Regulatory Affairs, 31*(2-4), 35–48. doi:10.3109/10601333.2014.962748

Pontes, H. M., & Griffiths, M. D. (2015). Measuring DSM-5 Internet gaming disorder: Development and validation of a short psychometric scale. *Computers in Human Behavior, 45*, 137–143. doi:10.1016/j.chb.2014.12.006

Prizant-Passal, S., Shechner, T., & Aderka, I. M. (2016). Social anxiety and Internet use—A meta-analysis: What do we know? What are we missing? *Computers in Human Behavior, 62*, 221–229. doi:10.1016/j.chb.2016.04.003

Przybylski, A. K., Murayama, K., DeHaan, C. R., & Gladwell, V. (2013). Motivational, emotional, and behavioral correlates of fear of missing out. *Computers in Human Behavior, 29*(4), 1841–1848. doi:10.1016/j.chb.2013.02.014

Ramirez Jr, A., & Zhang, S. (2007). When online meets offline: The effect of modality switching on relational communication. *Communication Monographs, 74*(3), 287–310.

Riggio, R., & Zimmerman, J. (1991). Social skills and interpersonal relationships: Influences on social support and support seeking. In W. H. Jones & D. Perlman (Eds.), *Advances in personal relationships* (Vol. 2, pp. 133–155). London: Jessica Kingsley Press.

Ryan, T., Chester, A., Reece, J., & Xenos, S. (2014). The uses and abuses of Facebook: A review of Facebook addiction. *Journal of Behavioral Addictions, 3*(3), 133–148. doi:10.1556/JBA.3.2014.016

Salovey, P., & Mayer, J. D. (1990). Emotional intelligence. *Imagination, Cognition, and Personality, 9*(3), 185–211.

Scherer, K. (1997). College life on-line: Healthy and unhealthy Internet use. *Journal of College Student Development, 38*(6), 655–665.

Schimmenti, A., Guglielmucci, F., Barbasio, C., & Granieri, A. (2012). Attachment disorganization and dissociation in virtual worlds: A study on problematic Internet use among players of online role-playing games. *Clinical Neuropsychiatry: Journal of Treatment Evaluation, 9*(5), 195–202.

Schimmenti, A., Passanisi, A., Gervasi, A. M., Manzella, S., & Famà, F. I. (2013). Insecure attachment attitudes in the onset of problematic Internet use among late adolescents. *Child Psychiatry & Human Development, 45*(5), 588–595. doi:10.1007/s10578-013-0428-0

Schneider, J. P. (2000). Effects of cybersex addiction on the family: Results of a survey. *Sexual Addiction & Compulsivity, 7*(1–2), 31–58. doi:10.1080/10720160008400206

Shaffer, H. J., Hall, M. N., & Vander Bilt, J. (2000). "Computer addiction": A critical consideration. *American Journal of Orthopsychiatry, 70*(2), 162–168. doi:10.1037/h0087741

Song, I., LaRose, R., Eastin, M. S., & Lin, C. A. (2004). Internet gratifications and Internet addiction: On the uses and abuses of new media. *CyberPsychology & Behavior*, 7(4), 384–394. doi:10.1089/cpb.2004.7.384

Spada, M. M., Langston, B., Nikčević, A. V., & Moneta, G. B. (2008). The role of metacognitions in problematic Internet use. *Computers in Human Behavior*, 24(5), 2325–2335. doi:10.1016/j.chb.2007.12.002

Starcevic, V., & Aboujaoude, E. (2016). Internet addiction: Reappraisal of an increasingly inadequate concept. *CNS Spectrums*, 22(1), 7–13. doi:10.1017/S1092852915000863

Stewart, M. C., Dainton, M., & Goodboy, A. K. (2014). Maintaining relationships on Facebook: Associations with uncertainty, jealousy, and satisfaction. *Communication Reports*, 27(1), 13–26. doi:10.1080/08934215.2013.845675

Sultan, A. (2014). Addiction to mobile text messaging applications is nothing to "lol" about. *The Social Science Journal*, 51(1), 57–69. doi:10.1016/j.soscij.2013.09.003

Teppers, E., Luyckx, K., Klimstra, T., & Goossens, L. (2014). Loneliness and Facebook motives in adolescence: A longitudinal inquiry into directionality of effect. *Journal of Adolescence*, 37(5), 691–699. doi:10.1016/j.adolescence.2013.11.003

Tokunaga, R. S. (2014). A unique problem or the manifestation of a preexisting disorder? The mediating role of problematic Internet use in the relationships between psychosocial problems and functional impairment. *Communication Research*, 41(4), 531–560. doi:10.1177/0093650212450910

Tokunaga, R. S. (2015). Perspectives on Internet addiction, problematic Internet use, and deficient self-regulation. *Annals of the International Communication Association*, 39(1), 131–161.

Tokunaga, R. S. (2016). An examination of functional difficulties from Internet use: Media habit. *Human Communication Research*, 42(3), 339–370. doi:10.1111/hcre.12081

Tokunaga, R. S. (2017). A meta-analysis of the relationships between psychosocial problems and Internet habits: Synthesizing Internet addiction, problematic Internet use, and deficient self-regulation research. *Communication Monographs*, 84(4), 423–446. doi:10.1080/03637751.2017.1332419

Tokunaga, R. S., & Rains, S. A. (2010). An evaluation of two characterizations of the relationships between problematic Internet use, time spent using the Internet, and psychosocial problems. *Human Communication Research*, 36(4), 512–545. https://doi.org/10.1111/j.1468-2958.2010.01386.x

Tokunaga, R. S., & Rains, S. A. (2016). A review and meta-analysis examining conceptual and operational definitions of problematic Internet use. *Human Communication Research*, 42(2), 165–199. doi:10.1111/hcre.12075

Van Deursen, A. J., Bolle, C. L., Hegner, S. M., & Kommers, P. (2015). Modeling habitual and addictive smartphone behavior: The role of smartphone usage types, emotional intelligence, social stress, self-regulation, age, and gender. *Computers in Human Behavior*, 45, 411–420. doi:10.1016/j.chb.2014.12.039

Van Rooij, A. J., & Kardefelt-Winther, D. (2017). Lost in the chaos: Flawed literature should not generate new disorders. *Journal of Behavioral Addictions*, 6(2), 128–132. doi:10.1556/2006.6.2017.015

Van Rooij, A. J., Schoenmakers, T. M., Van de Eijnden, R. J. J. M., & Van de Mheen, D. (2010). Compulsive Internet use: The role of online gaming and other Internet applications. *Journal of Adolescent Health*, 47(1), 51–57. doi:10.1016/j.jadohealth.2009.12.021

Vorderer, P., & Kohring, M. (2013). Permanently online: A challenge for media and communication research. *International Journal of Communication*, 7(1), 188–196. doi:1932-8086/2013FEA0002

Vorderer, P., Krömer, N., & Schneider, F. M. (2016). Permanently online—Permanently connected: Explorations into university students' use of social media and mobile smart devices. *Computers in Human Behavior*, 63, 694–703. doi:10.1016/j.chb.2016.05.085

Wallace, P. M. (1999). *The psychology of the Internet*. New York: Cambridge University Press.

Walther, J. B. (1996). Computer-mediated communication: Impersonal, interpersonal, and hyperpersonal interaction. *Communication Research*, 23(1), 3–43. doi:10.1177/009365096023001001

Wegmann, E., Oberst, U., Stodt, B., & Brand, M. (2017). Online-specific fear of missing out and Internet-use expectancies contribute to symptoms of Internet-communication disorder. *Addictive Behaviors Reports*, 5, 33–42. doi:10.1016/j.abrep.2017.04.001

Weinstein, A., & Lejoyeux, M. (2010). Internet addiction or excessive Internet use. *The American Journal of Drug and Alcohol Abuse*, 36(5), 277–283. doi:10.3109/00952990.2010.491880

Weinstein, A., Feder, L., Rosenberg, K. P., & Dannon, P. N. (2014). Internet addiction disorder: Overview and controversies. In K. P. Rosenberg & L. C. Feder (Eds.), *Behavioral addictions: Criteria, evidence, and treatment.* (pp. 99–117). San Diego, CA: Elsevier Academic.

Widyanto, L., & Griffiths, M. D. (2006). "Internet addiction": A critical review. *International Journal of Mental Health and Addiction*, 4(1), 31–51. https://doi.org/10.1007/s11469-006-9009-9

Widyanto, L., & Griffiths, M. D. (2007). Internet addiction: Does it really exist? (Revisited). In J. Gackenbach (Ed.), *Psychology and the Internet: Intrapersonal, interpersonal, and transpersonal implications* (2nd ed., pp. 141–163), San Diego, CA: Elsevier Academic Press.

Young, K. S. (1996). Psychology of computer use: XL. Addictive use of the Internet: A case that breaks the stereotype. *Psychological Reports*, 79(3, Pt 1), 899–902.

Young, K. S. (1998). Internet addiction: The emergence of a new clinical disorder. *CyberPsychology & Behavior*, 1(3), 237–244. https://doi.org/10.1089/cpb.1998.1.237

Young, K. S., & Rogers, R. C. (1998). The relationship between depression and Internet addiction. *CyberPsychology & Behavior*, 1(1), 25–28. doi:10.1089/cpb.1998.1.25

Chapter Three

Online Relational Transgressions

As social networking and mobile devices became integrated into our personal lives, the traditional media and press, along with researchers, began to ask how online social behaviors might pose relational risks to romantic couples and friends. A 2010 article in *The Daily Mail* described Facebook as "the marriage killer," noting that one in five American divorces involved Facebook (Gardner, 2010). In a 2010 study, 81% percent of the nation's top divorce attorneys reported seeing an increase in the number of divorce cases employing social networking evidence (American Academy of Matrimonial Lawyers, 2010). The study noted, "Facebook holds the distinction of being the unrivaled leader for online divorce evidence with 66% citing it as the primary source." *The Atlantic* indicated that lawyers had begun recommending people obtain prenuptial and postnuptial digital privacy contracts. Such agreements "prevent spouses from using personal texts, emails, or photos against each other should they wind up in divorce court" (Cottle, 2014, p. 60).

The online transgressions described in this chapter range from harmless and mundane annoyances to severe conflicts that may end a close relationship. In families, a parent's online relational transgression may not only harm the other spouse, but children are often affected by parent stress and conflict. Among friends, transgressions can cause conflict, hurt feelings, and end relationships. In romantic relationships, communication technology can facilitate affairs. Whether intentional or not, a variety of online behaviors can create, enhance, and help hide transgressions among romantic couples as well as among friends. When severe, relational transgressions may seriously hurt both the relationship and the people involved. Thus, research on online transgressions has made an essential contribution to broadening our understanding of problematic Internet use.

Relational transgressions on social networking sites create a strain on interpersonal relationships (Tokunaga, 2014). Fox, Osborn, and Warber (2014) reported results from a study indicating, "Facebook can generate or exacerbate relationship turmoil" (p. 532). Fox et al. (2014) conducted a focus group revealing college students' opinions about how online behavior may threaten romantic relationships. Responses included statements such as, "Facebook is a trap," "It's not going to make a relationship better, but it could make it worse," "It's ruining people," and "It's just a total, a total train wreck." Further, "in multiple groups, participants unanimously agreed that they would be better off without Facebook in their romantic relationships" (Fox et al., 2014, p. 533). The examples above illustrate the types of concerns people have about how online behavior might harm close relationships. What is less clear, however, is *how* and *why* particular actions create problems.

This chapter presents an interpersonal approach to examining online relationship transgressions. The chapter employs a relational rules perspective to empirical research on relational transgressions in both romantic and friendship relationships. The sections below first define online relational transgressions based on rule violations. Later sections examine online transgressions in both romantic and friendship contexts.

Throughout this chapter, the concept of relational transgressions is used to connect and organize different lines of research on online behavior that can create conflict and inflict harm on the other partner and the relationship. Online relational transgression is a useful concept for establishing theory-driven research lines on topics such as online infidelity, social networking jealousy, and partner surveillance, as well as research a friendship problems arising from online behavior. All of these are examples of what this chapter describes as online relationship transgressions. The communication research on offline relational transgressions provides both a conceptual and empirical starting point for better understanding how computer-mediated communication creates problems in close relationships. As the following sections will demonstrate, although infidelity is dramatically different from being embarrassed by a friend's Facebook post, the relational transgression concept provides a bridge and theoretical foundation for organizing previous research and guiding future scholarship.

Currently, there is more empirical data than there are clear and detailed theories explaining and connecting various online relational transgressions. The sections below use literature on interaction and relational rules, uncertainty reduction theory, politeness theory, and facework to organize and summarize these lines of research. This chapter examines the research into online relational transgressions and employs theories from interpersonal and relational communication research to help clarify and explain the observed effects. For example, research on interaction and relational rules (Argyle & Henderson, 1984, 1985) can help guide a conceptual narrative of online relational transgressions as rule violations. The rule approach also helps explain why specific behaviors have different meanings in different relationships and different contexts. Similarly, research into online transgressions among friends also can be explained by relational rules approach. Regardless of the technology or behavior, the relational rules perspective and politeness theory offer conceptual foundations to explain online relational transgressions. A rules approach helps explain what constitutes a transgression, and why. It also helps illuminate implicit rules that couples and friends develop around Internet use and technology. Face and politeness theory add further detail to what the rules are that govern social interaction.

Relational Rules and Transgressions

Relational transgressions, among friends or romantic partners, occur when one person engages in behavior that violates relational rules in a way that hurts the other partner (Afifi & Metts, 1998; Emmers-Sommer, 2003; Metts, 1994). Specifically, Metts defines transgressions as "violations of relationally relevant rules" (1994, p. 218). Relational transgressions may be intentional or accidental. For example, one may purposely engage in transgressions as strategies for initiating the termination of relationships (Vaughn, 1986). Unintentional violations occur when a partner accidentally breaks a rule, such as betraying a secret. Transgressions may be single incidents or may be incremental, involving a cumulative process in which a rule is slowly violated over time (Emmers-Sommer, 2003). Relational transgressions may result in a variety of adverse effects ranging from mild irritation to severe emotional distress and the end of the relationship. At the most severe end of the spectrum, behaviors such partner abuse and interpersonal violence are far worse than relational transgressions (e.g., cyber-relational abuse, cyberbullying, cyberstalking). Later chapters will examine more severe forms of online aggression and harassment. This chapter focuses on non-abusive online transgressions that cause conflict and threaten close relationships.

Rules for Interaction and Relationships

Understanding relational transgressions requires a closer examination of the rules that guide interpersonal interactions and relationships. Long before the Internet, social scientists noted the importance of rules in social interaction and relationships. Interaction rules about politeness guide our casual everyday exchanges (Brown and Levinson, 1987; Goffman, 1967). For example, Goffman (1959, 1967) argued that in all social interactions we have an obligation to uphold or help maintain the other's face. Thus, interaction rules include using behaviors that are validating and avoiding disconfirming behaviors. Goffman described an *interaction ritual* wherein people's interpersonal behaviors conform to rules about face and facework, such as, "don't embarrass the other," "don't put the other in an uncomfortable position," and "affirm the other's desire to be seen in a certain way." Brown and Levinson's (1987) politeness theory is an attempt to delineate these interaction rules.

Relational rules govern boundaries and expectations in close relationships such as friendships and romantic relationships (Argyle & Henderson, 1984; Argyle, Henderson, & Furnham, 1985). Further, relational rules guide partners toward long-term goals by helping to coordinate behavior, regulate levels of intimacy, and avoid relationship-specific courses of conflict (Argyle et al., 1985). Relational transgressions occur when these rules are violated. For example, friendships may be damaged by breaking a promise to keep something secret (the rule "friends keep secrets"). Kline and Stafford (2004) reported the quality of friendship relationships was related to the degree to which friends followed not only interaction rules, but also relational rules about how rewarding friendship should be ("friendship should offer emotional intimacy, support, and give help"), rules to minimize conflict ("don't criticize in public," "don't nag") and also about boundaries with third parties "keep secrets," "be loyal"). As later sections will elaborate, much of the emerging literature on Facebook-related relationship problems entails studies of relationship rule violations.

The rules that govern romantic relationship are distinct from those among friends. Argyle and Henderson (1985) argued that no other relationship is as rule-bound as marriage. As Emmers-Sommer (2003) explains, "these rules might be implicit or explicit" and "some rules generalize to most couples (monogamy) while others can be relationship specific" (p. 188). In romantic relationships, common relational rules include being faithful, respecting the other's privacy, paying attention to the other's face needs, and providing affirmation and validation. Relational rules also regulate divisions of labor, how the couple manages conflict, and how a couple deals with others who represent a threat to the relationship. Kline and Stafford (2004) discovered that marital quality was greater among couples employing interaction rules. In fact, the study indicated that 51% of the variance in marital satisfaction was accounted for by adherence to interaction rules.

Online Infidelity and Romantic Relationship Transgressions

Since the mid-1990s, researchers have examined the ways that online behaviors might constitute infidelity, or cheating, in romantic relationships. Early research on the effects of problematic online sexual behaviors on marriages grew into a significant line of inquiry into online infidelity (e.g., Cooper, 2002; Mahaeau & Subotnik, 2001; Whitty, 2004; Young, 1998). Beyond cheating, researchers have also identified other online relational transgressions in romantic relationships, such as unwanted relationship intrusion, partner surveillance, and Facebook-related conflict and jealousy (e.g., Elphinstone & Noller, 2011; Muise, Christofides, & Desmarias, 2009; Tokunaga, 2015; Valenzuela, Halpern & Katz, 2014). Collectively, the problems listed above reflect online romantic relational transgressions. Researchers have also begun to explore the ways in which people use online contexts, such as texting, Twitter, or Facebook to actually conduct relational conflict and relationship breakups (Clayton, 2014; Clayton, Nagurney, & Smith, 2013; Lefebvre, Blackburn, & Brody, 2015). For example, some partners reveal details of their relationship problems via social networks in order to retaliate against or hurt the other (Cravens & Whiting, 2014). Although breakups and conflict are not necessarily the result of transgressions, the use of technology, rather than in-person communication, to conduct conflict or initiate breakups may involve transgressive behaviors.

The most extensively studied online romantic transgression is infidelity. Early Internet technology did not permit people to do much else besides communicate with text from desktop machines. At the time, studying online versus offline relationship problems made sense since there was a clear distinction between online and offline relational behavior. Today, however, the two are entwined to the point in which our closest relationships integrate the most extensive variety of different communication channels (Caughlin & Sharabi, 2013; Haythornthwaite, 2005; Ledbetter, 2015; Sharabi & Caughlin, 2017). Thus, when reviewing older studies (i.e., those published before social networking and smartphones were widespread), it is essential to keep in mind that the technology and contexts continue to evolve.

Research on Internet infidelity emerged out of work on problematic online sexual behaviors. One of the earliest types of interpersonal problematic Internet use entailed using the Internet to engage in sexual or emotional intimacy outside of a relationship (e.g., Cooper, 2002). For the most part, this early research focused on people who had psychological problems with symptoms that manifested in problematic online sexual behavior. Initially, research in this area was concerned with compulsive or addictive online sexual behavior and the potential negative consequences of such behavior for people's relationships offline. In 2007, Docan-Morgan and Docan observed that Internet infidelity had "not been adequately studied outside of sexual addiction and compulsivity studies, in part because the Internet has only recently become a site for relationship initiation and development" (p. 320).

As more people started using the Internet in the mid-2000s, researchers began to identify online extradyadic romantic behaviors among people who were not cybersex addicts and did not exhibit pathological behaviors (Whitty, 2011). Today, online infidelity is no longer thought of as limited only to people with psychological disorders (Jones & Hertlein, 2012). It makes sense that, when Internet use was less common, early studies focused more on pathological correlates of online infidelity. Although Internet infidelity may have initially begun among relatively small portions of the population who also exhibited problematic online sexual behaviors, the problem has moved into the mainstream along with social networking and mobile device use. By 2011, Whitty observed, "there is general agreement that people can and do cheat on their partners on the Internet" (p. 194). Today, most extradyadic affairs likely involve a combination of in-person and mediated communication.

Defining Online Infidelity

Initially, one of the primary questions researchers sought to answer was whether or not various online sexual behaviors were acts of unfaithfulness (for reviews, see Jones & Hertlein, 2012; Whitty, 2011). Whitty (2011) explains that early studies speculated about whether or not Internet infidelity was real or possible since, in most cases, the involved parties were not physically together and frequently did not know one another offline (e.g., Cooper, 2002; Mahaeau & Subotnik, 2001; Whitty, 2004; Young, 1998). Schneider, Weiss, and Samenow (2012) recall that, in the mid-1990s, a person caught communicating with strangers online could easily push aside their spouse's concerns with comments like "how can you call it cheating when I've never met her (or him)? They're thousands of miles away, it's not real, so stop calling it cheating" (p. 124).

A significant line of online infidelity research has involved attempts to define the phenomenon. Some researchers sought to arrive at definitions by asking family therapists (e.g., Nelson, Piercy, & Sprenkle, 2005), some have attempted to define online Infidelity by distinguishing it from other forms of problematic Internet use (Jones & Hertlein, 2012), and others asked people what online behaviors they would consider to be acts of infidelity (e.g., Whitty, 2004).

Several scholars have noted the importance of rule violations when defining online infidelity. Whitty (2011) defined Internet infidelity as occurring "when the rules of the relationship are broken by acting inappropriately in an emotional and/or sexual manner with at least one person other than one's partner" (p. 195). In their definition of online infidelity, Docan-Morgan and Docan (2007) emphasized that it "constitutes a breach of trust and/or violation of agreed-upon norms (overt or covert) by one or both individuals in that relationship with regard to relational exclusivity" (p. 331). Using the concept of transgressions helps avoid the conceptual problem of definitions that go out of date when technology changes. Regardless of the device, application, or technology, the stable characteristic of online infidelity is the use of technology to violate relational boundary rules with another person.

As literature below elaborates, online romantic infidelity has four defining characteristics: (1) relationship rules are violated, (2) it includes online intimacy with a third party, (3) it involves secrecy and deception, and (4) the behavior hurts the betrayed partner and damages the primary relationship. The following paragraphs explore each of these characteristics in further detail.

Relational Norms and Rule Violations. Consistent with the rules approach presented earlier, one defining feature of online infidelity is that it violates relational rules or crosses a central relationship boundary. Emmers-Sommer (2003) argued that marriages have both implicit and explicit rules that are shared by most couples, such as monogamy. Whitty (2011) explains that the "the rules might differ for different couples, but there are some fundamental rules that are often unspoken and are typical expectations of most committed relationships" (p. 195). Indeed, researchers have defined online infidelity as a type of rule violation (Docan-Morgan & Docan, 2007; Whitty, 2011).

Most couples generally agree about which online behaviors are transgressions. Helsper and Whitty (2010) examined 920 married couples and uncovered high levels of agreement between spouses about the unacceptability of online infidelity (both emotional and sexual). The authors suggested that the result reflect the fact that higher emotional involvement online increases the likelihood of the online relationship moving offline. Ninety percent of the couples agreed that falling in love or engaging in cybersex with someone else was a serious rule violation. In terms of emotional intimacy, 79% agreed it is inappropriate to disclose intimate details about themselves to another person online. Flirting was also seen as a transgression, as 69% of couples agreed that online flirting would be upsetting.

Similarly, a study by Docan-Morgan and Docan (2007) revealed that emotional involvement (i.e., emotional affair) was perceived as a particularly problematic form of online infidelity. In this study, 208 undergraduates responded to questions about which types of online behaviors they considered to be the most severe examples of online infidelity. The participants identified "involving/goal-directed" behaviors as more severe than "informal/superficial" acts. Participants reported the most egregious online behavioral violations to be those intentionally crossing the boundaries of emotional and sexual intimacy. For example, some of the intentional transgressive behaviors included disclosing love to a third party, making plans to meet another person, having cybersex, and flirting online.

Interestingly, the study also revealed that people viewed behaviors as less severe if they were the person committing the act and more severe if their partner committed the behavior (Docan-Morgan & Docan, 2007). More specifically, the authors suggested, "relational partners seem to have a double-standard, self-motivated rules, and different expectations in terms of their own actions compared to their partner's actions when acting on relational alternatives. This finding provides us with an understanding as to why some people make the conscious choice to engage in Internet infidelity—they view their actions as less severe" (Docan-Morgan & Docan, 2007, p. 332). Similarly, Fricker and Moore (2008) found that 80% of people who had participated in extradyadic cybersex did not view it as unfaithful. Attribution theory (Miller & Ross, 1975) would explain this as a self-serving bias, attributing one's own transgressive behaviors to outside circumstances or momentary lapses in judgment.

Intimacy With A Third Party. Online infidelity occurs when people use mediated communication to have an intimate relationship with an outside third party who represents a potential romantic alternative. Here, "romantic alternative" describes people who might be romantically attracted to the cheating partner. If the third party were not a romantic threat, it would not be considered infidelity. In other words, a man going online to talk to his brother, despite it being intimate, is not an issue. However, if a man is texting an attractive coworker and hiding that from his partner, the situation now involves a potential threat to the relationship.

Whitty (2011) noted, "the Internet might be the exclusive, main, or partial space where the inappropriate emotional or sexual interactions take place" (p. 122). Extradyadic intimacy can be sexual, emotional, or some combination of the two (Luo, Cartun, & Snider, 2010; Martins et al., 2016; Whitty, 2011). Sexting, flirtatious or sexual chatting, and other forms of online sexual intimacy with another person are the most obvious forms of online infidelity. Although some studies identify pornography use as a type of online infidelity (e.g., Docan-Morgan & Docan, 2007), a review of the literature by Whitty (2011) reported that researchers have consistently found that "viewing pornography online or offline is considered by few to be an act of infidelity" (p. 196; also see Parker & Wampler, 2003). Whitty (2011) explains that unlike online interactions with a third party, viewing pornography is generally not viewed as infidelity because it is a passive act that has no possibility of leading to interactions with another person. In distinguishing online affairs from other problematic online sexual behaviors, Jones and Hertlein (2012) explained that Internet infidelity is primarily a relational activity, involving an identifiable third person whereas other problematic forms of online sexual behavior are primarily individual activities.

In addition to sexual transgressions, online *emotional* infidelity has also been identified as a severe relational transgression that can be just as damaging as sexual infidelity (Whitty, 2004, 2005, 2011; Whitty & Quigley, 2008). Luo et al. (2010) provided evidence that online extradyadic behavior was twice as likely to be described as emotional rather than sexual. As Helsper and Whitty (2010) noted, "emotional online betrayal, such as falling in love or self-disclosing intimate details about oneself or one's partner online, are also seen by many to be serious relationships transgressions" (p. 918). Henline, Lamke, and Howard (2007) surveyed 127 college students in committed relationships about perceptions of online infidelity and observed greater perceived distress in response to emotional rather than online sexual infidelity. Similarly, Docan-Morgan and Docan (2007) reported that online behaviors that were "non-sexual in nature such as sharing secrets, expressing care, flirting, and communicating before bed every night were viewed as considerable degrees of infidelity" (p. 331).

Secrecy. Despite disagreements about how to define online infidelity, most scholars identify secrecy as a central feature of online infidelity (Hertlein & Piercy, 2006; Jones & Hertlein, 2012; Shaw, 1997). In an early study of the consequences of Internet infidelity, Shaw (1997) observed that betrayed partners repeatedly mentioned being lied to as a significant cause of their distress. Young (2006) noted that although most spouses lie to protect their other types of problematic online behaviors, "those engaging in cyberaffairs have a higher stake in concealing the truth, which often triggers bigger and bolder lies" (p. 48).

Research by Cravens, Leckie, and Whiting (2013) describes the central roles of secrecy and concealment in betrayed partners' descriptions of their partner's online infidelity. One participant remarked, "I noticed she was spending a lot of time late at night hiding her chats, removed me (her husband) from her friend list, come to find out [sic] her own mother noticed her strange behavior for a married woman" (p. 81). Another participant said, "For years we were able to log into each other's email accounts. Now she's changed the passwords and has also put a password on her phone. We've always shared everything. This brought back a load of suspicion tonight" (p. 81). Cravens et al. (2013) reported a variety of types of secrecy and concealment including closing windows on computers when the partner came into the room, friending ex-relational partners on Facebook, deleting texts, and adding or changing passwords.

Although deception has always been part of online affairs, the types of deceptive behaviors involved have changed as mobile technology has developed. In the early days of the Internet, deception might have involved using a computer in another room, clearing one's browser history, or quickly closing a window when one's partner walked in the room. The widespread adoption of smartphones and other mobile devices has enabled greater secrecy and allowed online affairs to take place anywhere at any time. Today's online environment enables individuals to engage in both emotional and sexual affairs without ever leaving the kitchen table. Whereas affairs once took place entirely outside the home, or in a separate room where the computer was kept, the types of affairs that take place online today might actually occur while a husband is sitting in the same room as his wife and texting his affair partner on his smartphone. A 2014 article in the *Atlantic,* titled "The Adultery Arms Race," described the burgeoning industry of mobile technologies designed to help hide affairs from spouses (Cottle, 2014). For example, the app CoverMe offers military-grade encryption for phone calls. Another tool named CATE (the Call and Text Eraser) allows a user to hide texts and phone calls from specific contacts and offers a "quick clean" feature that allows the user to remove potentially incriminating evidence simply by shaking the smartphone. A program named "Gallery Lock" allows a smartphone user to hide pictures and videos inside a private "gallery" within the phone. At the same time, there is a growing list of products designed to help suspicious partners spy on potential cheaters. "Every new app that promises to make playing around safer and easier just increases the appetite for a cleverer way to expose such deception" (Cottle, 2014,

p. 59). For example, about 2 million subscribers pay between $20 and $70 per month for mSpy, a program that allows users to listen in on phone calls, review browsing history, and even track a smartphone's physical location. Interestingly, digital surveillance tools are increasingly being suggested by marital therapists as tools to facilitate reconciliation and rebuild trust in the wake of an online affair (Cottle, 2014; Schneider et al., 2012).

Harmful Effects of Online Infidelity

Research on traditional (offline) extramarital affairs indicates that they are often experienced as significant traumas for the betrayed partner and can destroy the trust and intimacy necessary to maintain the marriage (Dattilio, 2004; Glass, 2002; Hall & Fincham, 2006). Unfortunately, there is little research that specifically examines the consequences of Internet affairs—most of the literature includes other forms of potentially problematic online sexual behaviors in addition to online cheating. However, what evidence is available does suggest that the effects of online infidelity on betrayed partners and relationships appear to be similar in severity to the effects of more traditional affairs.

Online infidelity hurts betrayed partners and damages relationships (Atwood, 2005; Docan-Morgan & Docan, 2007; Nelson et al., 2005; Schneider 2000; Schneider et al., 2012). As with offline affairs, online infidelity takes away energy and resources from the primary relationship and often creates distance between partners (Atwood, 2005; Nelson et al., 2005; Shaw, 1997). Nelson et al. (2005) explain that relationship damage "is further exacerbated when one spouse pretends that this drain of energy will affect neither their partner nor the relationship, as long as it remains undiscovered" (p. 174). Young (2006) noted that online affairs result in "relational regression" (Carnes, 2001) whereby the cheating spouse demonstrates a declining investment in the marital relationship and distances from the betrayed spouse and others in the social network (Schneider, 2000; Young, 2006).

Researchers have sought to distinguish unique types of damage that online infidelity may create, as compared to traditional offline affairs. As technologies merge with in-person interaction, it is probably more useful to talk about how technology changes or alters the broader transgression of infidelity. Gerson (2011) suggested several ways that the pain associated with online betrayal may be especially damaging to the betrayed partner. First, Gerson noted that online betrayal is often *exposed in a sudden and abrupt manner* that is startling because it was conducted in secrecy. For example, a betrayed spouse may suddenly discover all of the messages his cheating partner has exchanged with an affair partner at one time. A second unique aspect of online betrayal is that it often has been conducted from *within the home* the cheating partner shares with the betrayed partner. On the other hand, offline affairs usually take place outside the home. Gerson (2011) noted a third unique feature of online betrayal is that there is often a *permanent record of the communication* between the cheating parties that, in some cases, may be stored forever online and reexamined by the betrayed partner when he or she feels anxious. This type of permanent preservation of the affair can make it very difficult for the primary relationship or betrayed partner to recover.

In addition to damaging the relationship itself, online infidelity hurts the betrayed partner. In one early study, Schneider (2000) surveyed people who had experienced severe adverse consequences because of their partner's cybersex involvement (which entailed a variety of cybersex problems including online affairs). Betrayed partners overwhelmingly reported that online affairs were just as emotionally painful as an offline betrayals. In this study, participants, most of whom were female, reported feeling betrayed, rejected, jealous, humiliated, angered, and having experienced diminished self-esteem as a result of their partner's online sexual activities. Participants also reported one or both partners losing interest in sex. Further, the participants repeatedly mentioned being lied to as a major source of their distress. The betrayed partners in this study reported that online affairs were just as emotionally painful as a traditional offline affair and considered their partner's online affair as adultery. Schneider's (2000) study also identified negative consequences for the children of a parent struggling with a cheating spouse's online sexual transgressions, including exposure to parental conflict, parents divorcing, and one parent's preoccupation with the other's online behavior.

In another study, Schneider et al. (2012) examined emotional reactions of betrayed partners to cybersex transgressions in relationships. The results revealed that 56% of betrayed partners reported feeling traumatized. The betrayed partners also reported losing trust in their mate, needing to seek counseling for their partner's behavior, and engaging in snooping and monitoring behaviors due to diminished trust in their partners. McDaniel, Drouin, and Cravens (2017) reported that engaging in infidelity-related behaviors on social media correlated with lower relationship satisfaction and higher relationship ambivalence. The researchers also reported relationships between greater attachment insecurity and engaging in infidelity related behaviors on social media.

As with other problems presented in this book, the computer-mediated context in which most online affairs take place offers a sense of anonymity and safety that may facilitate the development of these transgressions and give the cheating partner a sense that the behavior is less than real or less damaging than an in-person affair. The next section examines the features of online communication that might facilitate online affairs and also identifies some characteristics of individuals who are most likely to engage in them.

Explaining Online Infidelity

A critical area of interest among online infidelity researchers is identifying the factors that facilitate Internet infidelity. At the broadest level, the literature has focused on features associated with online communication technology that may contribute to online infidelity.

Technological Affordances. It is difficult to talk about Internet infidelity without acknowledging the rapidly evolving nature of the technology and the way people use it. With the rise of social networking sites, the emergence of websites that promote online affairs, smartphones, and other mobile technology, the line between device-mediated infidelity and traditional affairs is blurred and most affairs today likely involve some element of online interaction. In fact, Whitty (2011) argued, "digital technologies have made it easier for affairs to take place offline.

Snapchat or Instagram might be used for erotic exchanges of text, images, and videos. Additionally, with texting and messaging apps, subtle messages can be sent to an affair partner to organize a quick meeting. All this communication can easily take place in the home where one's spouse is present. So, it is important to note that digital technologies have changed the nature of even more traditional affairs" (p. 199).

As with research on other areas of problematic Internet use, studies suggest that computer-mediated communication environments offer affordances that may make it easier and less risky for individuals to initiate and conduct an affair online. Researchers in the 1990s and early 2000s emphasized anonymity and accessibility as the primary affordances that drew people to use the Internet for engaging in extradyadic relationships. Long before social networking and texting, early Internet users often used chatrooms, newsgroups, MOOs (Multi-User Dimensions, Object Oriented) and BBS (bulletin board systems) to meet strangers online and form relationships (see Parks & Floyd, 1996; Parks & Roberts, 1998; Rabby & Walther, 2003; Turkle, 1995). These online environments were mostly limited to text-based chat and messaging. For this reason, sharing images was much more difficult than it is today, which made it easy for users to easily conceal their identity, age, and gender from other users. At the time, Greenfield (1999) noted several features of the online environment that might promote extradyadic relationships, including increased disinhibition, a more intense sense of intimacy, accelerated intimacy development, dissociation (timelessness), and a loss of boundaries. Other researchers proposed models that identified unique Internet affordances thought to facilitate online infidelity, including the "Triple A Engine" (accessibility, affordability, and anonymity; Cooper, 2002), the "ACE model" (anonymity, convenience, escaping; Young, Griffin-Shelley, Cooper, Omara, & Buckingham, 2000) and the "Seven A's" (anonymity, accessibility, affordability, approximation, acceptability, ambiguity, accommodation; Hertlein & Stevenson, 2010). Although these early models have slight differences, they reflect some of the most common features thought to explain why online affairs might happen. Compared to face-to-face encounters, communicating online made it easier to hide one's identity, offered access to more potential affair partners, and was faster and cheaper than going to out to bars or other places to meet. The ambiguity of whether online interactions were actually violating relationship rules may have made it easier for people who would not otherwise have sought out an affair to become involved in one.

Additionally, communication researchers have noted that computer-mediated communication might change the way people communicate and develop intimacy, which also helps explain the appeal of online affairs. Walther (1996) characterized early computer-mediated communication contexts as hyperpersonal, suggesting that compared to traditional face-to-face conversations, online interpersonal exchanges enable participants to have greater control over self-presentation. When both partners engage in strategic self-presentation designed to impress the other and minimize negative perceptions, the result can be idealized perceptions of the other and overestimates of the similarity with the partner (Van Der Heide, Ramirez, Burgoon, & Peña, 2015; Walther, 1996, 2006). Another early theory, the Social Information and Deindividuation Theory (SIDE; Lea & Spears 1992; Lea, Spears & de Groot, 2001), argued the reduced nonverbal cues in early computer-mediated communication contexts (i.e., the inability to see the other person) led people to rely more heavily on social cues. In other words, SIDE theory suggested that impressions of conversational partners online might be based on prototypical beliefs about members of social groups and social norms rather than on unique characteristics of the individual partners. As a consequence, the theory suggests that people deindividuate their partners online. According to SIDE theory, deindividuation can result in perceptions of the other person that generate attraction that "may be (falsely) perceived to be personal in nature—an illusory reflection of interpersonal love—by the perceiver" (Rabby & Walther, 2003, p. 151). Online environments may enhance and exaggerate the development of intimacy. Research suggests that computer-mediated conversations among strangers contain a higher proportion of intimate self-disclosure and personal questions than comparable face-to-face interactions (Joinson, 2001; Tidwell & Walther, 2002).

Social Networking Affordances. Social networking sites, such as Facebook, have unique features that some researchers argue may facilitate online infidelity (Clayton, 2014; Clayton et al., 2013; Cravens & Whiting, 2014, 2015; Valenzuela et al., 2014). Cravens and Whiting (2014) explain that although Facebook infidelity is similar in many ways to other types of Internet infidelity, "what is unique about Facebook infidelity is the level of interaction that Facebook affords its users" (p. 328). Affair partners can use Facebook to exchange private messages, exchange pictures, share videos, and keep track of each other's status updates. Additionally, affair participants can block other users on Facebook so that the betrayed parties (the people being cheated on) will not be able to see any trace of them or their presence on Facebook.

Social networking sites offer a relatively easy and low-cost means for searching for an affair partner (Kendall, 2011). Valenzuela et al. (2014) noted that "Facebook in particular has a series of unique affordances that has helped to reduce these searching costs and consequently may contribute to cheating" (p. 95). For example, Facebook's search capabilities enable a user to find another person by name, email, workplace, mutual friends, location, hometown, and school. Additionally, they point out that using Facebook to search through friend lists of mutual friends enables users to find people they might be interested in pursuing a relationship with. Facebook also automatically suggests potential friends based on mutual friends.

Since social networking behaviors often take place between people who also know each other offline, research indicates that people view Facebook infidelity as especially threating. Cravens and Whiting (2014) claim that "a unique finding related to Facebook infidelity is the possibility of greater perceived threat of Facebook interactions due to the likelihood of the relationship occurring offline as well as online" (p. 328). Whereas early Internet technology may have enabled affairs among anonymous strangers, social networking sites facilitate reconnecting with a variety of past relationship partners (Ellison, Steinfield, & Lampe, 2007). Valenzuela et al. (2014) noted that Facebook can "support users' maintenance of relationships that may otherwise be only transitory, but could become problematic when juxtaposed to the marital relationship" (p. 95). Valenzuela et al. (2014) also suggested that Facebook's event invitation feature enables users to monitor if a particular person will be attending an event. Finally, Valenzuela et al. (2014)

observed that Facebook users could have multiple profiles, enabling a person to have one profile for family and friends and an entirely separate profile that lists them as single and interested in pursuing a relationship.

Affordances of Mobility. Mobile devices have taken online social interaction off the desktop and enabled us to be online everywhere, all the time. Additionally, apps such as Tinder and Grindr are using location-based data to help users connect with other people nearby who are seeking sexual or romantic interactions. Affair partners use mobile devices to keep in contact via text messaging and to engage in sexting, sending sexually explicit text, videos, and photos (e.g., Wysocki & Childers, 2011). Video technologies such as Facetime and Skype allow people to use their mobile devices or webcams to engage in real-time video interactions.

The topic of online infidelity is the most widely researched online relational transgression. Despite changes in communication technology and uses, online infidelity can be broadly described as a serious relational transgression in which one partner engages in secret intimacy with an outside party that harms the primary relationship. With the widespread adoption of social networking, additional online relational transgressions have emerged that reflect other ways that couples break relational rules with technology. The next section examines other types of online romantic transgressions and sources of conflict.

Other Romantic Relationship Transgressions and Conflicts

Beyond extradyadic behavior, there a varieties of other online transgressions that create conflict among romantic couples. For example, relational partners may argue about a social media posting that one partner finds embarrassing. Social networking behaviors can also create jealousy. Additionally, when jealous or anxious, romantic partners can use surveillance and intrusion to violate privacy boundaries (Elphistone & Noller, 2011; Fox, 2014; Fox, Warber, & Makstaller, 2013; Muise et al., 2009; Utz & Beukeboom, 2011). Romantic partners' surveillance of each other's Facebook activity may have negative impacts on the relationship (Tokunaga, 2011b, 2015). Another response to relational uncertainty or personal insecurity is to cross personal boundaries and violate a partner's privacy. Elphinstone and Noller (2011) noted that one partner's excessive Facebook use might lead the other partner to be hypervigilant for relationship threats, experience jealousy-related suspicions, and engage in interpersonal electronic surveillance. They add that "the tendency for Facebook to impinge on people's lives, together with the infinite number of available third-party threats, encourages the experience of jealous thoughts and engagement in surveillance behaviors, resulting in dissatisfying romantic relationships" (p. 634).

Tokunaga (2015) critiqued previous conclusions that Facebook surveillance leads to lower relationship satisfaction (e.g., Elphinstone & Noller, 2011; Muise et al., 2009). Instead, Tokunaga (2015) contended that relationship dissatisfaction leads to increased interpersonal electronic surveillance. Tokunaga (2015), in his critique of these earlier studies, argued, "dyadic distrust, jealousy, and (dis)satisfaction were characterized as unintended outcomes of surveillance over social networking sites. Little consideration was given to the possibility that these relational qualities instead motivated online surveillance" (p. 15). Tokunaga (2015) provided evidence that "dissatisfied partners and those who can readily envision viable alternatives to their current romantic partner are also the most likely to add online surveillance to their repertoire of currently enacted maintenance strategies. These individuals adopt negative working models of their partner, self, and relationship that impair their ability to avoid destructive communication patterns" (p. 13). Tokunaga (2015) also found that online surveillance transgressions are often motivated by distrust, anxiety, hypervigilance, and jealousy (also see Marshall, Bejanyan, & Ferenczi, 2013).

Romantic partners frequently engage in a variety of behaviors to reduce uncertainty about their partner and about the relationship. Long before the Internet, communication researchers recognized a fundamental need for individuals to reduce uncertainty about social partners and identified a variety of uncertainty reduction strategies people used in both new and established relationships (Baxter & Wilmot, 1984; Berger & Calabrese, 1975). Interpersonal communication research on uncertainty reduction has demonstrated that relational partners are motivated to reduce uncertainty about their partner and the relationship status. Research on face-to-face interactions reveals a variety of uncertainty reduction behaviors that couples use to gauge relationship status and commitment.

In earlier studies on uncertainty reduction in romantic couples, Baxter and Wilmot (1984) identified a number of dysfunctional and manipulative strategies romantic partners used to test one another's commitment, including separation tests (i.e., purposely distancing from the other in order to gauge their reaction) and jealousy tests (i.e., openly flirting with another person in order to see if one's partner gets jealous). Secret tests, such as purposely manipulating the partner and disguising one's motives, violate basic rules of romantic relationships and are often transgressions themselves. More recent research has revealed that romantic partners use Facebook to engage in uncertainty reduction with separation tests and jealousy checks. Moreover, these online versions of Baxter and Wilmot's secret tests create conflict and turmoil in the relationship (Fox & Anderegg, 2016). For example, Fox and Anderegg (2016) noted that romantic partners take advantage of the unique features (or affordances) of Facebook (i.e., visibility of their relationship status, ability to comment to make publicly visible comments to one's partner, visibility of one's friend list, and communication with others) to test the boundaries and status of their relationships (also see Fox & Anderegg, 2014).

In one study, participants mentioned situations in which network members intentionally induced doubt by posting comments or photos designed to create suspicion for their—or others'—partners (Fox et al., 2014). Fox et al. (2014) reported that romantic partners might change their Facebook relational status from "in a relationship" to "it's complicated" in order to worry their partner or to reveal relationship problems to other members of their social network. In the study, participants widely agreed that manipulating relationship status to publicly indicate relational distress was an "inappropriate way to deal with conflict and couples should opt for privacy during relational problems" (p.

532). From the perspective of uncertainty reduction theory, the status-changing behavior may be characterized as a type of separation test similar to those identified by Baxter and Wilmot (1984). One partner may induce separation or distance to gauge the other partner's reaction as an indication of relationship investment. The intentional manipulation of Facebook relationship status in order to evaluate the response exemplifies how Baxter and Wilmot's typology of uncertainty reduction tests during in-person interactions can help also explain online relational transgressions.

Another source of Facebook-related relational conflict involves public displays of relational distress or instability. For example, Muscanell, Guadagno, Rice, and Murphy (2013) observed that participants reported that they would feel angry, hurt, and jealous if their romantic partner did not post photos of them as a couple on Facebook, perhaps suggesting that one's partner does not acknowledge the relationship or may be trying to hide their relational status. Papp, Danielewicz, and Cayemberg (2012) observed that relationship conflicts occur when couples disagree about how to present their relationship on Facebook. Moreover, they learned that how couples display relational status plays a role in relationship satisfaction, whereby "disagreements over the Facebook relationship status was associated with lower level of females' but not males' relational satisfaction, after accounting for global conflict" (p. 85).

The fact that many of these behaviors are displayed publicly and viewable by other members of the social network can make the problems even more severe (Bryant & Marmo, 2012; Tokunaga, 2011b). When couples become "Facebook official" by indicating their relationship status publicly, the Facebook status is seen "as a tie-sign indicating that the couple is 'out of the market' and can promote their unity as a 'digital wedding ring'" (Orosz, Szekeres, Kiss, Farkas, & Roland-Lévy, 2015, n.p.). Fox et al.'s (2014) participants noted that relational transgressions that might have been ignored or downplayed if they took place offline become more serious when played out on Facebook—"it is the expression enabled through Facebook, as well as the act of distributing this information online versus offline, that creates distress that may have otherwise been avoided" (p. 83). More directly, disgruntled relationship partners may post information intentionally revealing internal relational distress to other members of the social network, often as retaliation for a perceived transgression (Cravens & Whiting, 2014).

Summary of Online Transgressions in Romantic Relationships

The primary focus of online romantic transgression research has been on extradyadic relationships, or online infidelity. The sections above conceptually defined online infidelity by identifying several of its essential characteristics including, intimacy with an outside third party, secrecy, concealment, violation of relational rules and norms, and damage to the relationship or victim if revealed. Social networking and mobile technology have characteristics that facilitate online infidelity. Today, most infidelity is multimodal, rather than online or offline. Uncertainty reduction theory can help explain intrusions and other transgressions that often occur in response to jealousy and anxiety about the relationship.

Although most of the literature on Internet-related relational transgressions pertains to romantic relationships, there is a growing interest among researchers in the problems Facebook presents for friendships. The next section provides an overview of this new area of research on Internet-related friendship transgressions.

Online Friendship Transgressions

In addition to online transgressions in romantic relationships, interpersonal technology is also a source of conflict among friends. Although a variety of online technologies may be used to enact friendship transgressions, most of the research has focused on problems involving social networking services such as Facebook. According to Tokunaga (2011a), "Despite the numerous benefits associated with the use of social networking sites, these technologies have also harmed interpersonal relationships by providing a forum for negative events that result in relational strain to occur" (p. 425). Whether they take place in person or online, behaviors that violate friendship rules often result in conflict and, in some cases, termination of the relationship (Argyle & Henderson, 1984; Henderson & Argyle, 1986).

Many common in-person friendship transgressions also occur in technology-mediated communication. For example, both offline or online, friends embarrass each other, exclude one another, gossip, and betray secrets. The more interesting online friendship transgressions are those that are unique to the online environment of social network sites and do not have offline counterparts, such as defriending, having a tag or post removed, or not receiving a like on an important post. Tokunaga (2011a) asked participants to recall adverse events involving online social networking sites that caused interpersonal strain in their relationships. The three most commonly reported negative events were (1) being defriended or having a friend request denied, (2) having one's message or tag deleted by a friend, and (3) ranking disparities on "top friend" applications (indicating incongruity in how each friend values the other). Tokunaga (2011a) observed that "all three activities are tied to context-specific social norms that are neither intuitive nor exist in offline contexts" (p. 430). Although these types of behaviors exist only online, rules for their use reflect a broader and deeper set of guidelines that help maintain friendship relationships.

Although the types of friendship transgressions that take place online are unique in many ways, they also share important similarities to offline transgressions. Online friendship transgressions usually involve the violation of expectations and of friendship relational rules (Bevan, Ang, & Fearns, 2014; Bryant & Marmo, 2012). Bevan et al. (2014), for example, found that being unfriended on Facebook constituted a negative and moderately-to-highly significant expectancy violation that was especially upsetting when the ties to the unfriended were close. Unfriending an ex-romantic partner is also seen as a transgression after a breakup. Fox et al. (2014) discovered that de-friending a former partner, when friend networks overlapped, was perceived as socially unacceptable and "it would be perceived as rude or cruel unless the breakup was particularly vicious" (p. 532).

This section reviews the newly emerging literature on social-networking-related conflict and transgressions among friends. First, the section explores the contextual characteristics of social networking sites that may encourage transgressions and reviews research on types of online behaviors that create problems among friends. Following sections present research on the unique rules that guide friendship interactions on social networking sites and explore the negative consequences when friends break those rules.

Social Networking and Online Friendship Transgressions

While Facebook is a popular venue for self-disclosure, it also allows others to share information about us, which can lead to embarrassment. A study by Oeldorf-Hirsch, Birnholtz, and Hancock (2017) investigated the effects of shared face-threatening information on emotional and nonverbal indicators of embarrassment. In this research, pairs of friends posted about each other on Facebook. Results show that face-threatening information shared by others produced a powerful emotional and nonverbal embarrassment response. However, it was not the content of the face-threatening post that produced this effect. Instead, the level of embarrassment depend primarily on whether that information violated the individual's identity and if the individual perceived that unknown members of their audience could see it. In response, individuals were most likely to joke about the post, although those who were most embarrassed were more likely to delete it. These results inform our understanding of how the process of embarrassment works online. The emotional embarrassment response is similar offline but is affected by the features of these sites, such as a large invisible audience and the need for ideal self-presentation. This finding has significant implications for treating online social networks and their effects to be as "real" as those offline.

According to Tokunaga (2011a), "there are several characteristics of social networking sites that have the potential to create or intensify problems in relationships, which make social networking sites an ideal forum for studying negative event types arising from Internet use" (p. 426). Tokunaga identified three specific contextual characteristics of social networking sites that may contribute to, or deepen, friendship problems.

First, Tokunaga suggests that social networks have unclear norms for interaction that are "loosely articulated" and "equivocal" (2011a, p. 426). Although there are rules and expectations that friends adhere to in Facebook interactions (e.g., Bryant & Marmo, 2012; Peña & Brody, 2014), they are less well articulated and developed than the types of rules that govern offline interaction. Bryant and Marmo (2012) argued that friendship rules on Facebook do exist but are more complicated because of the multiple audiences involved. The researchers asserted, "Facebook users might come to hold a different set of behavioral expectations because they simultaneously use the site to manage friendships of a close, casual, and acquaintance nature. The diversity of relationships present on the venue therefore suggests a more complex structure of rules" (Bryant & Marmo, 2012, p. 1018). To add to the confusion and ambiguity, Bryant and Marmo (2012) also noted that many of the expectations governing Facebook behavior are unspoken and implicit.

The second characteristic of social networking sites that Tokunaga suggested may contribute to relational problems among friends is the "ambiguous and elastic" meaning of the term "friend" on these sites (Tokunaga, 2011a, p. 426). Tokunaga explained, "interpersonal problems can sometimes stem from the use of the word 'friends' because certain expectations about interaction norms accompany such labels" (p. 426). For example, one might feel slighted or upset that a distant acquaintance who is one's Facebook "friend" did not post a happy birthday message or comment on a graduation picture, despite the fact that one would not expect such attention from that person offline. Neglecting friends' online posts or being non-responsive to friends' online actions can be hurtful and threaten a person's self-esteem (Greitmeyer, Mügge, & Bollermann, 2014). Additionally, Tokunaga (2011a) noted that Facebook creates a dichotomous social world in which people are either friend or non-friend, which can lead to interpersonal difficulties. For example, rejecting or ignoring a friend request may be perceived as a transgression, despite the fact that the person making the request is not someone one would consider a friend offline. In Tokunaga's (2011a) study, participants were asked to recall specific episodes in which they experienced interpersonal strain while using social networking sites.

The most frequently reported adverse event was having one's friend request denied or ignored.

The third contextual feature of social networking sites that Tokunaga (2011a) suggested can create relational problems is the reduced social presence during online interaction. The lack of physical proximity and visual feedback, along with the asynchronous nature of some Facebook communication, may increase the damage caused when a person unintentionally upsets a friend. Tokunaga (2011a) explained that in cases of unintentional hurtful behaviors, the reduced social presence on social networking sites can create barriers to reconciliation, and in some cases, prevent the offending party from even knowing that the other person is upset. Additionally, Tokunaga (2011a) argued that the reduced social presence can increase psychological distance between users and, consequently, make it easier to engage in purposeful behavior that hurts or embarrasses a friend and damages a relationship.

Taken together, the contextual characteristics of social networking applications outlined above all contribute to creating a potentially risky environment for friendship interaction. Unclear rules, ambiguous relational definitions, and diminished social presence can worsen common types of problems among friends and also give rise to unique problems that might not otherwise occur offline. Tokunaga argued, "the collection of these functional characteristics creates a social medium that encourages social problems" (2011a, p. 426).

The public nature of social networking sites and the vast audiences involved present other opportunities for friendship transgressions. Although Facebook does have private messaging and audience filtering features, much of what happens is viewable to a broad audience of other users. As the next section explains, the public nature of friendship interaction on Facebook increases the necessity that friends carefully consider how their online actions may affect the other's image and also increases the potential damage to individuals and relationships resulting from online face threats. The very fact that researchers have identified online friendship rules highlights the risk of online relational transgressions and importance of face maintenance among friends.

Facework and Face Threats Among Friends Online

Politeness theory suggests that the public nature of online social networking can facilitate embarrassing a friend or threatening their face. The rules guiding friendship, as well as social interaction in general, are based on the expectation that partners will uphold each other's face, or positive self-image, and avoid behaviors that might threaten the other's face (Brown & Levinson, 1987; Goffman, 1959, 1967). According to Brown and Levinson (1987), social actors have face needs that include both a positive self-image (positive face) and a sense of independence or autonomy (negative face). Although face threats certainly occur offline, when they take place online, they may be more damaging and problematic because they are often visible to a much wider audience and preserved online in a way that creates a sense of permanence (Bryant & Marmo, 2012; Litt et al., 2014; Peña & Brody, 2014; Tokunaga, 2011b). As Goffman (1959, 1967) noted, the harmful effects of embarrassment are worse when it occurs in front of an audience.

Social networking increases the size of the possible audience who might see or read something embarrassing that a friend posted. Goffman suggested that we employ facework, or politeness strategies, to minimize the potential damage of engaging in a face-threatening act. A lack of politeness or attention to someone's face online violates the basic relational rule to help uphold a friend's face, at least publicly.

Although online face threats may be self-inflicted, others are friend-generated. A variety of face-threatening acts can occur on social networking apps (Bryant & Marmo, 2012). Some typical examples of online face threating acts that occur among friends include posting embarrassing information about a friend, tagging a friend in an embarrassing picture, revealing something that was supposed to be held in confidence in a Facebook post, or posting something about one's self that might embarrass a friend just by association (Litt et al., 2014). Peña & Brody (2014) explain that on Facebook, "users may threaten receiver's face when bragging or when discussing sex, alcohol drinking [sic], or politics in their status updates ... SNS users may also threaten receiver's autonomy and goals when asking for favors or giving unwanted advice" (pp. 144–145). According to Bryant and Marmo

(2012), "Facebook friends are highly concerned about the appropriateness of various communication channels as well as the importance of facework and impression management" (p. 1026).

One study asked participants to recall a recent experience of friend-generated Facebook face threat and to rate its severity (Litt et al., 2014). The results revealed four types of friend-generated face threats that were commonly experienced on Facebook. The most commonly reported type of threat was *norm violation* (45%), in which a friend posted content on Facebook showing a participant's norm-violating behavior. For example, one participant recalled a situation in which a friend posted a picture of the participant intoxicated at a party. The researchers noted that although being drunk at a party was normative for young adults, one participant was concerned that other members of his Facebook audience, such as family and potential future employers, might form negative impressions of him based on the picture. Litt et al. (2014) also mentioned "an asymmetry in consequences between the poster and target [in which] poor judgment in posting content by others can have serious consequences for the target" (p. 454).

The second type of friend-generated online face threat involved *idealized self-presentation violations* (Litt et al., 2014). Here, participants were upset by a friend posting content that was incongruent with the participant's desired self-presentation, even though the post did not reveal any norm violation. In other words, the target was not engaging in any embarrassing behavior, but the information posted was upsetting because it still compromised her self-presentational efforts. The most commonly reported example of idealized self-presentation violations involved a friend posting an unflattering picture of a participant. Although Facebook users can be highly strategic and selective about the pictures they post of themselves, they must rely on their friends to exercise similar judgment.

The third type of friend-generated face-threatening act was what Lin et al. (2015) described as an *association effect*. About 21% of the participants reported being embarrassed by their friend's own self-presentation on Facebook. In these situations, the posting did not directly involve or mention the participant but "he/she worries that others will negatively judge him/her because of the other's behavior"

(p. 454). For example, one participant reported "a friend posted a link to an image that she thought was funny on my wall ... I was slightly embarrassed because I did not find the image funny and I was worried about how my other Facebook friends would think of me for having the link on my wall. I did not want my friends to think I was the type of person to find the image funny" (Litt et al., 2014, p. 454).

The fourth type of face-threat identified in Litt et al.'s (2014) study, *aggregate effect*, was the least common. Aggregate effect face-threats occur when a friend's Facebook behavior draws unwanted attention to something from the other friend's the past. On Facebook, when a friend comments on, or "likes," an older post or picture, the activity brings the original material back to the top of the newsfeed. In some cases, this caused embarrassment, such as when one participant's friend "liked" an old picture of the participant with an ex-romantic partner, causing the picture to display in the participant's newsfeed. Litt et al. (2014) explained, "this example highlights that even simple behavior by multiple others acting independently—such as commenting or liking—can have significant effects in the aggregate. The others in this case likely felt that they were being polite and flattering in responding positively to the photo, and had no idea that their behaviors were contributing to an aggregation that became embarrassing" (p. 455).

Taken together, Litt et al.'s (2014) work reveals that one's Facebook friends can threaten one's desired self-image by neglecting to exercise judgment about how postings might compromise one's public image or failing to consider how people may experience face threats associated with their friend's online activities. The unique way Facebook preserves posts also creates the possibility of face threats due to how information might be viewed by future audiences or how older material can quickly be revived at the top of a newsfeed by another person's action.

The Litt et al. (2014) study offered a second valuable contribution to the literature by identifying factors that affect how targets perceived their friends' face-threatening behaviors. Participants rated the perceived severity of a friend's face threat according to how much the event embarrassed them, made them feel awkward, made them look bad, made them feel exposed, and made them uncomfortable. The results revealed that face threats were more severe when participants saw them as being intentional and when participants placed a high value on how they are seen by others. Face threat severity was also related to the diversity of a participant's Facebook audience, such that more diverse audiences were associated with more severe perceptions of face threat. Here, Litt et al. (2014) noted that "people with more groups represented in their Facebook networks experienced face threats as more severe, thus suggesting that information crossing group boundaries is potentially an ongoing and stressful issue" (p. 457).

The results from the Litt et al. (2014) study represent an essential contribution to the emerging literature on friendship transgressions involving Facebook; they illustrate the complicated considerations of how one's online behavior affects one's friends' self-presentational goals. Regardless of intention, however, Litt et al. (2014) emphasize that the Facebook audience plays a major role in other-generated face threats, suggesting that "the majority of other-generated face threats described by our participants occurred primarily because others had difficulty navigating and/or lacked motivation in understanding the targets' diverse audiences ... not knowing who is in the potential audience for a post or the norms for different groups in an audience makes it particularly difficult to know whether or not shared content is likely to present a face-threatening scenario" (p. 457).

Thus, available data indicate that the face-maintenance expectations that govern offline interactions also apply to online contexts such as Facebook. The study also shows how the unique communicative context of social networking can make face maintenance more difficult for friends and facilitates a variety of unique types of face threats. As the next section illustrates, researchers have begun to identify specific rules that friends employ to guide interaction on Facebook and that, when violated, constitute Facebook-related friendship transgressions.

Distinct Friendship Rules on Social Networks

Research on emerging friendship rules for social networking (Bryant & Marmo, 2012) helps illustrate how prevalent and impactful these online friend transgressions are. There are many old transgressions in new packages with the popularity of technology (e.g., indfidelity). Nevertheless, the technology does offer some features that create new types of violations and also change the repercussions of violations by virtue of the audience or other aspects that alter the communication process.

Bryant and Marmo (2012) hypothesized that friends might expect different behaviors online than in offline interactions. For example, they proposed, "Facebook users likely possess unspoken behavioral codes regarding the appropriate use of synchronous/asynchronous and public/private Facebook communication tools in various types of friendships" (p. 1018). Bryant and Marmo argued that although earlier studies had demonstrated that friendships are guided by interaction rules (e.g., Argyle & Henderson, 1984), online interactions on social networking sites might change the nature of friend interactions in ways that require unique or different sets of rules. Moreover, given Facebook's semi-public nature, users might require friends to follow different rules for online interaction. Bryant and Marmo (2012) also noted that interaction rules for Facebook might differ from face-to-face expectations because users simultaneously use the site to manage friendships that vary in intimacy. Consequently, the researchers argued that "Facebook users must attempt to negotiate friendships of varying levels of closeness using mediated interaction, and might therefore come to understand a distinct set of Facebook friendship rules" (p. 1018).

Bryant and Marmo (2012) conducted two studies to identify Facebook friendship rules, determine which rules were most important, identify categories of rules, and assess whether rules differed based on the closeness of the friendship. In the first study, a focus group of college students was asked to generate a list of Facebook-specific rules that govern interactions among friends online. A second study asked another group of participants to identify the most important friendship rules. Bryant and Marmo (2012) observed that "participants were cognizant that Facebook interactions could produce negative consequences, and therefore endorsed rules that could prevent Facebook friends from hurting each other's public image" (p. 1026). The five most important rules were responsiveness ("I should expect a response from this person if I post on his/her profile"), respect ("I should not say anything disrespectful about this person on Facebook"), considering consequences ("I should consider how a post might negatively impact this person's relationships"), avoid reposting deleted material ("If I post something that this person deletes, I should not repost"), and maintaining offline contact ("I should communicate with this person outside of Facebook").

Taken together, Bryant and Marmo (2012) identified general categories of rules guiding friendship behaviors on social networks: rules about communication channels, rules about deception and control, rules about relationship maintenance, rules considering negative consequences for self, and an awareness of how one's own behavior might embarrass a friend. Channel rules specified which particular Facebook components were most appropriate to use to communicate with a friend (i.e., write on a friend's wall, send a private message, comment on a photo, use messenger to chat). Rules governing deception and control pertained to controlling the friend's access to one's profile, deleting or blocking a person who did something to embarrass the user, and being aware that people can lie on Facebook. Relational maintenance rules involved using Facebook for relationship preservation, such as wishing a friend happy birthday or using Facebook to learn more about the friend. The last two categories of rules involved being aware of the way that Facebook interactions with friends might adversely affect one's own image or embarrass a friend. For example, rules in this category included "do not post information a person could use against me," "project myself in a manner that the other would want to be associated with," "don't embarrass the other, " "protect the other's image when posting," and "consider how my post might negatively affect the relationship." Bryant and Marmo's (2012) Facebook friendship rules reveal an underlying categorical structure that functions to maintain relationship stability and minimize conflict.

In a second phase of the study, Bryant and Marmo (2010) asked 593 participants to rate the list of rules for how important they were in one of three types of friendships (close, casual, or acquaintance). The importance of four of the five rule categories was different for close friends, casual friends, and acquaintances. In general, Facebook users more strongly endorsed rules that protected the image of close friends. The authors interpreted this finding as indicating that offline relational norms for loyalty and protecting one's close friends also apply on Facebook. The results also revealed that Facebook rules about deception and control were different depending on relational closeness. Participants reported being more willing to work out rule violations with close friends where they may unfriend or block a more casual acquaintance for a similar transgression.

Whereas the research reviewed above examined the rules friends use to avoid online transgressions, other studies have examined the consequences of breaking Facebook friendship rules. Peña and Brody (2014) asked participants to view examples of online face-threating behaviors and to report how likely they would be to unfriend or hide the transgressor from their Facebook feed. The results indicated that posts that threatened the participants' desired self-image were more strongly linked to the receiver's intention to hide the friend from the Facebook feed, compared to other types of face threats (e.g., threats to the desire to be seen as independent and autonomous). Moreover, the perceived degree of severity of the posted face threats was associated with intention to hide the sender. Hiding a friend was conceptualized as a *relatively moderate negative response* whereas unfriending was conceptualized as a *significantly more extreme negative response*. According to Peña and Brody "Hiding and unfriending are online strategies that imply avoidance and relational dissolution" (2015, p. 147). Thus, friends have also developed online strategies for responding to transgressions.

Summary of Online Friendship Transgressions

Online behaviors can transgress friendship rules. Some of the transgressions are not new and existed long before the technology made it possible to amplify the audience. Today, however, a rumor is enough to destroy a reputation. Politeness theory and the concepts of face threat are useful theoretical tools for organizing and guiding research into online friendship transgressions. The small, but growing, research indicates that online face threats are common transgressions among friends. Research reviewed above revealed that young adult friends are aware of the potential relational transgressions and have established "Facebook rules" to help guide behavior and minimize conflict. Future research might consider what predicts whether people are able to mitigate or lessen the impact of their transgressions, and how social skill is related to the ability to minimize perceived threats or transgressions.

Future Research on Online Relational Transgressions

The research reviewed in this chapter reveals a rapidly changing face of problematic Internet use. Beyond the online habits that the term usually refers to, this chapter indicates another type of problem: the wide variety of online relational rule transgressions that create distress and harm relationships. Today, people must try to avoid online relational transgressions ranging from minor annoyances to severe relationship disruptions. Although early research questioned the very possibility of "online infidelity," that idea is quickly becoming obsolete since virtually any infidelity is now likely to entail media multiplexity (Haythornthwaite, 2005; Ledbetter, 2015) and modality switching (Caughlin & Sharabi, 2013; Sharabi & Caughlin, 2017).

That being said, it is more important than ever that research begin to examine the ways that couples handle online boundary violations. Far more common than infidelity, mundane transgressions have emerged along with social networking and mobile devices. Partners use technology in both functional and less-than-functional ways to reduce uncertainty about the other. Future research here should consider factors that might determine whether a person engages in more functional or dysfunctional online uncertainty reduction (e.g., directly asking versus spying or playing games). The rich literature on relational rules and transgressions, uncertainty reduction, and politeness in face-to-face settings can help guide development of models of online transgressions.

Technology has become deeply embedded in our close relationships and, as a consequence, people have developed complex types of relational rules. Yet, today's online relational transgressions closely resemble issues friends and couples have always fought about. Although technology changes rapidly, the basic rules and expectations in close interpersonal relationships are relatively stable. Earlier research on relational rules and transgressions in face-to-face contexts can help organize and guide the newer study of online transgressions. Relational rules are the common conceptual thread that ties together the wide variety of transgressions covered in this chapter. Rather than studying these in isolation, the research areas of romantic and friend transgressions can inform one another. For example, although romantic rules are more complicated, some of the friendship rules about Facebook also guide romantic partners.

Though technology and its role in our lives continue to change, the basic rules of close interpersonal relationship remain relatively stable. Using interpersonal and relational communication theory and research as a guide for studying transgressions allows for changes in how technology is used. Secrecy is a transgression, regardless of whether it involves Facebook or an old-fashioned email exchange. Approaching online relational problems from an interpersonal perspective means putting relational dynamics ahead of whatever the present technology is. Channel characteristics change, but expectations about how to treat friends and romantic partners are enduring.

References

Afifi, W. A., & Metts, S. (1998). Characteristics and consequences of expectation violations in close relationships. *Journal of Social and Personal Relationships*, 15(3), 365–392. doi:10.1177/0265407598153004

American Academy of Matrimonial Lawyers (2010, February 10). Big surge in social networking evidence says survey of nation's top divorce lawyers. Retrieved from https://www.aaml.org/about-the-academy/press/press-releases/e-discovery/big-surge-social-networking-evidence-says-survey-

Argyle, M., & Henderson, M. (1984). The rules of friendship. *Journal of Social and Personal Relationships*, 1(2), 211–237.

Argyle, M., Henderson, M., & Furnham, A. (1985). The rules of social relationships. *British Journal of Social Psychology*, 24(2), 125–139. doi:10.1111/j.2044-8309.1985.tb00671.x

Atwood, J. D. (2005). Cyber-Affairs: "What's the big deal?" Therapeutic considerations. *Journal of Couple and Relationship Therapy*, 4(2–3), 117–134.

Baxter, L. A., & Wilmot, W. W. (1984). "Secret tests": Social strategies for acquiring information about the state of the relationship. *Human Communication Research*, 11(2), 171–201. doi:10.1111/j.1468-2958.1984.tb00044.x

Berger, C. R., & Calabrese, R. J. (1975). Some explorations in initial interaction and beyond: Toward a developmental theory of interpersonal communication. *Human Communication Research, 1*(2), 99–112. doi:10.1111/j.1468-2958.1975.tb00258.x

Bevan, J. L., Ang, P. C., & Fearns, J. B. (2014). Being unfriended on Facebook: An application of expectancy violation theory. *Computers in Human Behavior, 33*, 171–178. doi:10.1016/j.chb.2014.01.029

Bevan, J. L., Pfyl, J., & Barclay, B. (2012). Negative emotional and cognitive responses to being unfriended on Facebook: An exploratory study. *Computers in Human Behavior, 28*(4), 1458–1464. doi:10.1016/j.chb.2012.03.008

Brown, P., & Levinson, S. C. (1987). *Politeness: Some universals in language usage.* New York: Cambridge University Press.

Bryant, E. M., & Marmo, J. (2012). The rules of Facebook friendship: A two-stage examination of interaction rules in close, casual, and acquaintance friendships. *Journal of Social and Personal Relationships, 29*(8), 1013–1035. doi:10.1177/0265407512443616

Carnes, P. (2001). Cybersex, courtship, and escalating arousal: Factors in addictive sexual desire. *Sexual Addiction & Compulsivity 8*(1), 45–78. doi:10.1080/10720160127560

Caughlin, J. P., & Sharabi, L. L. (2013). A communicative interdependence perspective of close relationships: The connections between mediated and unmediated interactions matter. *Journal of Communication, 63*(5), 873–893. doi:10.1111/jcom.12046

Clayton, R. B. (2014). The third wheel: The impact of Twitter use on relationship infidelity and divorce. *Cyberpsychology, Behavior, and Social Networking, 17*(7), 425–430. doi:10.1089/cyber.2013.0570

Clayton, R. B., Nagurney, A., & Smith, J. R. (2013). Cheating, breakup, and divorce: Is Facebook use to blame? *Cyberpsychology, Behavior, and Social Networking, 16*(10), 717–720. doi:10.1089/cyber.2012.0424

Cooper, A. (2002). *Sex and the Internet: A guidebook for clinicians.* New York: Routledge.

Cottle, M. (2014, November). The adultery arms race. *The Atlantic, 314*(4), 58–62. Retrieved from https://www.theatlantic.com/magazine/archive/2014/11/the-adultery-arms-race/380794/

Cravens, J. D., & Whiting, J. B. (2014). Clinical implications of Internet infidelity: Where Facebook fits in. *The American Journal of Family Therapy, 42*(4), 325–339. doi:10.1080/01926187.2013.874211

Cravens, J. D., & Whiting, J. B. (2015). Fooling around on Facebook: The perceptions of infidelity behavior on social networking sites. *Journal of Couple & Relationship Therapy, 15*(3), 1–21. doi:10.1080/15332691.2014.1003670

Cravens, J. D., Leckie, K. R., & Whiting, J. B. (2013). Facebook infidelity: When poking becomes problematic. *Contemporary Family Therapy, 35*(1), 74–90. doi:10.1007/s10591-012-9231-5

Dattilio, F. M. (2004). Extramarital affairs: The much overlooked PTSD. *Behavior Therapist, 27*(4), 76–78.

Docan-Morgan, T., & Docan, C. A. (2007). Internet infidelity: Double standards and the differing views of women and men. *Communication Quarterly, 55*(3), 317–342. doi:10.1080/01463370701492519

Ellison, N. B., Steinfield, C., & Lampe, C. (2007). The benefits of Facebook "friends:" Social capital and college students' use of online social network sites. *Journal of Computer-Mediated Communication, 12*(4), 1143–1168. doi:10.1111/j.1083-6101.2007.00367.x

Elphinstone, R. A., & Noller, P. (2011). Time to face it! Facebook intrusion and the implications for romantic jealousy and relationship satisfaction. *Cyberpsychology, Behavior, and Social Networking, 14*(11), 631–635. doi:10.1089/cyber.2010.0318

Emmers-Sommer, T. M. (2003). When partners falter: Repair after a transgression. In D. J.Canary & M. Dainton (Eds.), *Maintaining relationships through communication: Relational, contextual, and cultural variations* (pp. 185–205). Hillsdale, NJ: Lawrence Erlbaum Associates.

Fox, J., & Anderegg, C. (2014). Romantic relationship stages and social networking sites: Uncertainty reduction strategies and perceived relational norms on Facebook. *Cyberpsychology, Behavior, and Social Networking, 17*(11), 685–691. doi:10.1089/cyber.2014.0232

Fox, J., & Anderegg, C. (2016). Turbulence, turmoil, and termination: The dark side of social networking sites for romantic relationships. In E. Gilchrist & S. Long (Eds.), *Contexts for dark side communication* (269–280). New York, NY: Peter Lang Publishing.

Fox, J., Osborn, J. L., & Warber, K. M. (2014). Relational dialectics and social networking sites: The role of Facebook in romantic relationship escalation, maintenance, conflict, and dissolution. *Computers in Human Behavior, 35*, 527–534. doi:10.1016/j.chb.2014.02.031

Fox, J., Warber, K. M., & Makstaller, D. C. (2013). The role of Facebook in romantic relationship development: An exploration of Knapp's relational stage model. *Journal of Social and Personal Relationships, 30*(6), 771–794. doi:10.1177/0265407512468370

Fricker, J., & Moore, S. (2008). Internet infidelity and its correlates. *Australian Journal of Counseling Psychology, 9*(2), 15–22.

Gardner, D. (2010, December 2). The marriage killer: One in five American divorces now involve Facebook. *The Daily Mail*. Retrieved from https://www.dailymail.co.uk/news/article-1334482/The-marriage-killer-One-American-divorces-involve-Facebook.html

Gerson, M. J. (2011). Cyberspace betrayal: Attachment in an era of virtual connection. *Journal of Family Psychotherapy, 22*(2), 148–156. doi:10.1080/08975353.2011.578039

Glass, S. P. (2002). Couple therapy after the trauma of infidelity. In A. S. Gurman & N. S. Jacobson (Eds.), *Clinical handbook of couple therapy* (pp. 488–507). New York: Guilford Press.

Goffman, E. (1959). *The presentation of self in everyday life*. New York: Doubleday Anchor Books.

Goffman, E. (1967). *Interaction ritual: Essays on face-to-face behavior*. New York: Doubleday Anchor Books.

Greenfield, D. (1999). Psychological characteristics of compulsive Internet use: A preliminary analysis. *CyberPsychology & Behavior, 2*(5), 403–412. doi:10.1089/cpb.1999.2.403

Greitemeyer, T., Mügge, D. O., & Bollermann, I. (2014). Having responsive Facebook friends affects the satisfaction of psychological needs more than having many Facebook friends. *Basic & Applied Social Psychology, 36*(3), 252–258. doi:10.1080/01973533.2014.900619

Hall, J. H., & Fincham, F. D. (2006). Relationship dissolution following infidelity: The roles of attributions and forgiveness. *Journal of Social & Clinical Psychology, 25*(5), 508–522. doi:10.1521/jscp.2006.25.5.508

Haythornthwaite, C. (2005). Social networks and Internet connectivity effects. *Information, Communication & Society, 8*(2), 125–147. doi:10.1080/13691180500146185

Helsper, E. J., & Whitty, M. T. (2010). Netiquette within married couples: Agreement about acceptable online behavior and surveillance between partners. *Computers in Human Behavior, 26*(5), 916–926. doi:10.1016/j.chb.2010.02.006

Henline, B. H., Lamke, L. K., & Howard, M. D. (2007). Exploring perceptions of online infidelity. *Personal Relationships, 14*(1), 113–128. doi:10.1111/j.1475-6811.2006.00144.x

Hertlein, K. M., & Piercy, F. P. (2006). Internet infidelity: A critical review of the literature. *The Family Journal, 14*(4), 366–371. doi:10.1177/1066480706290508

Hertlein, K. M., & Stevenson, A. (2010). The seven "As" contributing to Internet-related intimacy problems: A literature review. *Cyberpsychology: Journal of Psychosocial Research on Cyberspace, 4*(1). Retrieved from https://cyberpsychology.eu/article/view/4230/3273

Joinson, A. N. (2001). Self-disclosure in computer-mediated communication: The role of self-awareness and visual anonymity. *European Journal of Social Psychology, 31*(2), 177–192. doi:10.1002/ejsp.36

Jones, K. E., & Hertlein, K. M. (2012). Four key dimensions for distinguishing Internet infidelity from Internet and sex addiction: Concepts and clinical application. *The American Journal of Family Therapy, 40*(2), 115–125. doi:10.1080/01926187.2011.600677

Kline, S. L., & Stafford, L. (2004). A comparison of interaction rules and interaction frequency in relationship to marital quality. *Communication Reports, 17*(1), 11–26. doi:10.1080/08934210409389370

Lea, M., & Spears, R. (1992). Paralanguage and social perception in computer-mediated communication. *Journal of Organizational Computing, 2*(3–4), 321–341.

Lea, M., Spears, R., & de Groot, D. (2001). Knowing me, knowing you: Anonymity effects on social identity processes within groups. *Personality and Social Psychology Bulletin, 27*(5), 526–537. doi:10.1177/0146167201275002

Ledbetter, A. M. (2015). Media multiplexity theory: Technology use and interpersonal tie strength. In D. O. Braithwaite & P. Schrodt (Eds.), *Engaging theories in interpersonal communication: Multiple perspectives* (2nd ed., pp. 363–376). Thousand Oaks, CA: Sage.

LeFebvre, L., Blackburn, K. M., & Brody, N. (2015). Navigating romantic relationships on Facebook: Extending the relationship dissolution model to social networking environments. *Journal of Social and Personal Relationships, 32*(1), 78–98. doi:10.1177/0265407514524848

Litt, E., Spottswood, E., Birnholtz, J., Hancock, J. T., Smith, M. E., & Reynolds, L. (2014). Awkward encounters of an "other" kind: Collective self-presentation and face threat on Facebook. *Proceedings of the 17th ACM conference on computer supported cooperative work & social computing* (pp. 449–460). New York, NY: ACM. doi:10.1145/2531602.2531646

Luo, S., Cartun, M. A., & Snider, A. G. (2010). Assessing extradyadic behavior: A review, a new measure, and two new models. *Personality and Individual Differences, 49*(3), 155–163. doi:10.1016/j.paid.2010.03.033

Maheu, M. M., & Subotnik, R. (2001). *Infidelity on the Internet: Virtual relationships and real betrayal*. Naperville, IL: Sourcebooks.

Marshall, T. C., Bejanyan, K., & Ferenczi, N. (2013). Attachment styles and personal growth following romantic breakups: The mediating roles of distress, rumination, and tendency to rebound. *PLOS ONE, 8*(9). doi:10.1371/journal.pone.0075161

Martins, A., Pereira, M., Andrade, R., Dattilio, F. M., Narciso, I., & Canavarro, M. C. (2016). Infidelity in dating relationships: Gender-specific correlates of face-to-face and online extradyadic involvement. *Archives of Sexual Behavior, 45*(1), 193–205. doi:10.1007/s10508-015-0576-3

McDaniel, B. T., Drouin, M., & Cravens, J. D. (2017). Do you have anything to hide? Infidelity-related behaviors on social media sites and marital satisfaction. *Computers in Human Behavior, 66*, 88–95. doi:10.1016/j.chb.2016.09.031

Metts, S. (1994). Relational transgressions. In W. R.Cupach & B. H. Spitzberg (Eds.), *The dark side of interpersonal communication* (pp. 217–239). Hillsdale, NJ: Lawrence Erlbaum Associates.

Miller, D. T., & Ross, M. (1975). Self-serving biases in the attribution of causality: Fact or fiction? *Psychological Bulletin, 82*(2), 213–225. doi:10.1037/h0076486

Muise, A., Christofides, E., & Desmarias, S. (2009). More information than you ever wanted: Does Facebook bring out the green-eyed monster of jealousy? *CyberPsychology & Behavior, 12*(4), 441–444. doi:10.1089/cpb.2008.0263

Muscanell, N. L., Guadagno, R. E., Rice, L., & Murphy, S. (2013). Don't it make my brown eyes green? An analysis of Facebook use and romantic jealousy. *Cyberpsychology, Behavior, and Social Networking, 16*(4), 237–242.

Nelson, T., Piercy, F. P., & Sprenkle, D. H. (2005). Internet infidelity: A multiwave Delphi Study. *Journal of Couple and Relationship Therapy, 4*(2–3), 173–194. doi:10.1300/J398v04n02

Oeldorf-Hirsch, A., Birnholtz, J., & Hancock, J. T. (2017). Your post is embarrassing me: Face threats, identity, and the audience on Facebook. *Computers in Human Behavior, 73*, 92–99. doi:10.1016/j.chb.2017.03.030

Orosz, G., Szekeres, Á., Kiss, Z. G., Farkas, P., & Roland-Lévy, C. (2015). Elevated romantic love and jealousy if relationship status is declared on Facebook. *Frontiers in Psychology*. Retrieved from https://journal.frontiersin.org/article/10.3389/fpsyg.2015.00214

Papp, L. M., Danielewicz, J., & Cayemberg, C. (2012). "Are we Facebook official?" Implications of dating partners' Facebook use and profiles for intimate relationship satisfaction. *Cyberpsychology, Behavior, and Social Networking, 15*(2), 85–90. doi:10.1089/cyber.2011.0291

Parker, T. S. & Wampler, K. S. (2003). How bad is it? Perceptions of the relationship impact of different types of Internet sexual activities. *Contemporary Family Therapy, 25*(4), 415–429.

Parks, M. R., & Floyd, K. (1996). Making friends in cyberspace. *Journal of Communication, 46*(1), 80–97. doi:10.1111/j.1460-2466.1996.tb01462.x

Parks, M. R., & Roberts, L. D. (1998). 'Making Moosic': The development of personal relationships online and a comparison to their off-line counterparts. *Journal of Social and Personal Relationships, 15*(4), 517–537. doi:10.1177%2F0265407598154005

Peña, J., & Brody, N. (2014). Intentions to hide and unfriend Facebook connections based on perceptions of sender attractiveness and status updates. *Computers in Human Behavior, 31*, 143–150. doi:10.1016/j.chb.2013.10.004

Rabby, M. K., & Walther, J. B. (2003). Computer-mediated communication effects on relationship formation and maintenance. In D. J. Canary & M. Dainton (Eds.), *Maintaining relationships through communication* (pp. 141–162). Mahwah, NJ: Lawrence Erlbaum Associates.

Schneider, J. P. (2000). Effects of cybersex addiction on the family: Results of a survey. *Sexual Addiction & Compulsivity, 7*(1–2), 31–58. doi:10.1080/10720160008400206

Schneider, J. P., Weiss, R., & Samenow, C. (2012). Is it really cheating? Understanding the emotional reactions and clinical treatment of spouses and partners affected by cybersex infidelity. *Sexual Addiction & Compulsivity, 19*(1–2), 123–139. doi:10.1080/10720162.2012.658344

Sharabi, L. L., & Caughlin, J. P. (2017). What predicts first date success? A longitudinal study of modality switching in online dating. *Personal Relationships, 24*(2), 370–391. doi:10.1111/pere.12188

Shaw, J. (1997). Treatment rationale for Internet infidelity. *Journal of Sex Education and Therapy, 22*(1), 29–34. doi:10.1080/01614576.1997.11074168

Tidwell, L. C., & Walther, J. B. (2002). Computer-mediated communication effects on disclosure, impressions, and interpersonal evaluations: Getting to know one another a bit at a time. *Human Communication Research, 28*(3), 317–348. doi:10.1111/j.1468-2958.2002.tb00811.x

Tokunaga, R. S. (2011a). Friend me or you'll strain us: Understanding negative events that occur over social networking sites. *Cyberpsychology, Behavior, and Social Networking, 14*(7–8), 425–432. doi:10.1089/cyber.2010.0140

Tokunaga, R. S. (2011b). Social networking site or social surveillance site? Understanding the use of interpersonal electronic surveillance in romantic relationships. *Computers in Human Behavior, 27*(2), 705–713. doi:10.1016/j.chb.2010.08.014

Tokunaga, R. S. (2014). Relational transgressions on social networking sites: Individual, interpersonal, and contextual explanations for dyadic strain and communication rules change. *Computers in Human Behavior, 39*, 287–295. doi:10.1016/j.chb.2014.07.024

Tokunaga, R. S. (2015). Interpersonal surveillance over social network sites: Applying a theory of negative relational maintenance and the investment model. *Journal of Social and Personal Relationships, 33*(2), 171–190. doi:10.1177/0265407514568749

Turkle, S. (1995). *Life on the screen: Identity in the age of the Internet.* New York: Simon & Schuster.

Utz, S., & Beukeboom, C. J. (2011). The role of social network sites in romantic relationships: Effects on jealousy and relationship happiness. *Journal of Computer-Mediated Communication, 16*(4), 511–527. doi:10.1111/j.1083-6101.2011.01552.x

Valenzuela, S., Halpern, D., & Katz, J. E. (2014). Social network sites, marriage well-being and divorce: Survey and state-level evidence from the United States. *Computers in Human Behavior, 36,* 94–101. doi:10.1016/j.chb.2014.03.034

Walther, J. B. (1996). Computer-mediated communication impersonal, interpersonal and hyperpersonal interaction. *Communication Research, 23*(1), 3–43. doi:10.1177/009365096023001001

Walther, J. B. (2006). Nonverbal dynamics in computer-mediated communication. In V. Manusov & M. L. Patterson (Eds.), *The Sage handbook of nonverbal communication* (pp. 461–480). Thousand Oaks, CA: Sage.

Walther, J. B., Van Der Heide, B., Ramirez, A., Burgoon, J. K., & Peña, J. (2015). Interpersonal and hyperpersonal dimensions of computer-mediated communication. In S. Shyam Sundar (Ed.), *The handbook of the psychology of communication technology* (pp. 3–22). Hoboken, NJ: John Wiley & Sons.

Whitty, M. T. (2004). Pushing the wrong buttons: Men's and women's attitudes toward online and offline infidelity. *CyberPsychology & Behavior, 6*(6), 569–579. doi:10.1089/109493103322725342

Whitty, M. T. (2005). The realness of cybercheating: Men's and women's representations of unfaithful Internet relationships. *Social Science Computer Review, 23*(1), 57–67. doi:10.1177/0894439304271536

Whitty, M. T. (2011). Internet infidelity: A real problem. In K. S. Young & C. N. de Abreu (Eds.), *Internet addiction: A Handbook and guide to evaluation and treatment* (pp. 191–204). Hoboken, NJ: John Wiley & Sons.

Wysocki, D. K., & Childers, C. D. (2011). "Let my fingers do the talking": Sexting and infidelity in cyberspace. *Sexuality & Culture, 15*(3), 217–239. doi:10.1007/s12119-011-9091-4

Young, K. S. (1998). Internet addiction: The emergence of a new clinical disorder. *CyberPsychology & Behavior, 1*(3), 237–244. doi:10.1089/cpb.1998.1.237

Young, K. S. (2006). Online infidelity. *Journal of Couple & Relationship Therapy, 5*(2), 43–56. doi:10.1300/J398v05n02_03

Young, K. S., Griffin-Shelley, E., Cooper, A., O'mara, J., & Buchanan, J. (2000). Online infidelity: A new dimension in couple relationships with implications for evaluation and treatment. *Sexual Addiction & Compulsivity, 7*(1–2), 59–74. doi:10.1080/10720160008400207

Chapter Four

Cyberbullying and Online Interpersonal Aggression

Interpersonal aggression has always been part of online behavior. From the earliest days of computer-mediated communication, members of text-based messaging systems and online communities engaged in "flaming," verbal expressions of hostility and insults (Lea, O'Shea, Fung, & Spears, 1992). Given that so few people were using the Internet at the time, and that most flaming occurred between anonymous users, online aggression was relatively non-threatening compared to modern online interpersonal aggression. As mobility and social networking became commonplace, people began using these platforms to engage in intentional, repeated aggression towards other people. Today, young people's lives are entirely enmeshed in online social behavior (Lenhart, Smith, & Anderson, 2015) and concerns about the effects of cyberbullying victimization motivate both scholarly and public interest in the problem.

In their review of "cyberbullying myths" Sabella, Patchin, and Hinduja (2013) noted that mass media headlines often describe cyberbullying as far more common and prevalent than empirical research suggests. Sabella et al. (2013) present several examples of news stories claiming that cyberbullying had become an "epidemic," with headlines such as "Cyberbullying a National Epidemic" (*Education Insider*, 2010) and "It's Time to Stop the Cyberbullying Epidemic" (McGraw, 2015). Sabella et al. (2013) argued, "Recent headlines can serve to fuel what may be a distorted and artificially-inflated view of cyberbullying" (p. 2704). Similarly, as Mitchell and Jones (2015) observed, "The amount of public and academic attention to cyberbullying sometimes overshadows the consistent finding that in-person peer victimization and bullying happens to youth at substantially higher rates than online victimization experiences" (p. 473). Indeed, perhaps one of the most consistent findings that researchers have reported is that *traditional, in person, bullying is far more common and frequent than cyberbullying* (Sabella et al., 2013). A meta-analysis of cyberbullying studies revealed that cyberbullying occurs about half as often as traditional bullying (Modecki, Minchin, Harbaugh, Guerra, & Runions, 2014).

Cyberbullying is the most widely studied form of online interpersonal aggression. Between, 2000 and 2016, researchers published over 1,000 articles on cyberbullying.[1] Across studies, cyberbullying victimization is associated with psychological and social problems (see Nixon, 2014). Despite the seriousness of cyberbullying, researchers have made little progress toward developing *theory-driven* empirical research. Research and media reports on cyberbullying reveal a state of confusion, exaggerated claims, and inaccurate information (see Olweus 2012; Sabella et al., 2013).

The primary reason for the inconsistent and ambiguous literature on cyberbullying is that scholars struggle with conceptualizing and measuring the phenomenon (Kowalski, Giumetti, Schroder, & Lattanner, 2014; Menesini, Calussi, & Nocentini, 2012; Olenik, 2012; Thomas, Connor, & Scott, 2015; Tokunaga, 2010). Conceptual definitions are the foundation of any theory-based research program. Inconsistent definitions and measures make it difficult to compare findings across studies and to draw conclusions about the prevalence, causes, and effects of cyberbullying (Tokunaga, 2010).

Today, the most common definition of cyberbullying is based on a well-established definition of traditional bullying (Olweus, 1993).

Cyberbullying is, "an aggressive, intentional act carried out by a group or individual, using electronic forms of contact, repeatedly and over time against a victim who cannot easily defend him or herself" (Smith et al., 2008, p. 376). This definition, along with similar ones from other researchers (e.g., Kowalski, Giumetti, Schroeder & Lattanner, 2014; Kowalski, Limber, & Agatston, 2012; Patchin & Hinduja, 2012; Savage & Tokunaga, 2017), is based on the defining features of traditional bullying: intentionality, repetition of behavior, and presence of a power imbalance (Olweus, 1993).

Though cyberbullying and traditional bullying share many characteristics, one problem with the definitions above is that they do not address how cyberbullying differs from traditional bullying. Researchers have struggled with the question of whether cyberbullying is distinct enough from other forms of bullying to warrant separate study and definitions (Popović-Ćitić, Djurić, & Cvetković, 2011; Roberto & Eden, 2010; Sourander et al., 2010; Tokunaga, 2010; Wade & Beran, 2011). Although it shares similarties with traditional bullying, cyberbullying also has unique qualities afforded by technology.

To help understand the interpersonal aspects of cyberbullying, this chapter emphasizes the importance of approaching it as a communication problem. The similarities between traditional and cyberbullying can assist in distinguishing cyberbullying from other types of online harassment. Further, examining the communicative differences can illuminate how technology alters bullying.

Similarities Between Cyberbullying and Traditional Bullying

Identifying the similarities between cyberbullying and traditional bullying can help outline how cyberbullying is distinct from other types of online harassment. For example, both conventional bullying and cyberbullying involve intentional aggressive behavior, behavior repeated over time, and a power difference between aggressor and victim. However, these characteristics do not apply to other forms of online aggression and harassment, such as cyberstalking or hostile comments on a Twitter post.

The repetitive behavior criterion distinguishes bullying as a cyclical pattern, distinct from other aggressive acts that may only occur once (Olweus, 1993). The repetition criterion is also important because the recurring victimization involved in bullying contributes to a unique victim experience that differs from the experience of a single-occurrence of aggression. Finally, the traditional bullying definition highlights the difference in power between bully and victim. A bully's overwhelming power is not only limited to physical strength, but may also involve higher social status, control over rewards and punishment for the victim (e.g., a boss or supervisor), or more significant relational influence over the victim. Together, these characteristics help conceptually connect cyberbullying with the broader traditional bullying research. According to Thomas et al. (2015), "There is considerable support that these three key criteria defining traditional bullying are largely applicable to cyberbullying" (p. 137). Patchin and Hinduja (2006) make a similar argument, stating "The constructs of malicious intent, violence, repetition, and power differential appear most salient when building a comprehensive definition of traditional bullying and are similarly appropriate when attempting to define this new permutation" (p. 152).

Another conceptual similarity between traditional bullying and cyberbullying is the distinction between direct versus indirect forms of the bullying behaviors (Aftab, 2011). In traditional bullying research, direct bullying refers to physical and verbal aggression whereas indirect bullying involves more passive or subversive forms of relational hostility, such as spreading rumors behind the victim's back (Scheithauer, Hayer, Petermann, & Jugert, 2006; Smith et al., 2012). Although it does not occur in-person, cyberbullying can still be described as *direct* when the bully interacts with the victim using texts, instant messages, emails, social networking. On the other hand, cyberbullying can be indirect when a bully uses interpersonal technologies to spread rumors, impersonate the victim online, or post media intended to embarrass a victim.

Additionally, "cyberbullying by proxy" is another type of indirect cyberbullying using accomplices to facilitate the bullying behavior, either with or without their knowledge. Kowalski, Limber, and Agatston (2012) and Atfab (2011) note that cyberbullying by proxy also occurs when a perpetrator hacks a victim's account and then sends out inappropriate, embarrassing, or upsetting messages to the victim's friends and family, who assume the victim sent the offensive message. Consequently, in these cases, victims face social or relational harms such as angering their friends and experiencing humiliation.

In addition to examining communicative similarities between cyberbullying and traditional bullying, research also benefits from examining how the two interpersonal phenomena differ. As the next section elaborates, there are essential communicative differences between traditional and cyberbullying that make cyberbullying a unique phenomenon. In fact, the differences between online and in-person bullying reveal how mediated communication may change the experience for the bully and the victim. The differences are of interest to communication researchers since most of the variations are due to the communicative context of online interaction.

Differences Between Cyberbullying and Traditional Bullying

Despite the similar conceptual definitions presented above, advancing the research requires scholars to consider how cyberbullying and traditional bullying differ. The differences become apparent when we recognize that cyberbullying is not another *type* of bullying (e.g., physical, verbal, online) or another *environment* in which bullying occurs (e.g., in school or online), but instead it is a *particular mode of communication through which bullying occurs* (e.g. face-to-face, social networking, online, text messaging; Ybarra, Boyd, Korchmaros, & Oppenheim, 2012). Ybarra et al. (2012) contend cyberbullying becomes a "distinct and meaningful category" once we recognize it a unique communication mode. Dooley, Pyzalski, and Cross (2009) made a similar argument that, "Considering cyberbullying as merely the electronic form of face-to-face bullying may overlook intricacies of these behaviors" (p. 183).

What is unique about cyberbullying is the communicative context and how it may change the experience for the victim and the bully.

Indeed, researchers have identified a myriad of important distinctions between traditional bullying and cyberbullying that further support the argument that conceptualizing cyberbullying as a distinct communicative context, rather than just another type of traditional bullying, is essential for fully capturing and understanding the phenomenon. Viewing cyberbullying as a communication process emphasizes those unique contextual features which may help researchers better understand how cyberbullying differs from traditional face-to-face bullying. The sections below examine the meaningful communicative differences between cyberbullying and traditional bullying. These differences emphasize the importance of treating cyberbullying as a communicative phenomenon.

Repetition Versus Persistence of Hurtful Messages

Smith (2012) contends that the traditional bullying criterion of repeated behavior (Olweus, 1993) is not a necessary condition for cyberbullying. Smith cautioned that, "Due to the nature of cyberbullying, the act, or behavior may repeat itself without the contribution of the cyberbully" (p. 95). For example, a single aggressive act, such as posting an embarrassing image of the victim on Instagram, could arguably be construed as repetitive because online material can repeatedly be shared and reposted by others. As a result, Smith (2012) argues "the use of repetition as a criterion for serious bullying may be less suitable for cyberbullying" (p. 97) since a single act of aggression can be shared and repeated by others besides the original bully. Dooley, Pyżalski, & Cross (2009) noted, "Repetition in cyberbullying is especially problematic to operationalize, as there can be differences between the perpetrator and victim regarding perceptions of how many incidences occur and the potential consequences" (p. 183). For instance, a single act, such as posting the message on a website, "can result in continued and widespread ridicule and humiliation for the victim. Whereas the aggressive act is not repeated the damage caused by the act is relieved through the ongoing humiliation" (Dooley et al., 2009, p. 183). Thus, a single instance of online behavior may meet the criterion of repetition since online material spreads quickly and people may repeatedly view and share it.

One solution to the disagreements about repetition in definitions of cyberbullying would be to reframe the criterio as *persistence over time*. In other words, although a behavior may only occur once, the hurtful message may persist online indefinitely, it may be distributed widely, and it could come back at any time. These characteristics of online message persistence may create victim experiences analogous to being repeatedly victimized by traditional bullying. The distinction between the concepts of repetition and persistence illustrates the point that *communicative processes are central to understanding cyberbullying*. Indeed, to ignore the unique features of message persistence online would miss part of what is especially upsetting about cyberbullying.

Power Imbalance

Traditional bullying involves a power imbalance where a perpetrator may possess more social capital or physical strength than the victim (Olweus, 1993). Traditional bullies derive power by being bigger, stronger, or more popular than their target. Among adults in the workplace, bullies may hold greater institutional status than victims (Glendinning, 2002). In addition to the types of power imbalances above, power imbalances also arise from the communicative features unique to cyberbullying.

First, a cyberbully might hold power over victims by virtue of the bully's technological expertise. Dooley et al. (2009) note that although simple cyberbullying requires little technical skill (e.g., posting a picture or sending a text), advanced technical skill may represent a type of power unique to cyberbullying. For example, a cyberbully with computer skill may be able to engage in more serious online aggression (e.g., manipulating or modifying pictures, spreading rumors across sites, hijacking social networking accounts).

In situations where a cyberbully may not have greater power than the victim, the *communication medium itself creates a power imbalance*. Dooley et al. (2009) note that by its very nature, cyberbullying creates a situation that victims cannot escape as readily as face-to-face situations. Put differently, technology is more powerful than the victim is. If embarrassing materials spread online, there is little that the victim can do to stop or minimize the damage. Although the aggressor might not have more physical or social power, the cyberbully attains power by proxy of the technology. As the next sections elaborate, although traditional and cyberbullying both involve power imbalances, the unique context of online harassment may further exacerbate the power imbalance.

Time and Space Boundaries

Cyberbullying transcends the ordinary time and space limits of in-person interaction and traditional bullying. Cappadocia, Craig, and Peplar (2013) explain cyberbullying is "widening the scope of bullying beyond the school environment and leaving victimized youth without a safe haven" (p. 172). For example, being at home used to be a respite for adolescents bullied at school. Today, online communication easily defies the physical and social barriers that once protected people at home (Slonje & Smith, 2008). A. Dempsey, Sulkowski, J. Dempsey, and Storch (2011) add that online, bullies have greater control over social interaction including the choices of "when to harass a peer, in what medium they will send their message, and whether they want bystanders to witness the harassment" (p. 298).

Anonymity, Reduced Social Presence, and Disinhibition

The possibility of anonymity and diminished social presence online create an experience that is different from traditional bullying for both victims and perpetrators (Bartlett, 2015; Bryce & Faser, 2013; A. Dempsey et al., 2011; Dooley et al., 2009; Menesini et al, 2012; Thomas et al., 2015; Tokunaga, 2010; Ybarra & Mitchell, 2004b). The various degrees of anonymity available online contribute to the power imbalance between bully and victim. The bully's ability to remain unknown represents a source of power in that the victim is not able to identify the origin of the aggression (Cappadocia et al., 2013; Hinduja & Patchin, 2008; Menesini et al., 2012; Ybarra & Mitchell, 2004b). Victims may feel more powerless when they do not know who is harassing them. More broadly, as the next section explains, anonymity also represents a crucial interpersonal difference between traditional bullying and cyberbullying.

Traditional bullying lacks the opportunities for anonymity that cyberbullies may exploit. Many victims report that they do not know the identity of their cyberbullies. In an early study, Ybarra and Mitchell (2004a) found that a majority of cyberbullying aggressors (84%) indicated knowing the identity of their victim, whereas a majority of the victims (69%) reported they did not know their aggressor. In a sample of over 3,000 students in grades 6 through 8, almost half of victims did not know the identity of their cyberbully (Kowalski & Limber, 2007). In another study that employed focus groups of adolescents, those who admitted engaging in cyberbullying "had mostly operated anonymously or disguised themselves," despite knowing their victims personally offline (Vandenbosch & van Cleemput, 2008, p. 501).

Anonymity may affect both victims' and aggressors' experiences in a cyberbullying relationship. For the victim, not knowing the identity of the cyberbully may worsen already painful experiences. Sticca and Perren (2013) sought to isolate and identify the role anonymity might play in the impact of cyberbullying on victims. The results revealed that adolescents perceived cyberbullying cases as more harmful when the bully's identity was unknown. Additionally, the influence of anonymity itself was seen as more harmful in cyberbullying than in traditional bullying scenarios. In other words, participants perceived anonymous cyberbullies as more dangerous than they perceived anonymous traditional bullies.

For bullies, the reduced social presence and potential anonymity may lower inhibitions that inhibit aggression (Bryce & Fraser, 2013; Vandebosch & van Cleemput, 2009; Udris, 2014). Bartlett (2015) argues that, in a computer-mediated context, an "aggressor's anonymity may enhance the frequency of which cyberbullying (vs. traditional bullying) occurs" (p. 71).

From the earliest days of research on computer-mediated communication, scholars have suggested the psychological distance, diminished social presence, and lack of visual and identifying cues inherent in many forms of online interaction may foster *disinhibition* whereby people act out in ways that are less restrained and more intense than they would in face-to-face contexts (e.g., Joinson, 1998; Lapidot-Lefler, & Barak, 2012; Suler, 2004). Online disinhibition is not necessarily harmful. For example, in an online support group, disinhibition may help people disclose more easily than in person. Suler (2004) introduced the concept of a *toxic disinhibition effect* to describe ways in which online disinhibition could cause harm, such as cyberbullying.

For cyberbullies, *feeling* anonymous may be more important than *being* anonymous. Even if the cyberbully's identity *is known*, the computer-mediated communication context may still foster disinhibition due to the reduced social presence, lack of eye contact, sense of invisibility, and the asynchronous nature of online interaction (Lapidot-Lefler & Barak, 2012; Suler, 2004; Udris, 2014). As Barlett (2015) argued, "Feeling anonymous and being anonymous are not identical, and even if the cyber victim can identify their aggressor, the bully may still feel anonymous, which may predict cyberbullying frequency" (p. 71). Lapidot-Lefler and Barak (2012) revealed that anonymity, lack of eye contact, and perceived invisibility all predicted online disinhibition. Yet, the study also reported the lack of eye contact in computer-mediated contexts might have a stronger impact on disinhibition than the impact of anonymity alone.

Lack of eye contact may be a strong disihibitor because it minimizes a bully's awareness of the how their aggression affects victims, thus minimizing guilt (Raskauskas & Stolz, 2007). Slojne and Smith (2008) observed, "Compared to most traditional bullying, the person carrying out the cyberbullying may be less aware or even unaware of the consequences caused by his or her actions. Without such direct feedback, there may be fewer opportunities for empathy or remorse" (p. 148). Heirman and Walrave (2008) describe cyberbullies' lack of awareness of how their aggression harms a victim as the *"cockpit effect,"* explaining that "due to absent face-to-face-cues, the bully sitting in front of his/her computer display, like a pilot in a cockpit, feels disinhibited and is facilitated in his/her bullying behavior since he/she cannot directly observe the emotional reaction of his/her target" (para. 29). In other words, they argued, "Communication technology has created distance between perpetrator and target and thereby has eliminated pity and empathy as powerful inhibitions for human aggression" (para. 29).

Consistent with the arguments above, a study by Udris (2014) revealed that online disinhibition was a significant predictor of cyberbullying. In a sample of 887 Japanese students, group means for disinhibition were higher for students who engaged in cyberbullying than their non-involved peers. Further, those students who reported higher levels of online disinhibition were more likely than peers to have engaged in cyberbullying in the previous six months. Most importantly for the current discussion of anonymity, the scale item representing 'invisibility' on the disinhibition measure was a significant predictor of cyberbullying; students who endorsed this item were more likely to cyberbully others.

In sum, the literature reviewed in this section suggests that the computer-mediated communication context that enables cyberbullying creates an experience that is distinct from traditional bullying due to the potential for increased social distance, anonymity, and reduced social presence. These factors may create toxic disinhibition that leads young people to act more aggressively and more intensely than they might otherwise in a face-to-face situation. Moreover, the decreased social presence and lack of visual cues may minimize empathy for victims and awareness of the impact on the victims that might help stop or lessen aggression in a face-to-face setting. The research also suggests that people perceive the effects of cyberbullying to be more harmful to victims when the aggressor is anonymous.

Audience and Dispersal

The communication technologies used in cyberbullying create another significant difference from traditional bullying regarding the scope of the audience and the speed that information can disperse. Whereas traditional bullying requires an audience to be physically present to witness the aggression, cyberbullying may play out in front of much broader audience who are not physically present, and the audience can quickly grow larger over time (Cappadocia et al., 2013; Dooley et al., 2009; Sabella et al., 2013; Slojne & Smith, 2008; Sticca & Perren, 2013; Thomas et al., 2015). Sabella et al. (2013) observed, "With modern technology, cyberbullying can occur at the speed of thought" (p. 2704). Similarly, Dooley et al. (2009) noted that with cyberbullying, "the potential audience is limitless" (p. 187).

Goffman (1967) asserted that people seek to maintain face and experience adverse emotional reactions when their face is threatened in social situations. The ways that cyberbullying increases the audience presents a unique type of face threat to victims, compared to the face threats inherent in traditional bullying.

Several researchers have suggested that the features of audience and speed of dispersal make cyberbullying especially distressing for victims. Dooley et al. (2009) argued that "Given how quickly and extensively images can be distributed to groups using mobile phones or the Internet, it is not surprising that the effect of such an act would be more distressing and damaging to a victim than being bullied in a face-to-face interaction which only a small group of individuals would observe" (p. 187). Bauman and Newman (2013) made a similar point, arguing that, in cases of cyberbullying, "the size of the audience can amplify the humiliation" (p. 28). Additionally, cyberbullying victims' uncertainty about who viewed the offending messages or material may also contribute to cyberbullying victims' distress (Slojne & Smith, 2008).

In sum, this section presented two approaches to defining cyberbullying. First, research identifying how cyberbullying is like traditional bullying can help ground cyberbullying studies in an established research literature. Basing a definition of cyberbullying on more established models of traditional bullying helps illuminate how cyberbullying may differ from other types of online aggression. Noting the communicative differences between in-person and online bullying also contributes to the conceptual understanding of cyberbullying. Here, the unique features of computer-mediated communication may alter the bullying experience. Perhaps most importantly for this book, the research suggests that the *mode of communication* is what makes cyberbullying unique and worthy of consideration as a distinct phenomenon.

Estimating Cyberbullying Prevalence

There is little agreement in the literature regarding how often cyberbullying occurs or how many people it affects. The inconsistencies that characterize the research on cyberbullying prevalence stem from a variety of problems, including differences in how cyberbullying is measured and defined. The sections below describe the methodological and conceptual problems with estimating cyberbullying prevalence and then provide an overview of the different estimates of how often cyberbullying victimization and perpetration occur.

One challenge in measuring cyberbullying is that it can be difficult to separate bullies from victims. Cyberbullying research indicates that cases of bullying involve people who have been both bullies and victims, or "bully-victims" (Gámez-Guadix, Orue, Smith, & Calvete, 2013; Gradinger, Strohmeier, and Speil, 2009; Kowalski & Limber, 2013; Perren, Dooley, Shaw, & Cross, 2010; Sourander et al., 2010; Wang, Iannotti, & Luk, 2012; Wang, Iannotti, Luk, & Nansel, 2010). According to Görzig and Ólafsson (2013), "Cyberbullying might be a circular problem that does not merit a clear-cut differentiation of cyberbullies from cyber victims" (p. 10). In one study, for example, Cappadocia et al. (2013) found that about 5% of the students in their sample reported simultaneous involvement, being both a bully and being victimized. Hinduja and Patchin (2012) surveyed over 28,000 students and reported about 10% identified themselves as both cyberbullies and victims. Mishna, Khoury-Kassabri, Gadalla, and Daciuk (2012) surveyed 2,186 middle and high school students, observing that 25.7% reported having been both a cyberbully and victim during the previous three months.

Cyberbullying Victimization Estimates

Researchers have reported a wide range of cyberbully victimization estimates. One review of the research reported that 10–40% of adolescents have experienced some form of cyberbullying (Kowalski et al., 2014; Lenhart, 2007). A year-long longitudinal study by Cappadocia et al. (2013) revealed that about 10% of high school students reported being victims of cyberbullying. In Ybarra, Boyd, Korchmaros, and Oppenheim's (2012) study, 10% of children and adolescents sampled experienced cyberbullying on the Internet, and 8% had been bullied via texting. Williams and Guerra (2015) reported that, on average, about 9% of fifth to eleventh-grade students reported being cyberbullied. A recent multinational study of over 10,000 adolescents in six European countries reported that about 18% to 24% reported being victims of cyberbullying in the previous year (Tsitsika et al., 2015). In a review of 35 journal articles, Patchin and Hinduja (2012) reported an average of 24% of students had been cyberbullied and 17% engaged in cyberbullying. In a review of their own survey research, Hinduja and Patchin (2012) observed that "20% of the over 4,000 randomly selected 11- to 18-year-old students we surveyed in 2010 indicated they had been a victim at some point in their life" (p. 540). A meta-analysis of 80 separate studies revealed an average of 15% of participants reported being victims of cyberbullying (Modecki et al., 2014). A survey administered to over 28,000 adolescents revealed 25.6% reported being victims of cyberbullying (Waasdorp & Bradshaw, 2015). Toward the larger end of estimates, Mishna, Cook, Gadalla, Daciuk, and Solomon, (2010) found that 49.5% of middle and high school students reported having been cyberbullied. However, Mishna et al.'s estimate is substantially larger than the general pattern that emerges when one examines findings across the numerous studies mentioned above.

A longitudinal study by Gámez-Guadix, Gini, and Calvete (2015) investigated the stability of cyberbullying victimization among adolescents over time. In this study, researchers identified stable victims, (students who reported being victimized at both Times 1 and 2), victims who had only been cyberbullied at one of the two measurement times (students who reported being victimized at either Time 1 or 2) and non-victims who had never been cyberbullied. Results suggested that only about 6% of the adolescent sample were stable cyberbullying victims, between 14% and 18% were one-time victims, and 62% of the sample were not victims of cyberbullying at either time. Taken together, this research suggests that most cyberbullying victims are not stable victims whose victimization extends across time. Moreover, the data suggest relatively small victimization rates, with almost 62% of students having never been victimized.

Cyberbullying Perpetration Estimates

Estimates of engaging in cyberbullying are also widely divergent, with studies suggesting that between 10 to 40% of teenagers have engaged in some sort of cyberbullying behavior. Cappadocia et al. (2013) reported that roughly 10% of high school students admitted engaging in cyberbullying. Similarly, Modecki et al.'s (2014) meta-analysis of 80 studies concluded that about 16% of participants engaged in cyberbullying.

According to Raskauskas and Stoltz (2007), 21.4% of adolescent girls reported engaging in cyberbullying in the previous year. Mishna et al. (2010) found that 33.7% had cyberbullied someone in the last three months. In one study, Roberto, Eden, Savage, Ramos-Salazar, and Deiss (2014) reported that 35% of incoming college freshman engaged in cyberbullying at least one individual during their senior year of high school. Toward the higher end of estimates, 54% of teenagers sampled in a study by Gradinger et al. (2009) admitted they had engaged in cyberbullying.

Despite the disagreements and debates about prevalence estimates, one finding that researchers do seem to agree on is that cyberbullying is significantly less frequent than traditional bullying and usually occurs along with, or as part of, traditional bullying (Erdur-Baker, 2009; Juvoven & Gross, 2008; Katzer, Fetchenhauer, & Belschak, 2009; Kowalski & Limber, 2013; Kowalski et al. 2014; Olweus, 2013; Roberto et al., 2014; Slojne & Smith, 2008; Smith et al., 2008; Waasdorp & Bradshaw, 2015; Wang et al., 2010, Wang et al., 2012). In one review of the research, Tokunaga (2010) stated, "The statistical relationship between the frequency of traditional bullying and cyberbullying events is consistently documented in the literature" (p. 279).

Cyberbullying Happens Alongside Traditional Bullying

Cyberbully victims are likely to be victims of offline bullying as well. Smith et al.'s (2008) review notes "considerable overlap between pupil involvement in traditional bullying and involvement in cyberbullying" and emphasizes that "overlap is one of the most well-replicated findings in the relatively new area of cyberbullying" (p. 32). The meta-analysis by Modecki et al. (2014), revealed correlations between cyberbullying and traditional bullying perpetration and victimization. Salmivalli, Sainio, & Hodges (2013) sampled over 17,000 children and observed significant correlations between traditional and cyberbullying victimization.

Schneider, O'Donnell, Stueve, & Coulter (2012) surveyed 20,406 ninth- through twelfth-graders, observing 59.7% of cyberbullying victims were victims of traditional bullying. Waasdorp and Bradshaw (2015) found that 50.3% of bullying victims reported they were victims of both cyberbullying and traditional bullying, while only 4.6% reported being only cyberbullied. Similarly, 85% of cyberbullying victims also experienced traditional bullying in school (Juvonen & Gross, 2008). In another study, Ybarra, Diener-West, and Leaf (2007) reported that 35% students harassed online also reported being bullied at school.

Cyberbullying *perpetration* also co-occurs with traditional bullying behaviors. Hinduja and Patchin (2008) found that traditional bullies were more than twice as likely to be involved (as victim or perpetrator) in cyberbullying compared to students who did not engage in traditional bullying. Hinduja and Patchin (2012) presented data suggesting that almost two thirds of youth who reported being cyberbullies in the previous month were also bullied at school during the same period. Additionally, over three quarters of cyberbullies also admitted to bullying in school in the previous month.

Overall, the research on victimization and perpetration estimates is vague, but it does not suggest that cyberbullying is an "epidemic," as it has been characterized. In addition, the research notes the importance of recognizing that most cyberbullying also involves offline bullying, making estimations of both difficult.

Gender and Cyberbullying Prevalence

Researchers agree that boys engage in traditional bullying more than girls (e.g., Olweus, 1993; Olweus & Limber, 2010). However, the data on gender differences in cyberbullying are inconsistent and inconclusive (Ang & Goh, 2010; Giménez Gualdo, Hunter, Durkin, Arnaiz, & Maquilón 2015; Gradinger et al., 2009; Kowalski et al., 2014; Smith et al., 2008). To date, there is no clear picture in the literature about the relationship between sex and either cyberbullying behavior or victimization.

A review of some of the conflicting reports illustrates the difficulty researchers face trying to find a consistent pattern among the studies on gender and cyberbullying. Some studies have noted boys are more likely to perpetrate cyberbullying than girls (Erdur-Baker, 2009; Li, 2006). Yet, other data suggest girls are more likely to engage in cyberbullying behavior (e.g., Holfeld & Grabe, 2012). Moreover, a number studies have not found gender differences in either cyberbullying perpetration or victimization (Brown, Demaray, & Secord, 2014; Hindjua & Patchin, 2008; Jackson & Cohen, 2012; Monks, Robinson, & Worlidge, 2012; Slonje & Smith, 2008; Smith et al., 2008; Raskauska & Stolkz, 2007; Williams & Guerra, 2015; Ybarra & Mitchell, 2004a). In a two-study paper, Smith et al. (2008) found girls were more likely to be cyberbullying victims in the first study, but failed to find any gender difference in cyberbullying victims or aggressors in the second study. In a meta-analysis of 109 studies on sex-differences and cyberbullying, Barlett and Coyne (2014) only observed a small gender effect (males were slightly more likely to cyberbully than females), and this effect was moderated by age with girls more likely to report cyberbullying during early to mid-adolescence and boys more likely to engage in cyberbullying in mid to late adolescence. The meta-analysis also revealed that the publication status, year, continent, and country of the data collection each moderated the effects of gender on cyberbullying involvement.

Research on gender and cyberbullying victimization is also inconsistent. Several publications report girls are more likely than boys to be victims of cyberbullying (e.g., Cappadocia et al., 2013; Cénat et al., 2014; Cross, Lester, & Barnes, 2015; Elgar et al., 2014; Holfeld & Ledbetter, 2015; Mishna et al., 2012). Yet, other studies report the opposite, that boys are more likely to be victims (Erdur-Baker, 2009; Fanti, Demetrious & Hawa, 2012; Katzer et al. 2009; Wong, Chan & Cheng, 2014). Clearly, there is no widespread agreement on gender differences among victims.

Age and Cyberbullying Prevalence

Exploring the prevalence of cyberbullying among different age groups is difficult because most cyberbullying studies have limited their samples to children and adolescents. At best, researchers have been able to make some broad generalizations about age. In an extensive review and meta-analysis, Kowalski et al. (2014) noted that cyberbullying is especially prevalent among middleschool children. Similarly, Williams and Guerra (2007) observed that cyberbullying increases after fifth grade and peaks at eighth grade. According to Waasdorp and Bradshaw (2015) "cyberbullying may increase through high school" (p. 484). Overall, there is no clear or consistent pattern among findings.

More recent studies have examined cyberbullying among college students (e.g. Crosslin & Golman, 2014; Francisco, Veiga Simão, Ferreira, & Martins, 2015; Gahagan, Vaterlaus, & Frost, 2016; Kowalski, Morgan, Drake-Lavelle & Allison, 2016; Larrañaga, E., Yubero, S., & Ovejero 2015; Schenk & Fremouw, 2012; Schenk, Fremouw, & Keelan, 2013; Selkie, Kota, Chan, & Moreno, 2015). In one study, over 30% of college students reported their first experience of cyberbullying victimization occurred in college (Kowalski et al., 2014). Among those who had been cyberbullied in middle or high school, 43% of victims reported they experienced more cyberbullying while in college.

Even fewer studies have examined cyberbullying among non-student adult populations. One reason may be that when online aggression occurs among middle-aged or older adults, it may be considered harassment or stalking instead of bullying. Cassidy, Faucher, and Jackson (2014) surveyed 121 university faculty members and observed that 17% experienced cyberbullying by students and 9% were cyberbullied by colleagues in the previous year. In another study, the same researchers reported that 25% of faculty respondents had experienced cyberbullying from students (15%) and colleagues (12%); female faculty members were targeted more than males (Cassidy, Jackson, & Faucher, 2015). One significant limitation in the studies by Cassidy and colleagues is that the measure of cyberbullying included questions about cyberstalking, which confounded the two phenomena.

Although age is undoubtedly an essential variable for cyberbullying researchers to examine, more research is needed before drawing conclusions. To date, studies have not identified clear and consistent differences in the nature, predictors, or effects of cyberbullying in adults compared to the literature on children and adolescents.

Limitations of Cyberbullying Prevalence Estimates

As the review above illustrates, there are vast disparities in estimates of both cyberbullying victimization and perpetration. The inconsistencies in this line of research make it difficult to draw conclusions about how frequently cyberbullying occurs. This section examines some of the reasons for the inconsistencies in prevalence estimates. Estimations of cyberbullying prevalence rates are hindered by methodological and conceptual problems. There is a lack of consistency among cyberbullying measurement instruments (Berne et al., 2013). Additionally, some researchers question the measures' validity and reliability. Thomas et al. (2015) contend that "The majority of the measurement instruments designed to assess cyberbullying lack the minimum psychometric standards of scale development; only 12 of the 44 measures reviewed have been validated with confirmatory factor analysis" (p. 140).

Further, question types, survey wording, and even instructions to particpants affect measures of cyberbullying. A meta-analysis by Kowalski et al. (2014) concluded that "Prevalence rates are likely to be lower when using a single, global item to assess overall bullying behavior than when using multiple specific items to assess different forms of bullying behavior" (p. 1109). The prompts and instructions used in different survey instruments affect observed estimates of cyberbullying prevalence (Van Noorden, Haselager, Cillessen, & Bukowski, 2015). For example, Kert, Codding, Tryon, and Shiyko (2010) found that whether a survey presented participants with a definition of cyberbullying affected the number of people who reported being involved in cyberbullying. According to Ybarra et al. (2012), prevalence rates are higher when measures offer participants a behavioral list of bullying experiences without using a definition or using the word "bully."

In sum, the research on cyberbullying prevalence is fraught with inconsistent patterns of estimates that make it difficult to draw conclusions about how often cyberbullying happens and how many people it affects. Without consistent methods and measures, researchers cannot correctly compare results from different studies to understand or explain the discrepancies in results. An examination of the patterns of results in the literature clearly indicates that, although cyberbullying is a common occurrence, it occurs less frequently than traditional bullying. Moreover, cyberbullying often occurs along with traditional bullying. Finally, the evidence from studies reviewed here does not the support claim that cyberbullying is an "epidemic," as stories in the popular press often suggest (Sabella et al., 2013).

Correlates of Victimization

There is extensive literature documenting the association between cyberbullying victimization and a host of social, emotional, and behavioral problems. A majority of the research has employed cross-sectional designs which identify correlates of cyberbullying victimization. Unfortunately, these methods do not allow researchers to assess causal claims. The discussion below will first examine the correlation between victimization and three categories of variables: interpersonal problems, emotional problems, and behavioral problems (for an extensive review of this literature, see Nixon, 2014). Subsequent sections will then present findings from longitudinal and retrospective studies that shed light onto questions about causal effects of cyberbullying on victims.

Interpersonal Problems and Cyberbullying Victimization

Cyberbullying victimization is correlated with a number of interpersonal and relational difficulties. Victims of cyberbullying often report interpersonal relationship problems with peers, teachers, and with their families, appearing to be more socially isolated than peers both at school and at home (Campbell, Spears, Slee, Butler, & Kift, 2012; Dooley et al., 2012; Fredstrom, Adams, & Gilman, 2011; Katzer et al., 2009; Price & Dalgleish, 2010; Sourander et al., 2010). Cyberbullying victimization is correlated with loneliness (Brighi et al., 2012; Larrañaga, Yubero, Ovejero, & Navarro, 2016; Olenik-Shemesh, Heiman, & Eden, 2012; Van den Eijnden, Vermulst, van Rooij, Scholte, & van de Mheen, 2014). Jackson and Cohen (2012) observed that children who had been cyberbullied reported increased loneliness, lower peer acceptance, fewer friendships, and less optimism about peer relationships than other children. Similarly, cyberbullying victims report a diminished sense of belonging and are less popular in school, compared to non-victimized peers (Katzer et al., 2009; Wong et al., 2014).

A survey of 2,079 adolescents revealed strong parent-child relationships (i.e., healthy attachment and trust) were correlated with lower cyberbullying victimization. Additionally, cyberbullying victimization is related to other interpersonal deficits such as lower social skills (Dooley et al., 2012), lower empathy (Wong et al., 2014), and higher social anxiety (A. Dempsey et al., 2011; Pabian & Bandebosch, 2015; Van den Eijenden et al., 2014). Although these data cannot tell us whether cyberbullying caused these social problems or whether the problems are risk factors for being victimized, they clearly demonstrate that cyberbullying victims exhibit a variety of interpersonal deficits and social problems.

Emotional Problems and Cyberbullying Victimization

In addition to the interpersonal difficulties reviewed above, cyberbullying victimization is correlated with a number of indicators of psychological and emotional distress. For instance, one study found cyberbullying victims were 2.5 to 3 times more likely to report psychological distress than non-victims (Schneider et al., 2012). One of the most consistent and well-documented associations is between cyberbullying victimization and depression (Bonnano & Hymel, 2013; Campbell et al., 2012; Chang et al., 2013; Didden et al., 2009; Dooley et al., 2012; Kowalski & Limber 2013; Menesini et al., 2012; Mitchell, Ybarra, & Finkelhor. 2007; Perren, Dooley, Shaw, & Cross, 2010; Schenk & Fremouw, 2012; Schneider et al., 2012; Wang, Nansel, & Iannotti, 2011; Wigderson & Lynch 2013). Goebert, Else, Matsu, Chung-do, and Chang (2011) indicated that children who had been cyberbullied were 1.85 times more likely to be depressed than non-cyberbullied peers.

Other research reveals significant correlations between cyberbully victimization and both suicidal ideation (Bonanno & Hymel 2010; Hinduja & Patchin, 2010; Shenck & Fremouw, 2012) and suicidal behaviors (Hinduja & Patchin, 2010; Litwiller & Brausch, 2013; Schneider et al., 2012). In fact, Goebert et al., (2011) reported that cyberbullying victims had 3.22 times higher risk of suicidal behavior than peers. Similarly researchers have linked cyberbullying victimization with self-injuring behaviors (Schneider et al, 2012) and lower self-esteem (Brighiet al. 2012; Chang et al., 2013; Didden et al., 2009; Fredstrom et al., 2011; Katzer et al., 2009; Price & Dalglesih 2010; Wigderson & Lynch 2013).

Behavioral Problems and Cyberbullying Victimization

In addition to the interpersonal and mental health problems that are correlated with cyberbullying victimization, research has also identified a number of problematic, destructive, and antisocial behavioral correlates. Cyberbully victims often have problems at school such as truancy (Katzer et al., 2009; Ybarra et al., 2007) and poor academic performance (Price & Dalglesih 2010; Schneider et al. 2012; Wigderson & Lynch 2013; Ybarra et al. 2007). A number of studies suggest an association between victimization and behavior problems (Dooley et al., 2012; Hinduja & Patchin, 2007, 2008; Menesini et al., 2012; Mitchell et al., 2007). In one study, Ybarra et al. (2007) noted that 12.9% of students who had been cyberbullied reported carrying a weapon school in the previous month while only .6% of non-bullied students had brought a weapon to school.

Being a victim of cyberbullying is also associated with being a bully toward others (Wong et al., 2014). Cyberbully victimization is correlated with both violent behavior and substance abuse (Hinduja & Patchin 2008; Littwiller & Brausch, 2013; Mitchell et al., 2007; Pelfrey & Weber, 2013; Ybarra et al., 2007). Other data identify associations between being a victim of cyberbullying and risky sexual behavior (Litwiller & Brausch, 2013). In sum, cyberbullying victimization is associated with moderate to severe behavioral problems.

Taken together, the research reveals a robust pattern of associations between cyberbullying victimization and behavioral problems, emotional distress, and interpersonal difficulties. Although the cross-sectional data limit information about causality, the apparent pattern of findings across multiple studies using different methods is consistent with claims about the harms associated with being cyberbullied. As the next section will elaborate, evidence from longitudinal and retrospective studies provides better data about the harmful psychological effects of being cyberbullied.

Causes and Consequences of Cyberbullying Victimization

Despite identifying a broad range of interpersonal, emotional, and behavioral problems associated with victimization, research is less clear about whether those problems are causes or consequences. Gámez-Guadix et al. (2013) argued, "Only a few longitudinal studies have analyzed the relationship between cyberbullying and psychological and behavioral health problems. Furthermore, a majority of studies have used cross-sectional designs, which prevents the establishment of temporal and bidirectional relationships among these variables" (p. 447).

Van den Eijnden et al. (2014) describe two competing hypotheses to explain the association between victimization and psychosocial difficulties. First, the *vulnerability hypothesis* proposes that adolescents with psychosocial problems are more vulnerable to cyberbullying and more likely to be targets. Alternatively, the *effect hypothesis* argues that victimization creates psychosocial problems. Evidence from longitudinal data supports the vulnerability hypothesis. For example, cyberbullying victims' initial social anxiety scores predicted later cyberbullying victimization whereas victimization did not predict later social anxiety (Pabian & Vandebosch, 2016; Van den Eijnden et al., 2014). In another longitudinal study, adolescents' problems with close relationships predicted likelihood of being a victim of cyberbullying one year later (Fanti et al., 2012). Cross and Barnes (2015) tracked 1,119 secondary students for two years and found support for the vulnerability hypothesis; students' prior emotional difficulties, behavior problems, and peer problems predicted subsequent cybervictimization.

Although some of the studies reviewed here support the claim that prior psychosocial and behavioral problems increase one's vulnerability to subsequent cyberbullying victimization, the research in this area is far from conclusive. Future studies need to examine *why* some people are more vulnerable to victimization than others.

Effects of cyberbullying victimization. The adverse impacts of traditional bullying on victims are well documented. Studies consistently report that traditional bullying is harmful and its effects last into adulthood (Copeland, Wolke, Angold, & Costello, 2013; Olweus, 2013; Takizawa, Maughan & Arseneault, 2014). Victimization by bullies is "likely to result in serious long-term consequences and adjustment problems" (Olweus, 2013, p. 770). Ttofi, Farrington, Lösel, & Loeber (2011) conducted a meta-analysis of 36 longitudinal studies examining the link between traditional bullying and victim depression and reported traditional bullying victims had a higher probability for depression up to 36 years later, even when up to 20 other risk factors were controlled for. However, research is less clear about the impacts of cyberbullying on victims.

To date, a small number of cyberbullying studies have examined the consequences that victims experience. Some studies have employed longitudinal designs while others asked victims retrospective questions about their experiences (e.g., Agatstone, Kowalski, & Limber 2015).

Longitudinal studies support claims that cyberbullying victimization contributes to problems with depression and loneliness (Machmutow, Perren, Sticca, & Alsaker, 2012; Schultze-Krumbholz, Jäkel, Schultze & Scheithauer, 2102). Modecki et al. (2014) observed that cyberbully victimization predicted later problems with self-esteem, substance abuse, aggression, and delinquency. In a study by Cross and Barnes (2015) secondary students who were victims of cyberbullying were more likely to stay away from school in subsequent years.

Retrospective surveys and interviews that ask cyberbullying victims about their experiences consistently indicate that being cyberbullied results in emotional distress (Agatstone, Kowalski, & Limber 2015). Cyberbullying victims report experiencing a variety of distressing emotional effects including anger, frustration, fear, and anxiety (Campbell et al., 2012; Fredstrom et al., 2011; Goebert et al., 2011). In open-ended interviews, 93% of cyberbullying victims reported adverse effects such as helplessness, sadness, and powerlessness (Raskauskas & Stoltz, 2007). In another study, 60% of cyberbullying victims reported experiencing negative emotional, social, and behavioral effects from the experience (Dredge, Gleeson, & de la Piedad Garcia, 2014). Patchin and Hinduja (2006) found that 54% of children and teenagers who had been victims of cyberbullying reported that the experience had negative consequences; participants reported feeling angry (27%), frustrated (40%), and sad (31.9%). Additionally, cyberbully victims reported that the experience had negative effects on them at school (31.9%), at home (26.5%), and in their relationships with friends (20.4%).

Some data suggest that a pattern of ongoing, or repeated, cyberbullying is more predictive of later depression and substance abuse than one-time victimization or less-stable patterns of victimization. In a study on the stability of victimization across time, presented earlier, Gámez-Guadix et al. (2015) revealed that stable cyberbullying victims, students who had been victimized at both Times 1 and 2, displayed higher scores of depressive symptoms and problematic alcohol use over time than non-victims or students who had only reported victimization at one of the two times. This type of finding is key for developing more explicit theoretical accounts about the effects of cyberbullying in that it suggests that it may not be the bullying, per se, but rather the experience of repeated victimization, that contributes to harmful outcomes.

Not all longitudinal studies have yielded evidence of cyberbullying's harmful effects on victims. For example, Schultze-Krumbholz et al. (2012) observed that cybervictimization did not predict subsequent social withdrawal or psychopathology five months later. Researchers also note that the harmful effects of cyberbullying are moderated by experiences with traditional bullying. Salmivalli et al.'s (2013) longitudinal data from a sample of 7,850 elementary and middle school students revealed that cyberbullying victimization only led to subsequent increases in depression when the cyberbullying was accompanied by traditional bullying. In other words, cyberbullying victimization, alone, did not contribute to increased depression over time.

Longitudinal studies are best able to address questions about outcomes when they also control for influences of other variables. For example, Salmivalli et al.'s (2013) study demonstrated that the effects of cyberbullying can be confounded with the effects of traditional bullying victimization. This confound is especially likely given that most cyberbullying victims also experience traditional bullying (Mitchell &

Jones 2015; Waasdorp & Bradshaw, 2015). Distinguishing the effects of cyberbullying from those of traditional bullying would help researchers address the question of whether cyberbullying is relatively more benign or harmful than traditional bullying; the next section reviews research that offers some suggestions about how to answer this question.

Comparing Effects of Cyberbullying and Traditional Bullying. One of the myths about cyberbullying is that it is perceived as "more sinister than 'off-line' (i.e., traditional or school yard) bullying" (Sabella et al., 2013, p. 2074). The research reveals a more complicated picture because most victims experience both online and in-person bullying. Mitchell and Jones (2015) noted, "Given the large overlap between cyber and traditional bullying, how much can we attribute negative effects to the technology versus the fact that the youth was experiencing harassment and bullying in multiple places?" (p. 475). Waasdorp and Bradshaw (2015) explain that, although both types of victimization have similar consequences, "There is evidence that both forms of victimization have some distinct correlates and characteristics" (p. 484). In another study, researchers reported results from a factor analysis supporting the claim that, although cyberbullying is closely related to traditional bullying, the two forms of victimization are empirically distinct (Sumter, Valkenburg, Baumgartner, Peter, & van der Hof, 2015). Wigderson and Lynch's (2013) results revealed that cyberbullying victimization was uniquely associated with adolescent well-being and affected adolescents "above and beyond" traditional victimization (p. 297). Specifically, the study explained, "cyber-victimization accounted for a significant portion of the variance in both emotional problems and GPA, even after accounting for the contributions of physical and relational victimization" (p. 304). Similarly, Perren et al. (2010) reported cyberbullying victimization contributed to unique variation in depression scores above and beyond the influence of traditional victimization.

Menesini et al. (2012) argued there are unique "additive effects" of traditional and cyberbullying, and that cyberbullying needs to be looked at as a unique phenomenon. In their study, Menesini et al. (2012) reported robust evidence of additive effects for externalizing symptoms (aggressive and delinquent behaviors) and internalizing symptoms (somatic complaints and anxious-depressive symptoms). Other studies have recounted similar additive effects, illustrating the unique contribution cyberbullying made to outcomes when controlling for the effects of traditional bullying (Dooley, Pyżalski, & Cross, 2009; Gradinger et al., 2009).

Considering the earlier section of this chapter that explored differences between the communicative contexts of cyberbullying and traditional bullying, it is important for researchers to examine whether those differences might be reflected in different outcomes associated with the two types of bullying. In other words, are the damaging effects of cyberbullying and traditional bullying different because of the difference in the context and nature of the bullying (as discussed in an earlier section)? Or, do victims of cyberbullying and traditional bullying experience similar consequences (suggesting the differences in communication modes do not matter in terms of outcomes)?

There is some empirical evidence to support the claim that the unique properties of cyberbullying foster different, and perhaps more damaging, effects on the victim than traditional bullying. According to Dredge et al. (2014) "themes related to publicity, anonymity of perpetrators, features of the medium, presence of bystanders, and individual level factors [are] … potential influences upon impact severity" (p. 287). Smith et al. (2008) conducted a pair of studies examining adolescents' perceptions of the effects of various types of cyberbullying media. The findings revealed that adolescents perceived cyberbullying that involved pictures and videos as more harmful other types of cyberbullying and traditional bullying. Similarly, Slonje and Smith (2008) found adolescents viewed cyberbullying that involved pictures and videos as more hurtful than traditional bullying. Interestingly, the adolescent participants viewed cyberbullying as less hurtful than traditional bullying when cyberbullying was restricted to one-on-one communication, such as email and text messaging.

One explanation for the above results is that pictures and video can quickly be distributed to a broad audience whereas emails, instant messages, and chat are less likely to be spread to a potentially large audience. The authors explained that the findings suggested, "Cyberbullying is not a priori perceived as worse than traditional bullying.

Instead, bullying is perceived as worse if it is public (as opposed to private) and if it is anonymous (as opposed to not anonymous)" (Smith et al., 2008, pp. 748–749). In other words, it may not be that cyberbullying is worse, but rather than some of the communicative qualities involved have the potential to increase distress. The data may also indicate that victims' experiences are dependent on qualities of the communicative context such as "public/private" and "anonymous/identified."

In another study, Sticca and Perren (2013) sought to disentangle the effects of communication mode (online versus in-person) and the publicity of the bullying act. In their study, young participants rated the perceived severity of hypothetical bullying scenarios that varied by medium (in-person versus online), publicity (public versus private), and type of bullying (humiliation versus exclusion). Consistent with the claims above about the effects of a potentially large audience on cyberbullying victims, the results revealed that the public bullying was perceived as worse than private bullying in both traditional and cyberbullying. Moreover, public cyberbullying was rated as more severe than public traditional bullying (although, the effect size was small).

Not all studies support the claim that the communication mode involved in cyberbullying makes it more harmful than traditional bullying. For example, a study by Bauman and Newman (2013) did not find differences in perceived victim distress based on whether bullying vignettes involved online versus traditional communication modes. In another study, Mitchell, Jones, Turner, Shattuck, and Wolak (2016) reported, "Concern that technology involvement inherently amplifies harm to victims was not supported. Compared with in-person incidents, technology-only incidents were less likely to involve multiple episodes and power imbalances. They were seen by victims as easier to stop and had significantly less emotional impact" (p. 1). A study by Van Geel, Vedder, and Tanilon (2014) revealed that, while suicidal ideation was highest among victims who had experienced both types of bullying, the next highest level was among victims who had only been cyberbullied, and the lowest level was among victims who had only experienced traditional bullying.

When considered together, the studies reviewed above are generally consistent with the claim that the unique qualities of the interpersonal situation in cyberbullying are distinct from traditional bullying in ways that may enhance the negative effects of cyberbullying. More specifically, the studies suggest that the effects of cyberbullying may be worse than traditional bullying when the offensive material is widely distributed and available to a large audience. These distinctions are examples of how researchers can use communication variables to develop a conceptual narrative of cyberbullying.

It is hard to draw conclusions about the effects of cyberbullying and even harder to separate those effects from those of traditional bullying. Overall, research is consistent with claims that cyberbullying victimization is linked to subsequent emotional, behavioral, and social problems. However, the literature is less clear about the magnitude or intensity of the harmful effects. There is substantial evidence that bullying victimization is most detrimental to people who are victims of both cyberbullying and traditional bullying. The data also lend support to claims that the effects of cyberbullying are distinguishable from those of traditional bullying victimization. There are mixed results regarding the question of whether cyberbullying is relatively more harmful than traditional bullying. To advance cyberbullying literature, a critical agenda for cyberbullying researchers is to employ research designs that can formally address causal claims about the effects of victimization. Such designs would also help researchers disentangle the effects of cyberbullying from those of traditional bullying.

Characteristics of Cyberbullies

Beyond questions about victims, another primary line of research among cyberbullying scholars has attempted to identify risk factors that predict perpetration. The empirical picture of cyberbullies is based mostly on cross-sectional data that are not sufficient for assessing causal claims about the predictors or outcomes of engaging in cyberbullying. With that qualification in mind, however, the literature does reveal robust evidence that cyberbullying behavior is associated with a host of psychological, social, and behavioral problems. A smaller number of studies that have employed longitudinal designs offer more insight into the questions of predictors and outcomes. Before presenting the longitudinal studies, the following sections first review research from cross-sectional studies that have identified interpersonal, psychological, and behavioral risk factors correlated with cyberbullying perpetration.

Interpersonal Problems Among Cyberbullies

Numerous studies reveal that cyberbullies are likely to have been victims of traditional bullying and cyberbullying (Bauman, 2010; Pabian & Vandebosch, 2016; Sticca, Ruggieri, Alsaker, & Perren, 2013; Ybarra & Mitchell, 2004b; Zhou et al., 2013). A meta-analysis of 131 studies concluded that the most robust interpersonal correlate of cyberbullying perpetration was having been a victim of any type of bullying (Kowalski et al., 2014). Ybarra and Mitchell (2004a) hypothesized that, for victims of traditional bullying, "The Internet may be a place to assert dominance over others as compensation for being bullied in person" (p. 1313).

In another study, Ybarra and Mitchell (2004b) found cyberbullies were 1.65 times more likely than non-bullies to have been targets of traditional bullying and 5.44 times more likely to have been victims of cyberbullying. In a longitudinal study, Sticca et al. (2013) observed victims of traditional bullying were more than four times more likely to engage in cyberbullying behavior several months later. Roberto et al. (2014) reported that cyberbully victims were 12.63 times more likely to engage in cyberbullying than individuals who had not been victims. In addition to being victimized by other bullies, those who engage in cyberbullying are also more likely to have been subjected to physical or sexual abuse (Ybarra & Mitchell, 2004b).

Despite the robust findings linking prior bullying victimization to subsequent cyberbullying behavior, some studies have not found significant links between being victimized by traditional bullying and engaging in cyberbullying (e.g., Fanti et al., 2012; Gradinger et al., 2009; Raskauskas & Stoltz, 2007; Slonje & Smith, 2008). However, these studies are in the minority.

Cyberbullying behavior is associated with interpersonal and social problems. For example, cyberbullies are rated as less popular and socially acceptable by peers (Schoffstall & Cohen, 2011), have lower peer attachment (Wright et al., 2015), a decreased sense of belonging (Wong et al., 2014), and have more problems with peer relationships (Campbell, Slee, Spears, Butler, & Kift, 2013). Ybarra and Mitchell (2004b) noted that, compared to non-cyberbullies, cyberbullies were 2.57 times more likely to rate their parent-child emotional bond as poor, 2.2 times more likely to report that their parents used frequent discipline, and 1.84 times more likely to report infrequent parental monitoring. Thus, the evidence suggests cyberbullying perpetration is correlated with interpersonal and relational difficulties.

Emotional Problems Among Cyberbullies

Cyberbullying is correlated with many of the same emotional problems associated with cybervictimization. In fact, one study found that cyberbullies and cyberbully victims were equally likely to exhibit mental health problems (Beckman, Hagquist, & Hellstrom, 2012). Being a cyberbully is correlated with greater risk of mental health problems such as loneliness, stress, depression, and anxiety (Bonanno & Hymel, 2013; Campbell et al., 2013; Schenk et al., 2013; Schoffstall & Cohen, 2011). Researchers have noted that cyberbullying is associated with diminished self-esteem (Patchin & Hinduja, 2010) and lower self-worth (Schoffstall & Cohen, 2011). Compared to peers, cyberbullying perpetrators exhibit higher levels of suicidal ideation (Bonanno & Hymel, 2013), suicidal behavior (Hinduja & Patchin, 2010), and more strongly endorse items about suicidal behavior on surveys (Schenk et al., 2013).

Despite the similarities above, there are also psychological correlates of cyberbullying perpetration that distinguish it from cybervictimization. Cyberbullies exhibit stronger psychological traits and characteristics related to anger, narcissism, lack of empathy, moral disengagement, and misperceptions about how their aggression harms victims. A study by Ang, Tan, and Mansor (2011) reported that cyberbullies held different normative beliefs about aggression than their peers. Cyberbullies appear to be more likely than their peers to have anger as a personality trait, exhibit explosive expression of anger (Lonigro et al., 2015; Tanrikulu & Campbell, 2015) and have higher levels of hostility and paranoia (Schenk et al., 2013).

Consistent with the findings on anger and hostility, other research indicates that cyberbullies have lower emotional intelligence and more difficulty regulating their emotions (Baroncelli & Ciucci, 2014). Cyberbullying is also correlated with narcissistic personalities and narcissistic exploitativeness (Ang et al., 2011). In one recent study, Goodboy and Martin (2015) reported significant correlations between cyberbullying and each of the "dark triad" personality traits: psychopathy, Machiavellianism, and narcissism.

Given the well-documented link between psychopathy and low empathy (Blair, 2005), it is not surprising that cyberbullying is also correlated with callous unemotional traits (i.e., lack of guilt and concern for others) and deficits in empathy and remorse (Fanti et al. 2012). Cyberbullying is associated with moral disengagement, or the ability harm others without a guilty conscience (Bussey, Fitzpatrick, & Raman, 2015; Renati, Berrone, & Zanetti, 2012; Robson & Witenberg, 2013; Tanrikulu & Campbell, 2015; Wachs, 2012). In fact, Slonje, Smith & Frisén (2012) suggested cyberbullies may exhibit higher levels of moral disengagement than traditional bullies. One possible theoretical explanation is that the disinhibition, relative anonymity, and decreased social presence that characterize computer-mediated contexts make it easier for cyberbullies to aggress with less guilt or remorse than traditional bullies.

Consistent with the findings associating moral disengagement with cyberbullying, studies also suggest that cyberbullies have relatively lower empathy than their peers (Renati et al., 2012; Schulze-Krumbholz & Scheithauer, 2009, 2013; Steffgen, König, Pfetsch & Melzer, 2011) and lower empathic concern (Sticca et al., 2013). Moroever, Ang and Goh (2010) found cyberbullying was associated with lower affective empathy, the ability to experience what others are feeling.

Taken together the research indicates that cyberbullying is associated with many of the same psychological problems that cyberbully victims experience. Yet, cyberbullying also has several psychological correlates that are distinct from those associated with victimization. Personality characteristics, such as exploitative narcissism and trait anger, along with the motive to express anger and attain retaliation may explain why cyberbullies victimize their peers. Cyberbullying behavior is associated with a number of socio-emotional problems, such as decreased empathy and diminished affective empathy that might otherwise inhibit aggression towards victims. Finally, there is some evidence that cyberbullies may have more moral disengagement than traditional bullies, perhaps due to the unique qualities of the online social interaction.

Behavioral Characteristics of Cyberbullies

Cyberbullying correlates with other problematic behaviors. Studies have documented the relationship between cyberbullying and other forms of interpersonal aggression (Fletcher et al., 2014; Gradinger et al., 2009; Renati, Berrone & Zanetti, 2012; Roberto et al., 2014) and violent behavior (Pelfrey & Weber, 2013). In a study of cyberbullying among college students, Schenk et al. (2013) reported an association between engaging in cyberbullying and committing violent crimes. There is also robust evidence linking cyberbullying with engaging in traditional bullying behaviors (Fanti et al., 2012; Hinduja & Patchin 2008; Kowalski & Limber 2013; Pabian & Vandebosch, 2016; Pelfrey & Weber, 2013; Raskauskas & Stoltz 2007; Wong et al., 2014; Zhou et al., 2013).

In addition to aggression, cyberbullying is also associated with other behavioral problems including delinquency (Hinduja & Patchin 2008; Ybarra & Mitchell 2004a; Zhou et al., 2013), hyperactivity (Campbell et al., 2013; Fletcher et al., 2014), and drug and substance abuse (Hinduja & Patchin, 2008; Pelfrey & Webster, 2013; Sticca et al., 2013; Ybarra & Mitchell 2004a; Zhou et al. 2013). Cyberbullies' behavior problems also extend to difficulties at school, including lower academic achievement (see Kowalski et al., 2014) and an increased likelihood of serving detention or being suspended (Roberto et al., 2014).

Predictors and Consequences of Being a Cyberbully

As noted in other sections, there are numerous methodological obstacles preventing researchers from testing causal claims about what factors might *cause* cyberbullying perpetration and, similarly, what outcomes might be due to engaging in cyberbullying. To date, the best data for addressing these questions comes from research on motives for cyberbullying and longitudinal studies that capture the time-order of risk factors associated with later bullying. Results from these studies are presented below.

According to Kowalski et al.'s (2014) meta-analysis, little research has examined cyberbullying motives. However, the few studies that have assessed motives suggest that cyberbullying is most commonly motivated by anger (Gradinger, Strohmeier, & Spiel, 2012) and a desire to retaliate for being victimized by traditional bullying (Dooley et al. 2009; Hemphill et al. 2012; Raskauskas & Stoltz, 2007). Kowalski et al. (2014) speculate that cyberbullies may also be motivated by a desire to demonstrate technological skill or prowess.

A small number of studies have used longitudinal designs to examine predictors of subsequent cyberbullying perpetration. For example, one study tracked 7th graders and observed that prior bullying victimization predicted subsequent cyberbullying toward others (Sticca et al., 2013). Similarly, Pabian and Van Debosch (2015) noted that previous cyberbullying victimization and traditional bullying perpetration both predicted later cyberbullying behavior. Fanti et al. (2012) found that prior callous-unemotional traits (i.e., narcissism and impulsivity) and a lack of family social support predicted later cyberbullying. In another study, Cappadocia et al. (2013) observed more antisocial behavior and fewer prosocial peer influences predicted subsequent cyberbullying behavior. Finally, Schultze-Krumbholz and Scheithauer (2013) found that low affective empathy predicted cyberbullying perpetration five months later.

Conclusion

Questions about the causes and consequences of cyberbullying involvement are common topics addressed by both the popular press and scholarly research. Yet, as this chapter illustrated, the literature lacks sufficient data to answer those questions. Among the few studies with longitudinal designs that controlled for other variables, some clear patterns have emerged. Victims of cyberbullying report a variety of adverse emotional outcomes resulting from their experiences. Additionally, the longitudinal studies indicate that victimization predicts a variety of subsequent emotional, social, and behavioral problems. The cross-sectional studies shed further light on characteristics of victims. Broadly, cyberbullying victims tend to have a host of interpersonal, emotional, and behavioral problems. Although it is unclear whether the problems are causes or consequences, or both, the data clearly indicate that cyberbullying victimization is associated with a myriad of serious problems.

The research on cyberbullies reveals a similar pattern. Research on motives and studies using longitudinal data identify a number of risk factors that predict later cyberbullying. Cross-sectional studies have revealed similar patterns. Cyberbullying is correlated with many of the same interpersonal, emotional, and behavioral problems that victims exhibit. However, unlike most of the research on victims, cyberbullying behavior appears to be more closely related to problems with anger and aggression, lack of remorse, antisocial personality traits, and trouble with empathy and moral reasoning. Finally, the unique properties of online social interaction (e.g., reduced social presence, enhanced anonymity) may contribute to disinhibition among cyberbullies that, together with the traits mentioned above, may further enhance lack of remorse and inhibit feelings of guilt.

A review of the literature on cyberbullying reveals that while there is considerable debate and disagreement about how to define cyberbullying, there are also areas where many researchers do agree. Scholars have demonstrated that using conceptual definitions of traditional bullying is a useful way to approach defining cyberbullying. Here, Olweus' (1993) three characteristics of traditional bullying (intentionality, repetition, and power imbalance) have helped guide cyberbullying researchers in their efforts to characterize cyberbullying.

Exploring how cyberbullying differs from traditional bullying has also been an essential part of the debate. Here, researchers have argued that cyberbullying is a unique and distinct type of interpersonal aggression due to the communicative characteristics of the online environment. As noted in this chapter, cyberbullying is distinct from traditional bullying due to the fact that, in cyberbullying, the aggression may be quickly spread to a vast audience. And, in many cases, the harmful material cyberbullies send or post may persist online even after the initial aggressive act has ended. These features of online technology also serve to create a power imbalance between the victim and bully—the bully can spread hurtful information quickly to a broad audience before the victim is even aware of what has happened. Moreover, the persistent nature of online material, along with the fact that such material is difficult to delete, further enhances the cyberbully's power.

The research presented in this chapter suggests that the reduced social presence afforded by interpersonal technologies may function to disinhibit cyberbullies, making it easier for them to aggress and reducing potential feelings of guilt. For victims, the harms of being bullied may be intensified online where the aggression may be quickly dispersed to a vast audience and where the identity of the aggressor, in many cases, may not be known. Beyond that, the relative permanence of postings on the Internet and the fact that victims can receive messages anywhere at any time may increase victims' feelings of helplessness and powerlessness. Although cyberbullying is not the only type of online aggression, it is undoubtedly the most widely studied and perhaps widely publicized to date.

Note

1. Based on a 2017 search of the Scopus database for entries with "cyberbullying," "cyberbully," "cyberbullies," or "cyber-bullying" in the title, abstract, or keywords.

References

Agatston, P. W., Kowalski, R., & Limber, S. P. (2015). Students' perspectives on cyberbullying. *Journal of Adolescent Health*, 41(6 Suppl 1), S59–S60. doi:10.1016/j.jadohealth.2007.09.003

Ang, R. P., & Goh, D. H. (2010). Cyberbullying among adolescents: The role of affective and cognitive empathy, and gender. *Child Psychiatry & Human Development*, 41(4), 387–397. doi:10.1007/s10578-010-0176-3

Ang, R. P., Tan, K.-A., & Mansor, A. T. (2011). Normative beliefs about aggression as a mediator of narcissistic exploitativeness, and cyberbullying. *Journal of Interpersonal Violence*, 26(13), 2619–2634. doi:10.1177/0886260510388286

Atfab, P. (2011). A parent's guide to cyberbullying. Retrieved from https://www.wiredsafety.org/toolkitmedia/files/file/Parent_s_Articles/A_Parent_s_Guide_to_Cyberbullying_-_Extended.pdf

Barlett, C. P. (2015). Anonymously hurting others online: The effect of anonymity on cyberbullying frequency. *Psychology of Popular Media Culture, 4*(2), 70–79. doi:10.1037/a0034335

Barlett, C. P., & Coyne, S. M. (2014). A meta-analysis of sex differences in cyberbullying behavior: The moderating role of age. *Aggressive Behavior, 40*(5), 474–488. doi:10.1002/ab.21555

Baroncelli, A., & Ciucci, E. (2014). Unique effects of different components of trait emotional intelligence in traditional bullying and cyberbullying. *Journal of Adolescence, 37*(6), 807–815. doi:10.1016/j.adolescence.2014.05.009

Bauman, S. (2010). Cyberbullying in a rural intermediate school: An exploratory study. *The Journal of Early Adolescence, 30*(6), 803–833. doi:10.1177/0272431609350927

Bauman, S., & Newman, M. L. (2013). Testing assumptions about cyberbullying: Perceived distress associated with acts of conventional and cyberbullying. *Psychology of Violence, 3*(1), 27–38. doi:10.1037/a0029867

Beckman, L., Hagquist, C., & Hellström, L. (2012). Does the association with psychosomatic health problems differ between cyberbullying and traditional bullying? *Emotional & Behavioural Difficulties, 17*(3–4), 421–434. doi:10.1080/13632752.2012.704228

Berne, S., Frisén, A., Schultze-Krumbholz, A., Scheithauer, H., Naruskov, K., Luik, P., ... Zukauskiene, R. (2013). Cyberbullying assessment instruments: A systematic review. *Aggression and Violent Behavior, 18*(2), 320–334. doi:10.1016/j.avb.2012.11.022.

Blair, R. (2005). Responding to the emotions of others: Dissociating forms of empathy through the study of typical and psychiatric populations. *Consciousness and Cognition, 14*(4), 698–718. doi:10.1016/j.concog.2005.06.004

Bonanno, R., & Hymel, S. (2013). Cyberbullying and internalizing difficulties: Above and beyond the impact of traditional forms of bullying. *Journal of Youth and Adolescence, 42*(5), 685–697. doi:10.1007/s10964-013-9937-1

Brighi, A., Melotti, G., Annalisa, G., Genta, M., Ortega, R., Mora-Merchán, J., ... Thompson, F. (2012). Self-esteem and loneliness in relation to cyberbullying in three European countries. In Q. Li, D. Cross, & P. K. Smith (Eds.), *Cyberbullying in the global playground: Research from international perspectives* (pp. 32–56). Malden, MA: Blackwell.

Brown, C. F., Demaray, M. K., & Secord, S. M. (2014). Cyber victimization in middle school and relations to social emotional outcomes. *Computers in Human Behavior, 35*, 12–21. doi:10.1016/j.chb.2014.02.014

Bryce, J., & Fraser, J. (2013). "It's common sense that it's wrong": Young people's perceptions and experiences of cyberbullying. *Cyberpsychology, Behavior, and Social Networking, 16*(11), 783–787. doi:10.1089/cyber.2012.0275

Bussey, K., Fitzpatrick, S., & Raman, A. (2015). The role of moral disengagement and self-efficacy in cyberbullying. *Journal of School Violence, 14*(1), 30–46. doi:10.1080/15388220.2014.954045

Campbell, M. A., Slee, P. T., Spears, B., Butler, D., & Kift, S. (2013). Do cyberbullies suffer too? Cyberbullies' perceptions of the harm they cause to others and to their own mental health. *School Psychology International, 34*(6), 613–629. doi:10.1177/0143034313479698

Campbell, M., Spears, B., Slee, P., Butler, D., & Kift, S. (2012). Victims' perceptions of traditional and cyberbullying, and the psychosocial correlates of their victimization. *Emotional & Behavioural Difficulties, 17*(3–4), 389–401. doi:10.1080/13632752.2012.704316

Caplan, S. E. (2005). A social skill account of problematic Internet use. *Journal of Communication, 55*(4), 721–736. doi:10.1093/joc/55.4.721

Cappadocia, M. C., Craig, W. M., & Pepler, D. (2013). Cyberbullying: Prevalence, stability, and risk factors during adolescence. *Canadian Journal of School Psychology, 28*(2), 171–192. doi:10.1177/0829573513491212

Cassidy, W., Faucher, C., & Jackson, M. (2014). The dark side of the ivory tower: Cyberbullying of university faculty and teaching personnel. *Alberta Journal of Educational Research, 60*(2), 279–299.

Cassidy, W., Jackson, M., & Faucher, C. (2015). Gender differences and cyberbullying towards faculty members in higher education. In R. Navarro, S. Yubero, & E. Larrañaga (Eds.), *Cyberbullying across the globe: Gender, family, and mental health* (pp. 79–98). Switzerland: Springer International Publishing. doi:10.1007/978-3-319-25552-1_4

Cénat, J. M., Hébert, M., Blais, M., Lavoie, F., Guerrier, M., & Derivois, D. (2014). Cyberbullying, psychological distress, and self-esteem among youth in Quebec schools. *Journal of Affective Disorders, 169*, 7–9. doi:10.1016/j.jad.2014.07.019

Chang, F., Lee, C., Chiu, C., Hsi, W., Huang, T., & Pan, Y. (2013). Relationships among cyberbullying, school bullying, and mental health in Taiwanese adolescents. *Journal of School Health, 83*(6), 454–462. doi:10.1111/josh.12050

Copeland, W., Wolke, D., Angold, A., & Costello, E. (2013). Adult psychiatric outcomes of bullying and being bullied by peers in childhood and adolescence. *JAMA Psychiatry, 70*(4), 419–426. doi:10.1001/jamapsychiatry.2013.504

Cross, D., Lester, L., & Barnes, A. (2015). A longitudinal study of the social and emotional predictors and consequences of cyber and traditional bullying victimisation. *International Journal of Public Health, 60*, 207–217. doi:10.1007/s00038-015-0655-1

Crosslin, K., & Golman, M. (2014). "Maybe you don't want to face it"—College students' perspectives on cyberbullying. *Computers in Human Behavior, 41*, 14–20. doi:10.1016/j.chb.2014.09.007

Dempsey, A. G., Sulkowski, M. L., Dempsey, J., & Storch, E. A. (2011). Has cyber technology produced a new group of peer aggressors? *Cyberpsychology, Behavior and Social Networking, 14*(5), 297–302. doi:10.1089/cyber.2010.0108

Didden, R., Scholte, R. H. J., Korzilius, H., de Moor, J. M. H., Vermeulen, A., O'Reilly, M., ... Lancioni, G. E. (2009). Cyberbullying among students with intellectual and developmental disability in special education settings. *Developmental Neurorehabilitation*, *12*(3), 146–151. doi:10.1080/17518420902971356

Dooley, J. J., Pyżalski, J., & Cross, D. (2009). Cyberbullying versus face-to-face bullying. *Journal of Psychology*, *217*(4), 182–188. doi:10.1027/0044-3409.217.4.182

Dooley, J. J., Shaw, T., & Cross, D. (2012). The association between the mental health and behavioural problems of students and their reactions to cyber-victimization. *European Journal of Developmental Psychology*, *9*(2), 275–289. doi:10.1080/17405629.2011.648425

Dredge, R., Gleeson, J. F. M., & de la Piedad Garcia, X. (2014). Risk factors associated with impact severity of cyberbullying victimization: A qualitative study of adolescent online social networking. *Cyberpsychology, Behavior, and Social Networking*, *17*(5), 287–291. doi:10.1089/cyber.2013.0541

Education Insider (2010). Cyberbullying: A national epidemic. Retrieved from https://education-portal.com/articles/Cyberbullying_A_National_Epidemic.html

Elgar, F. J., Napoletano, A., Saul, G., Dirks, M., Craig, W., Poteat, V. P., ... Koenig, B. W. (2014). Cyberbullying victimization and mental health in adolescents and the moderating role of family dinners. *JAMA Pediatrics*, *168*(11), 1015–1022. doi:10.1001/jamapediatrics.2014.1223

Erdur-Baker, O. (2009). Cyberbullying and its correlation to traditional bullying, gender, and frequent and risky usage of Internet-mediated communication tools. *New Media & Society*, *12*(1), 109–125. doi:10.1177/1461444809341260

Fanti, K., Demetrious, A. & Hawa, V. (2012). A longitudinal study of cyberbullying: Examining risk and protective factors. *European Journal of Developmental Psychology*, *9*(2), 168–181. doi:10.1080/17405629.2011.643169

Fletcher, A., Fitzgerald-Yau, N., Jones, R., Allen, E., Viner, R. M., & Bonell, C. (2014). Brief report: Cyberbullying perpetration and its associations with socio-demographics, aggressive behaviour at school, and mental health outcomes. *Journal of Adolescence*, *37*(8), 1393–1398. doi:10.1016/j.adolescence.2014.10.005

Francisco, S. M., Veiga Simão, A., Ferreira, P. C., & Martins, M. (2015). Cyberbullying: The hidden side of college students. *Computers in Human Behavior*, *43*, 167–182. doi:10.1016/j.chb.2014.10.045

Fredstrom, B. K., Adams, R. E., & Gilman, R. (2011). Electronic and school-based victimization: Unique contexts for adjustment difficulties during adolescence. *Journal of Youth and Adolescence*, *40*(4), 405–415. doi:10.1007/s10964-010-9569-7

Gahagan, K., Vaterlaus, J. M., & Frost, L. R. (2016). College student cyberbullying on social networking sites: Conceptualization, prevalence, and perceived bystander responsibility. *Computers in Human Behavior*, *55*, 1097–1105. doi:10.1016/j.chb.2015.11.019

Gámez-Guadix, M., Gini, G., & Calvete, E. (2015). Stability of cyberbullying victimization among adolescents: Prevalence and association with bully-victim status and psychosocial adjustment. *Computers in Human Behavior, 53*, 140–148. doi:10.1016/j.chb.2015.07.007

Gámez-Guadix, M., Orue, I., Smith, P. K., & Calvete, E. (2013). Longitudinal and reciprocal relations of cyberbullying with depression, substance use, and problematic Internet use among adolescents. *Journal of Adolescent Health, 53*(4), 446–452. doi:10.1016/j.jadohealth.2013.03.030

Giménez Gualdo, A. M., Hunter, S. C., Durkin, K., Arnaiz, P., & Maquilón, J. J. (2015). The emotional impact of cyberbullying: Differences in perceptions and experiences as a function of role. *Computers & Education, 82*, 228–235. doi:10.1016/j.compedu.2014.11.013

Glendinning, P. M. (2002). Workplace bullying: Curing the cancer of the American workplace. *Public Personnel Management, 30*, 269–286.

Goebert, D., Else, I., Matsu, C., Chung-Do, J., & Chang, J. (2011). The impact of cyberbullying on substance use and mental health in a multiethnic sample. *Maternal and Child Health Journal, 15*(8), 1282–1286. doi:10.1007/s10995-010-0672-x

Goffman, E. (1959). *The presentation of self in everyday life*. New York: Doubleday Anchor Books.

Goffman, E. (1967). *Interaction ritual: Essays on face-to-face behavior*. New York: Doubleday Anchor Books.

Goodboy, A. K., & Martin, M. M. (2015). The personality profile of a cyberbully: Examining the dark triad. *Computers in Human Behavior, 49*, 1–4. doi:10.1016/j.chb.2015.02.052

Görzig, A., & Ólafsson, K. (2013). What makes a bully a cyberbully? Unravelling the characteristics of cyberbullies across twenty-five European countries. *Journal of Children and Media, 7*(1), 9–27. doi:10.1080/17482798.2012.739756

Gradinger, P., Strohmeier, D., & Spiel, C. (2009). Traditional bullying and cyberbullying: Identification of risk groups for adjustment problems. *Journal of Psychology, 217*(4), 205–213. doi:10.1027/0044-3409.217.4.205

Gradinger, P., Strohmeier, D., & Spiel, C. (2012). Motives for bullying others in cyberspace: A study on bullies and bully-victims in Austria. In Q. Li, D. Cross, & P. K. Smith (Eds.), *Cyberbullying in the global playground: Research from international perspectives* (pp. 263–284). Malden, MA: Wiley-Blackwell. doi:10.1002/9781119954484.ch13

Heirman, W., & Walrave, M. (2008). Assessing concerns and issues about the mediation of technology in cyberbullying. *Cyberpsychology: Journal of Psychosocial Research on Cyberspace, 2*(2), Article 1. Retrieved from https://cyberpsychology.eu/article/view/4214

Hemphill, S. A., Kotevski, A., Tollit, M., Smith, R., Herrenkohl, T. I., Toumbourou, J. W., & Catalano, R. F. (2012). Longitudinal predictors of cyber and traditional bullying perpetration in Australian secondary school students. *Journal of Adolescent Health, 51*(1), 59–65. doi:10.1016/j.jadohealth.2011.11.019.Longitudinal

Hinduja, S., & Patchin, J. W. (2007). Offline consequences of online victimization. *Journal of School Violence, 6*(3), 89–112. doi:10.1300/J202v06n03_06

Hinduja, S., & Patchin, J. W. (2008). Cyberbullying: An exploratory analysis of factors related to offending and victimization. *Deviant Behavior*, *29*(2), 129–156. doi:10.1080/01639620701457816

Hinduja, S., & Patchin, J. W. (2010). Bullying, cyberbullying, and suicide. *Archives of Suicide Research*, *14*(3), 206–221. doi:10.1080/13811118.2010.494133

Hinduja, S., & Patchin, J. W. (2012). Cyberbullying: Neither an epidemic nor a rarity. *European Journal of Developmental Psychology*, *9*(5), 539–543. doi:10.1080/17405629.2012.706448

Holfeld, B., & Grabe, M. (2012). Middle school students' perceptions of and responses to cyberbullying. *Journal of Educational Computing Research*, *46*(4), 395–413.

Jackson, C. L., & Cohen, R. (2012). Childhood victimization: Modeling the relation between classroom victimization, cyber victimization, and psychosocial functioning. *Psychology of Popular Media Culture*, *1*(4), 254–269. doi:10.1037/a0029482

Joinson, A. (1998). Causes and implications of disinhibited behavior on the Internet. In J. Gackenbach (Ed.), *Psychology and the Internet: Intrapersonal, interpersonal, and transpersonal implications.* (pp. 43–60). San Diego, CA: Academic Press.

Juvonen, J., & Gross, E. F. (2008). Extending the school grounds? Bullying experiences in cyberspace. *The Journal of School Health*, *78*(9), 496–505. doi:10.1111/j.1746-1561.2008.00335.x

Katzer, C., Fetchenhauer, D., & Belschak, F. (2009). Cyberbullying: Who are the victims? A comparison of victimization in Internet chatrooms and victimization in school. *Journal of Media Psychology: Theories, Methods, and Applications.* doi:10.1027/1864-1105.21.1.25

Kert, A. S., Codding, R. S., Tryon, G. S., & Shiyko, M. (2010). Impact of the word "bully" on the reported rate of bullying behavior. *Psychology in the Schools, 47(2),* 193–204. doi:10.1002/pits.20464

Kowalski, R. M., & Limber, S. P. (2007). Electronic bullying among middle school students. *Journal of Adolescent Health*, *41*(6), S22–S30.

Kowalski, R. M., & Limber, S. P. (2013). Psychological, physical, and academic correlates of cyberbullying and traditional bullying. *Journal of Adolescent Health*, *53*(1, Suppl.), S13–S20. doi:10.1016/j.jadohealth.2012.09.018

Kowalski, R. M., Giumetti, G. W., Schroeder, A. N., & Lattanner, M. R. (2014). Bullying in the digital age: A critical review and meta-analysis of cyberbullying research among youth. *Psychological Bulletin*, *140*(4), 1073–137. doi:10.1037/a0035618

Kowalski, R. M., Limber, S. P., & Agatston, P. W. (2012). *Cyberbullying: Bullying in the digital age* (2nd ed.). Malden, MA: John Wiley & Sons.

Kowalski, R. M., Morgan, C. A., Drake-Lavelle, K., & Allison, B. (2016). Cyberbullying among college students with disabilities. *Computers in Human Behavior*, *57*, 416–427. doi:10.1016/j.chb.2015.12.044

Lapidot-Lefler, N., & Barak, A. (2012). Effects of anonymity, invisibility, and lack of eye contact on toxic online disinhibition. *Computers in Human Behavior*, *28*(2), 434–443. doi:10.1016/j.chb.2011.10.014

Larrañaga, E., Yubero, S., & Ovejero, A. (2015). Gender variables and cyberbullying in college students. In R. Navarro, S. Yubero, & E. Larrañaga (Eds.), *Cyberbullying across the globe: Gender, family, and mental health* (pp. 63–77). Cuenca, Spain: Springer International Publishing. doi:10.1007/978-3-319-25552-1_3

Larrañaga, E., Yubero, S., Ovejero, A., & Navarro, R. (2016). Loneliness, parent-child communication, and cyberbullying victimization among Spanish youths. *Computers in Human Behavior, 65*, 1–8. doi:10.1016/j.chb.2016.08.015

Lea, M., O'Shea, T., Fung, P., & Spears, R. (1992). 'Flaming' in computer-mediated communication: Observations, explanations, implications. In M. Lea (Ed.), *Contexts of computer-mediated communication* (pp. 89–112). Hertfordshire, England: Harvester Wheatsheaf.

Lenhart, A. (2007). Cyberbullying and online teens. Pew Research Center. Retrieved from https://www.pewinternet.org/2007/06/27/cyberbullying/

Lenhart, A., Smith, A., & Anderson, M. (2015). Teens, technology and romantic relationships. Pew Research Center. Retrieved from https://www.pewinternet.org/files/2015/10/PI_2015-10-01_teens-technology-romance_FINAL.pdf

Li, Q. (2006). Cyberbullying in schools: A research of gender differences. *School Psychology International, 27*(2), 157–170. doi:10.1177/0143034306064547

Litwiller, B., & Brausch, A. (2013). Cyberbullying and physical bullying in adolescent suicide: The role of violent behavior and substance use. *Journal of Youth & Adolescence, 42*(5), 675–684. doi:10.1007/s10964-013-9925-5

Lonigro, A., Schneider, B. H., Laghi, F., Baiocco, R., Pallini, S., & Brunner, T. (2015). Is cyberbullying related to trait or state anger? *Child Psychiatry and Human Development, 46*(3), 445–454. doi:10.1007/s10578-014-0484-0

Machmutow, K., Perren, S., Sticca, F., & Alsaker, F. D. (2012). Peer victimisation and depressive symptoms: Can specific coping strategies buffer the negative impact of cybervictimisation? *Emotional & Behavioural Difficulties, 17*(3–4), 403–420. doi:10.1080/13632752.2012.704310

McGraw, P. (2015, May 6). It's time to stop the cyberbullying epidemic. *Huffington Post*. Retrieved from https://www.huffingtonpost.com/dr-phil/stop-cyberbullying_b_6647990.html.

Menesini, E. (2012). Cyberbullying: The right value of the phenomenon. Comments on the paper "Cyberbullying: An overrated phenomenon?" *European Journal of Developmental Psychology, 9*(5), 544–552. doi:10.1080/17405629.2012.706449

Menesini, E., Calussi, P., & Nocentini, A. (2012). Cyberbullying and traditional bullying: Unique, additive, and synergistic effects on psychological health symptoms. In Q. Li, D. Cross, & P. K. Smith (Eds.), *Bullying goes to the cyber playground: Research on cyberbullying from an international perspective* (pp. 245–262). London: Wiley-Blackwell.

Mishna, F., Cook, C., Gadalla, T., Daciuk, J., & Solomon, S. (2010). Cyberbullying behaviors among middle and high school students. *American Journal of Orthopsychiatry, 80*, 362–374.

Mishna, F., Khoury-Kassabri, M., Gadalla, T., & Daciuk, J. (2012). Risk factors for involvement in cyberbullying: Victims, bullies, and bully-victims. *Children & Youth Services Review, 34*(1), 63–70. doi:10.1016/j.childyouth.2011.08.032

Mitchell, K. J., & Jones, L. M. (2015). Cyberbullying and bullying must be studied within a broader peer victimization framework. *Journal of Adolescent Health, 56*(5), 473–474. doi:10.1016/j.jadohealth.2015.02.005

Mitchell, K. J., Jones, L. M., Turner, H. A., Shattuck, A., & Wolak, J. (2016). The role of technology in peer harassment: Does it amplify harm for youth? *Psychology of Violence, 6*(2), 193–204. doi:10.1037/a0039317

Mitchell, K. J., Ybarra, M., & Finkelhor, D. (2007). The relative importance of online victimization in understanding depression, delinquency, and substance use. *Child Maltreatment, 12*(4), 314–324. doi:10.1177/1077559507305996

Modecki, K. L., Minchin, J., Harbaugh, A. G., Guerra, N. G., & Runions, K. C. (2014). Bullying prevalence across contexts: A meta-analysis measuring cyber and traditional bullying. *Journal of Adolescent Health, 55*(5), 602–611. doi:10.1016/j.jadohealth.2014.06.007

Monks, C. P., Robinson, S., & Worlidge, P. (2012). The emergence of cyberbullying: A survey of primary school pupils' perceptions and experiences. *School Psychology International, 33*(5), 477–491. doi:10.1177/0143034312445242

Nixon, C. L. (2014). Current perspectives: The impact of cyberbullying on adolescent health. *Adolescent Health, Medicine, and Therapeutics, 5*, 143–158. doi:10.2147/AHMT.S36456

Olenik-Shemesh, D., Heiman, T., & Eden, S. (2012). Cyberbullying victimisation in adolescence: Relationships with loneliness and depressive mood. *Emotional & Behavioural Difficulties, 17*(3–4), 361–374. doi:10.1080/13632752.2012.704227

Olweus, D. (1993). *Bullying at school: What we know and what we can do*. Malden, MA: Blackwell.

Olweus, D. (2012). Cyberbullying: An overrated phenomenon? *European Journal of Developmental Psychology, 9*(5), 520–538. doi:10.1080/17405629.2012.682358

Olweus, D. (2013). School bullying: Development and some important challenges. *Annual Review of Clinical Psychology, 9*, 751–80. doi:10.1146/annurev-clinpsy-050212-185516

Olweus, D., & Limber, S. P. (2010). Bullying in school: Evaluation and dissemination of the Olweus Bullying Prevention Program. *American Journal of Orthopsychiatry, 80*(1), 124–134. doi:10.1111/j.1939-0025.2010.01015.x

Pabian, S., & Vandebosch, H. (2016). An investigation of short-term longitudinal associations between social anxiety and victimization and perpetuation of traditional bullying and cyberbullying. *Journal of Youth and Adolescence, 45*(2), 328–339. doi:10.1007/s10964-015-0259-3

Patchin, J. W., & Hinduja, S. (2006). Bullies move beyond the schoolyard: A preliminary look at cyberbullying. *Youth Violence and Juvenile Justice, 4*(2), 148–169. doi:10.1177/1541204006286288

Patchin, J. W., & Hinduja, S. (2010). Cyberbullying and self-esteem. *Journal of School Health, 80*(12), 614–621. doi:10.1111/j.1746-1561.2010.00548.x

Patchin, J. W., & Hinduja, S. (2012). *Preventing and responding to cyberbullying: Expert perspectives.* Thousand Oaks, CA: Routledge.

Pelfrey, W. V., & Weber, N. L. (2013). Keyboard gangsters: Analysis of incidence and correlates of cyberbullying in a large urban student population. *Deviant Behavior, 34*(1), 68–84. doi:10.1080/01639625.2012.707541

Perren, S., Dooley, J., Shaw, T., & Cross, D. (2010). Bullying in school and cyberspace: Associations with depressive symptoms in Swiss and Australian adolescents. *Child and Adolescent Psychiatry & Mental Health, 4*(28), 1–10. doi:10.1186/1753-2000-4-28

Popović-Ćitić, B., Djurić, S., & Cvetković, V. (2011). The prevalence of cyberbullying among adolescents: A case study of middle schools in Serbia. *School Psychology International, 32*(4), 412–424.

Price, M., & Dalgleish, J. (2010). Cyberbullying: Experiences, impacts and coping strategies as described by Australian young people. *Youth Studies Australia, 29*(2), 51–59.

Raskauskas, J., & Stoltz, A. D. (2007). Involvement in traditional and electronic bullying among adolescents. *Developmental Psychology, 43*(3), 564–575. doi:10.1037/0012-1649.43.3.564

Renati, R., Berrone, C., & Zanetti, M. A. (2012). Morally disengaged and unempathic: Do cyberbullies fit these definitions? An exploratory study. *Cyberpsychology, Behavior, and Social Networking, 15*(8), 391–398. doi:10.1089/cyber.2012.0046

Roberto, A. J., & Eden, J. (2010). Cyberbullying: Aggressive communication in the digital age. In T. Avtgis & A. S. Rancer (Eds.), *Arguments, aggression, and conflict: New directions in theory and research* (pp. 198–216). New York: Routledge.

Roberto, A. J., Eden, J., Savage, M. W., Ramos-Salazar, L., & Deiss, D. M. (2014). Prevalence and predictors of cyberbullying perpetration by high school seniors. *Communication Quarterly, 62*(1), 97–114. doi:10.1080/01463373.2013.860906

Robson, C., & Witenberg, R. T. (2013). The influence of moral disengagement, morally based self-esteem, age, and gender on traditional bullying and cyberbullying. *Journal of School Violence, 12*(2), 211–231. doi:10.1080/15388220.2012.762921

Sabella, R. A., Patchin, J. W., & Hinduja, S. (2013). Cyberbullying myths and realities. *Computers in Human Behavior, 29*(6), 2703–2711. doi:10.1016/j.chb.2013.06.040

Salmivalli, C., Sainio, M., & Hodges, E. V. E. (2013). Electronic victimization: Correlates, antecedents, and consequences among elementary and middle school students. *Journal of Clinical Child & Adolescent Psychology, 42*(4), 442–453. doi:10.1080/15374416.2012.759228

Savage, M. W., & Tokunaga, R. S. (2017). Moving toward a theory: Testing an integrated model of cyberbullying perpetration, aggression, communication skills, and Internet self-efficacy. *Computers in Human Behavior, 71*, 353–361. doi:10.1016/j.chb.2017.02.016

Scheithauer, H., Hayer, T., Petermann, F., & Jugert, G. (2006). Physical, verbal, and relational forms of bullying among German students: Age trends, gender differences, and correlates. *Aggressive Behavior, 32*(3), 261–275. doi:10.1002/ab.20128

Schenk, A. M., & Fremouw, W. J. (2012). Prevalence, psychological impact, and coping of cyberbully victims among college students. *Journal of School Violence, 11*(1), 21–37. doi:10.1080/15388220.2011.630310

Schenk, A. M., Fremouw, W. J., & Keelan, C. M. (2013). Characteristics of college cyberbullies. *Computers in Human Behavior, 29*(6), 2320–2327. doi:10.1016/j.chb.2013.05.013

Schneider, S. K., O'Donnell, L., Stueve, A., & Coulter, R. W. S. (2012). Cyberbullying, school bullying, and psychological distress: A regional census of high school students. *American Journal of Public Health, 102*(1), 171–177. doi:10.2105/AJPH.2011.300308

Schoffstall, C. L., & Cohen, R. (2011). Cyber aggression: The relation between online offenders and offline social competence. *Social Development, 20*(3), 587–604. doi:10.1111/j.1467-9507.2011.00609.x

Schultze-Krumbholz, A., & Scheithauer, H. (2009). Social-behavioral correlates of cyberbullying in a German student sample. *Journal of Psychology, 217*(4), 224–226. doi:10.1027/0044-3409.217.4.224

Schultze-Krumbholz, A., & Scheithauer, H. (2013). Is cyberbullying related to lack of empathy and social-emotional problems? *International Journal of Developmental Science, 7*(3–4), 161–166

Schultze-Krumbholz, A., Jäkel, A., Schultze, M., & Scheithauer, H. (2012). Emotional and behavioural problems in the context of cyberbullying: A longitudinal study among German adolescents. *Emotional & Behavioural Difficulties, 17*(3–4), 329–345. doi:10.1080/13632752.2012.704317

Selkie, E. M., Kota, R., Chan, Y., & Moreno, M. (2015). Cyberbullying, depression, and problem alcohol use in female college students: A multisite study. *Cyberpsychology, Behavior, and Social Networking, 18*(2), 79–86. doi:10.1089/cyber.2014.0371

Slonje, R., & Smith, P. K. (2008). Cyberbullying: Another main type of bullying? *Scandinavian Journal of Psychology, 49*(2), 147–154. doi:10.1111/j.1467-9450.2007.00611.x

Slonje, R., Smith, P. K., & Frisén, A. (2012). Processes of cyberbullying, and feelings of remorse by bullies: A pilot study. *European Journal of Developmental Psychology, 9*(2), 244–259. doi:10.1080/17405629.2011.643670

Smith, H., Polenik, K., Nakasita, S., & Jones, A. P. (2012). Profiling social, emotional, and behavioural difficulties of children involved in direct and indirect bullying behaviours. *Emotional & Behavioural Difficulties, 17*(3–4), 243–257. doi:10.1080/13632752.2012.704315

Smith, P. K. (2012). Cyberbullying and cyber aggression. In S. Jimerson & M. J. Furlong (Eds.), *Handbook of school violence and school safety: From research to practice* (2nd ed., pp. 93–103). New York: Routledge.

Smith, P. K., Mahdavi, J., Carvalho, M., Fisher, S., Russell, S., & Tippett, N. (2008). Cyberbullying: Its nature and impact in secondary school pupils. *Journal of Child Psychology and Psychiatry, and Allied Disciplines, 49*(4), 376–85. doi:10.1111/j.1469-7610.2007.01846.x

Sourander, A., Klomek, A. B., Ikonen, M., Lindroos, J., Luntamo, T., Koskelainen, M., ... Helenius, H. (2010). Psychosocial risk factors associated with cyberbullying among adolescents: A population-based study. *Archives of General Psychiatry, 67*(7), 720–728. doi:10.1001/archgenpsychiatry.2010.79

Steffgen, G., König, A., Pfetsch, J., & Melzer, A. (2011). Are cyberbullies less empathic? Adolescents' cyberbullying behavior and empathic responsiveness. *Cyberpsychology, Behavior, and Social Networking, 14*(11), 643–648. doi:10.1089/cyber.2010.0445

Sticca, F., & Perren, S. (2013). Is cyberbullying worse than traditional bullying? Examining the differential roles of medium, publicity, and anonymity for the perceived severity of bullying. *Journal of Youth and Adolescence, 42*(5), 739–750. doi:10.1007/s10964-012-9867-3

Sticca, F., Ruggieri, S., Alsaker, F., & Perren, S. (2013). Longitudinal risk factors for cyberbullying in adolescence. *Journal of Community and Applied Social Psychology, 23*(1), 52–67. doi:10.1002/casp.2136

Suler, J. (2004). The online disinhibition effect. *CyberPsychology & Behavior, 7*, 321–326. doi: 10.1089/1094931041291295.

Sumter, S. R., Valkenburg, P. M., Baumgartner, S. E., Peter, J., & van der Hof, S. (2015). Development and validation of the Multidimensional Offline and Online Peer Victimization Scale. *Computers in Human Behavior, 46*, 114–122. doi:10.1016/j.chb.2014.12.042

Takizawa, R., Maughan, B., & Arseneault, L. (2014). Adult health outcomes of childhood bullying victimization: Evidence from a five-decade longitudinal British birth cohort. *American Journal of Psychiatry, 171*. doi:10.1176/appi.ajp.2014.13101401

Tanrikulu, I., & Campbell, M. (2015). Correlates of traditional bullying and cyberbullying perpetration among Australian students. *Children & Youth Services Review, 55*, 138–146. doi:10.1016/j.childyouth.2015.06.001

Thomas, H. J., Connor, J. P., & Scott, J. G. (2015). Integrating traditional bullying and cyberbullying: Challenges of definition and measurement in adolescents. A review. *Educational Psychology Review, 27*(1), 135–152. doi:10.1007/s10648-014-9261-7

Tokunaga, R. S. (2010). Following you home from school: A critical review and synthesis of research on cyberbullying victimization. *Computers in Human Behavior, 26*(3), 277–287. doi:10.1016/j.chb.2009.11.014

Tsitsika, A., Janikian, M., Wójcik, S., Makaruk, K., Tzavela, E., Tzavara, C., ... Richardson, C. (2015). Cyberbullying victimization prevalence and associations with internalizing and externalizing problems among adolescents in six European countries. *Computers in Human Behavior, 51*, 1–7. doi:10.1016/j.chb.2015.04.048

Ttofi, M. M., Farrington, D. P., Lösel, F., & Loeber, R. (2011). Do the victims of school bullies tend to become depressed later in life? A systematic review and meta-analysis of longitudinal studies. *Journal of Aggression, Conflict and Peace Research, 3*(2), 63–73. doi:10.1108/17596591111132873

Udris, R. (2014). Cyberbullying among high school students in Japan: Development and validation of the online disinhibition scale. *Computers in Human Behavior, 41*, 253–261. doi:10.1016/j.chb.2014.09.036

Van den Eijnden, R., Vermulst, A., van Rooij, A. J., Scholte, R., & van de Mheen, D. (2014). The bidirectional relationships between online victimization and psychosocial problems in adolescents: A comparison with real-life victimization. *Journal of Youth and Adolescence, 43*(5), 790–802. doi:10.1007/s10964-013-0003-9

Van Geel, M., Vedder, P., & Tanilon, J. (2014). Relationship between peer victimization, cyberbullying, and suicide in children and adolescents: A meta-analysis. *JAMA Pediatrics, 168*(5), 435–442. doi:10.1001/jamapediatrics.2013.4143

Van Noorden, T. J., Haselager, G. T. J. T., Cillessen, A. N. H. N., & Bukowski, W. M. (2015). Empathy and involvement in bullying in children and adolescents: A systematic review. *Journal of Youth & Adolescence, 44*(3), 637–657. doi:10.1007/s10964-014-0135-6

Vandebosch, H., & Van Cleemput, K. (2008). Defining cyberbullying: A qualitative research into the perceptions of youngsters. *CyberPsychology & Behavior, 11*(4), 499–503. doi:10.1089/cpb.2007.0042

Waasdorp, T. E., & Bradshaw, C. P. (2015). The overlap between cyberbullying and traditional bullying. *Journal of Adolescent Health, 56*(5), 483–488. doi:10.1016/j.jadohealth.2014.12.002

Wachs, S. (2012). Moral disengagement and emotional and social difficulties in bullying and cyberbullying: Differences by participant role. *Emotional & Behavioural Difficulties, 17*(3–4), 347–360. doi:10.1080/13632752.2012.704318

Wade, A., & Beran, T. (2011). Cyberbullying: The new era of bullying. *Canadian Journal of School Psychology, 26*(1), 44–61.

Wang, J., Iannotti, R. J., & Luk, J. W. (2012). Patterns of adolescent bullying behaviors: Physical, verbal, exclusion, rumor, and cyber. *Journal of School Psychology, 50*(4), 521–534. doi:10.1016/j.jsp.2012.03.004

Wang, J., Iannotti, R. J., Luk, J. W., & Nansel, T. R. (2010). Co-occurrence of victimization from five subtypes of bullying: Physical, verbal, social exclusion, spreading rumors, and cyber. *Journal of Pediatric Psychology, 35*(10), 1103–1112. doi:10.1093/jpepsy/jsq048

Wang, J., Nansel, T. R., & Iannotti, R. J. (2011). Cyber and traditional bullying: Differential association with depression. *The Journal of Adolescent Health, 48*(4), 415–417. doi:10.1016/j.jadohealth.2010.07.012

Wigderson, S., & Lynch, M. (2013). Cyber- and traditional peer victimization: Unique relationships with adolescent well-being. *Psychology of Violence, 3*(4), 297–309. doi:10.1037/a0033657

Williams, K. R., & Guerra, N. G. (2015). Prevalence and predictors of Internet bullying. *Journal of Adolescent Health, 41*(6), S14–S21. doi:10.1016/j.jadohealth.2007.08.018

Wong, D. S. W., Chan, H. C. & Cheng, C. H. K. (2014). Cyberbullying perpetration and victimization among adolescents in Hong Kong. *Children and Youth Services Review, 36*, 133–140. doi:10.1016/j.childyouth.2013.11.006

Wright, M. F., Aoyama, I., Kamble, S. V., Li, Z., Soudi, S., Lei, L., & Shu, C. (2015). Peer attachment and cyber aggression involvement among Chinese, Indian, and Japanese adolescents. *Societies, 5*(2), 339–353. doi:10.3390/soc5020339

Ybarra, M. L., & Mitchell, K. J. (2004a). Online aggressor/targets, aggressors, and targets: A comparison of associated youth characteristics. *Journal of Child Psychology and Psychiatry, and Allied Disciplines, 45*(7), 1308–16. doi: 10.1111/j.1469-7610.2004.00328.x

Ybarra, M. L., & Mitchell, K. J. (2004b). Youth engaging in online harassment: Associations with caregiver-child relationships, Internet use, and personal characteristics. *Journal of Adolescence, 27*(3), 319–336. doi:10.1016/j.adolescence.2004.03.007

Ybarra, M. L., Boyd, D. M., Korchmaros, J. D., & Oppenheim, J. K. (2012). Defining and measuring cyberbullying within the larger context of bullying victimization. *Journal of Adolescent Health, 51*(1), 53–58. doi:10.1016/j.jadohealth.2011.12.031

Ybarra, M. L., Diener-West, M., & Leaf, P. J. (2007). Examining the overlap in Internet harassment and school bullying: Implications for school intervention. *Journal of Adolescent Health, 41*(6), S42–S50. doi:10.1016/j.jadohealth.2007.09.004

Zhou, Z., Tang, H., Tian, Y., Wei, H., Zhang, F., & Morrison, C. M. (2013). Cyberbullying and its risk factors among Chinese high school students. *School Psychology International, 34*(6), 630–647. doi:10.1177/0143034313479692

Chapter Five

Cyberstalking, Unwanted Pursuit, and Relational Intrusion

Stalking is an interpersonal phenomenon that entails pursuit, intrusion, and harassment. Westrup and Fremouw (1998) define stalking as "unwelcome, repetitive, and intrusive harassing and threatening behavior directed towards a specific individual" (p. 255). Tokunaga and Aune (2015) define cyberstalking as "repeated unwanted relational pursuit of an individual through communication technologies, such as computers, tablets, and smart phones" (p. 3; also see Reyns, 2012; Spitzberg & Hoobler, 2002).

Initial concerns about cyberstalking began to enter public and scholarly discourse in the mid-1990s. In 1994, the Baltimore Sun printed one of the first news stories on cyberstalking titled, "Criminals Lurk in Alleys of Cyberspace" (Rosenlind, 1994). Two of the earliest scholarly papers on cyberstalking appeared in 1995, addressing concerns about people using email to harass others (Barton, 1995; Ross, 1995). In 1999, Vice President Gore asked the U.S. Justice Department to provide guidance on how to address the emerging issue of cyberstalking. The subsequent Attorney General's report examined the prevalence of cyberstalking, reviewed legislation and practices for dealing with cyberstalking, and made policy recommendations for handling cyberstalking in the future (Reno, 1999). The report noted, "The lack of comprehensive data on the nature and extent of cyberstalking makes it difficult to develop effective response strategies." Further, the report's general recommendations suggested, "Future surveys and research studies on stalking should, where possible, include specific information on cyberstalking" (n.p.).

In the decades since the Attorney General's report, social and mobile technologies have become tools for online pursuit and harassment. By 2016, the Justice Department had successfully prosecuted the first case of cyberstalking resulting in the death of victims (and bystanders) and life sentences for family members of the killer (U. S. Justice Dept., 2016). Consistent with cyberstalking research, the case involved relational partners rather than strangers. In 2013, a Delaware man and his family members engaged in a campaign of cyberstalking and harassment against his ex-wife that ended when he shot her and several others. Two family members of the killer received life sentences for participating in the cyberstalking and planning the murder. Few states explicitly have cyberstalking laws, and the criteria differ among states. In other cases, cyberstalking cases are prosecuted using existing stalking, harassment, and electronic communication laws.

Unfortunately, cyberstalking is a common occurrence, especially if we include relational forms such as obsessive relational intrusion and unwanted pursuit (Dardis & Gidycz, 2016; Spitzberg & Cupach, 2014). One review of the literature explained "Cyberstalking happens, it is potentially widespread, it is serious, and it has real consequences for victims" (Reyns, 2012, p. 11). In a more recent analysis of the literature, Tokunaga and Aune (2015) stated, "Numerous cases of cyberstalking are reported each year, signaling the importance of studying this phenomenon" (p. 2).

Despite the high visibility of cyberstalking in the popular press and government legislation, scholars have devoted relatively little attention to the problem. Cyberstalking is a challenging phenomenon to study; researchers struggle to define and measure cyberstalking, to estimate its prevalence, to describe its effects on victims, to characterize victims and perpetrators, and to explain how it relates to other forms of stalking and online aggression. As Reyns (2012) observed, "It is striking how little progress has been made toward understanding cyberstalking" (p. 11). In their review of the cyberstalking research, Pereira and Matos (2016) mentioned, "knowledge about the nature, complexity, and impact of this problem remains insufficient" (p. 254).

The research that does exist lacks guiding theories and conceptual narratives. Cyberstalking research is often more descriptive than theory-driven. Because of the legal interest in the topic, definitions and clear descriptions are important. Thus, existing studies tend to focus on cyberstalking victimization rates, characteristics of victims, and characteristics of perpetrators. These are important data to help move research forward but they do not adequately address the important theoretical questions of *how* and *why*. According to Spitzberg and Cupach (2014), "With few exceptions, there is little theory to guide [cyberstalking] research" (p. 102). Without theory, it is difficult for researchers to build upon previous cyberstalking studies and refine conceptual models.

Defining Cyberstalking

Although there are several major challenges in cyberstalking research, perhaps the most central one is conceptually defining cyberstalking. Inconsistent definitions hinder researchers' abilities to measure cyberstalking and to develop conceptual models explaining the phenomenon. Consequently, a theme that dominates cyberstalking literature is the difficulty researchers have had trying to define and measure it (Fox, Nobles, & Fisher, 2011; Reyns, 2012).

This chapter employs Spitzberg and Cupach's (2014) work on unwanted pursuit and obsessive relational intrusion to conceptualize cyberstalking as an interpersonal and relational process (Spitzberg & Hoobler, 2002). Examining the communicative process of cyberstalking can help advance efforts to distinguish cyberstalking form other forms of online aggression.

Cupach and Spitzberg (1998) defined obsessive relational intrusion (ORI) as a pattern of "repeated and unwanted pursuit and invasion of one's sense of physical or symbolic privacy by another person, either stranger or acquaintance, who desires and presumes an intimate relationship" (p. 234). One important feature of ORI is that the goal is primarily to attain or maintain a relationship with the victim, rather than to hurt or threaten the victim. Of course, a benign intention may still result in scaring or harming the victim.

Chaulk and Jones (2011) argued that the functionality of Facebook provides a platform for relational intrusive behaviors. In a study examining whether and how people use obsessive relational intrusion on Facebook, Chaulk and Jones noted, "Not only are the types of behaviors inherent in offline ORI comparable to those found on Facebook, but so are the contexts in which they occur." Chaulk and Jones argued that many ORI and stalking behaviors "are facilitated by the Facebook application" (p. 250).

More specifically, most of the offline ORI tactics can also take place on Facebook (e.g., sharing embarrassing information or pictures, leaving unwanted messages, making dramatic displays of affection, intrusion into a victim's social circle, monitoring and surveilling the victim). On Facebook, for example, a pursuer might "follow" the victim by joining the same Facebook groups as the victim. Exaggerated displays of affection can be conveyed in a variety of ways on Facebook using text, images, and video. The pursuer might also leave unwanted messages on a victim's Facebook page, or on pages of the victim's family and friends. The study also identified more dangerous types of online obsessive intrusion on Facebook including leaving threatening messages, spreading rumors about the victim, and posting embarrassing or altered photos of the victim.

Taking a relational approach to cyberstalking, Spitzberg and Hoobler (2002) identified four types of cyberobsessional pursuit, or unwanted relational pursuit involving technology. *Hyperintimacy* describes a type of cyberobsessional pursuit where a stalker uses interpersonal technology in pursuit of a desired intimate relationship. The hallmark of hyperintimacy is that the pursuer repeatedly sends messages about the desired relationship, despite several attempts by the victim to reject the overtures. In some cases, hyperintimate pursuit may include unwanted expressions of affection, unsolicited compliments, or sexual messages. Additionally, hyperintimate behaviors can include expressing a desire to rekindle a previous relationship.

It is important to note that most of these behaviors would be considered desirable in a normal relationship, but in the context of cyberobsessional pursuit, they are threatening and disturbing. Thus, the key to identifying cyberstalking is in how the victim perceives the meaning of the pursuer's actions.

Spitzberg and Hoobler identified *threats* as a second type of cyberobsessional pursuit. Threats occur when pursuit messages suggest a desire to harm the victim. Cyberstalkers may threaten to harm victims' reputations or to embarrass victims on the Internet. At the most extreme, cyberobsessional pursuit can involve threats of physical harm or even death.

A third type of cyberobsessional behavior is *sabotage*. Spitzberg and Hoobler (2002) explain sabotage refers to an assault on the victim's character or reputation in which the perpetrator spreads rumors about the victim to the victim's peers. Similarly, cyberstalkers can sabotage a victim's public image by posting embarrassing material on social media or sending it to a victim's coworkers, friends, family, or romantic partner.

The most menacing type of cyberobsessional pursuit is *invasion*, where the pursuer's actions "profoundly interfere with victims' livelihoods" (Spitzberg & Hoobler, 2002, p. 5). The two main types of invasion behaviors are identity theft/impersonation and technological surveillance. Here, a cyberstalker may use the Internet or engage in hacking to gather personal or private information about the victim (Bocij, 2004). Another type of invasion occurs when cyberstalkers impersonate the victim online and assume the victim's identity while communicating with the victim's family and friends (McFarlane & Bocij, 2003). Cyberstalkers may also use GPS technology, keyloggers, and other surveillance tools to monitor and track the victim in real time.

At first, it seems strange that a pursuer would use threats and sabotage if their goal is to obtain a close relationship with their victim. The difference here is that, once rebuffed or asked to stop, most people move on. On the other hand, moving on may be especially difficult for the type of person who continues to pursue. At some point, after attempts are continually rebuffed, cyberobsessional pursuers' motivations may shift from a desire for intimacy to resentment over rejection.

Consequently, cyberobsessional pursuers may begin to respond with angry threats or sabotage.

Another reason cyberstalking is hard to define is that the term is used loosely in everyday conversations to connote a wide array of behaviors ranging from the ordinary and harmless to the criminal and damaging. Tokunaga and Aune (2015) noted that popular culture employs terms such as "Facebook stalking" or "creeping" that, despite their names, are often relatively harmless and mundane observations of a person's Facebook page. In fact, the target of "Facebook stalking" may have no idea that someone is paying extra attention to the target's profile.

Another reason that cyberstalking is difficult to define is that it shares many similarities with cyberbullying. Researchers have also debated whether cyberstalking merits special consideration or whether they should approach cyberstalking as a subset of the broader concept of stalking, in general. Before examining the conceptual and methodological challenges facing cyberstalking scholars, the next section summarizes empirical research on the prevalence of cyberstalking, characteristics of the victims, effects on victims, and characteristics of cyberstalkers. As one might expect, when studies employ different methods and measures, results vary dramatically.

Empirical Findings in Cyberstalking Research

Compared to research on other topics in this book, the cyberstalking literature is small and difficult to generalize. Conceptual ambiguity about cyberstalking creates problems for measurement and observation (Fox et al., 2011). Owens (2016) explained, "variations in the definition of stalking may change who is defined as a victim and thereby limit the generalizability of findings across previous studies" (p. 2196). In one review, Reyns, Henson, and Fisher (2012) observed, "researchers need to continue their efforts to better define and measure this type of pursuit-based victimization (p. 8; also see Parsons-Pollard & Moriarty, 2009). Until researchers begin to use consistent definitions and measures, the empirical data on cyberstalking should be interpreted cautiously (Fox et al., 2011). With these caveats in mind, the following paragraphs summarize the scant empirical literature on cyberstalking prevalence and characteristics of cyberstalkers and their victims.

Cyberstalking Prevalence

Questions about how frequently cyberstalking occurs, or how many people experience, it are difficult to answer. In one review, Cavezza and McEwan (2014) conclude, "no reliable estimates of the prevalence of cyberstalking exist" (p. 956). Likewise, Lee and O'Sullivan (2014) argued there is "very little recent data upon which to draw [cyberstalking prevalence] estimates" (p. 95). These problems derive, in part from researchers using different definitions and measures of cyberstalking (Reyns, 2012; Spitzberg & Cupach, 2014). Spitzberg and Cupach (2014) noted that the "prevalence of cyberstalking might be more difficult to operationalize than ordinary stalking" and "consequently, prevalence estimates are considered problematic" (p. 102).

A study by Dreßing, Bailer, Anders, Wagner, and Gallas (2014) demonstrated that prevalence rates vary depending on the *operational criteria used to define cyberstalking*. For example, 40% of the sample experienced "unwanted Internet contacts/harassment." However, when two other criteria were included in the definition of cyberstalking, "duration greater than two weeks" and "harassment causing fear," the prevalence estimate dropped to 6.3 percent. These results illustrate the dramatic effects that operational definitions have on measurement and subsequent data.

Even when using the same data, researchers report differing estimates of cyberstalking (see Spitzberg & Cupach 2014; Owens, 2016). Three studies analyzed the 2006 National Crime Victimization Survey and reported different estimates: 26% (Baum, Catalano, Rand, & Rose, 2009), 19% (Nobles, Reyns, Fox, & Fisher, 2014) and 18% (Truman, 2010). These studies each used different operational criteria for labeling a case as cyberstalking (Spitzberg & Cupach, 2014). For example, Nobles et al. (2014) used strict criteria for labeling cases as cyberstalking, including the victim had experienced fear and the behaviors were repeated. Other researchers employed more liberal and less exclusive criteria (Baum et al., 2009).

In general, cyberstalking appears to occur to a significant number of people, but estimates of that number are not reliable enough to draw detailed conclusions. The variability in definitions and inconsistencies in measurement produce an unreliable estimate of cyberstalking prevalence or victimization rates.

Cyberstalker Characteristics

Some studies indicate more men than women engage in cyberstalking. Ménard and Pincus (2012) noted men had significantly higher mean scores than women on both overt and cyberstalking. Cavezza and McEwan (2014) reported 94% of cyberstalkers were male. Reyns et al. (2012) observed that, among college students, nearly 7% of males compared to almost 4% of females admitted to engaging in cyberstalking. Conversely, Strawhun, Adams, and Huss (2013) found that women were more likely to report having engaged in cyberstalking. Here, the researchers note, "further research on frequency and motivation for cyberstalking among the sexes is necessary" (Strawhun et al., 2013, p. 715).

Cyberstalkers are commonly former relational partners or individuals desiring a romantic relationship with their victim (Cavezza & McEwan, 2014; Dardis & Giddy, 2016; Dreßing et al., 2014; Spitzberg & Cupach, 2007, 2014). Alexy, Burgess, Baker, Baum, and Smoyak (2005) reported that, among college students, cyberstalking is most likely to "emerge from a pre-existing relationship rather than a lunatic obsession of a complete stranger" (p. 350). Similarly, Cavezza and McEwan (2014) reported that 75% of their sample of cyberstalking victims were pursued by a former rejected relationship partner. Empirical data suggest that among former relational partners, those who also suffer from psychological problems may be more likely to engage in cyberstalking. Cavezza and McEwan (2014) found 61% of cyberstalkers were "diagnosed with a personality disorder or exhibited marked problematic personality traits" (p. 964).

In addition to psychopathologies, researchers have also noted interpersonal and relational difficulties among cyberstalkers. Cyberstalking appears to arise frequently from failed relationships and rejections (Alexy et al., 2005). Consistent with these claims, Strawhun et al. (2013)

reported that interpersonal and relational problems including insecure attachment, jealousy, and relationship violence were all significant correlates of cyberstalking behaviors. A study on traditional stalking revealed that rejection was most likely to motivate obsessive relational intrusion when the pursuer had a heightened sensitivity (or vulnerability) to rejection. In other words, those who can handle rejection are less likely to be motivated to seek intimacy through stalking.

Cyberstalkers' motivations vary from the desire to punish, retaliate, and seek revenge to a desire for reestablishing or starting an intimate relationship (Cavezza & McEwan, 2014; Spitzberg & Hoobler, 2002). In a study on cyberstalkers' motivations, Cavezza and McEwan (2014) observed resentment over romantic rejection most often. Similarly, Dreßing et al. (2014) observed most cyberstalking victims believed the pursuer was motivated by insult/injury, the result of jealousy, a desire to initiate a love relationship, or to exact revenge. The study reported a minority of victims perceived their cyberstalkers were motivated by a desire to initiate a friendship or restore a previous relationship.

McFarlane and Bocij (2003) proposed a typology of cyberstalkers based on motivations, behaviors, and relationship to the victim. An essential contribution of McFarlane and Bocij's typology is that the types of cyberstalking are organized along conceptual dimensions (motivation, behavior, relationship, etc.), offering some theoretical structure to the typology. McFarlane and Bocij identified five types of cyberstalking including, vindictive, composed, intimate, infatuated, and collective.

First, *vindictive* cyberstalkers are motivated by a desire to frighten and intimidate their victims. McFarlane and Bocij (2003) reported vindictive cyberstalkers threatened their victims more than any other group of stalkers and used the most extensive variety of communication technologies. Additionally, most victims received disturbing messages from vindictive stalkers, including bizarre comments, rambling conversations, and intimidating images (such as pictures of corpses). Vindictive cyberstalkers frequently engaged in offline stalking behaviors as well.

Next, a *composed* cyberstalker's motivation is to annoy, irritate, and upset the victim. McFarlane and Bocij (2003) observed that composed cyberstalkers were less likely than other types to have criminal records, psychiatric histories, or to have previously stalked another victim. Here, the typology is vague about how composed cyberstalkers differ from the vindictive type.

MacFarlane and Bocij (2003) describe *intimate* cyberstalkers as driven by a desire to "win" the affections of their target and to be closer to the victim. According to the study, intimate cyberstalkers are often former relational partners. Intimate cyberstalkers' behaviors range from messages intended to restore a previous relationship to threats against the victim. Tokunaga and Aune (2015) also used the term intimate cyberstalking to describe "psychological intimidation and threats made between people in existing relationships, but individuals not involved in a relationship can also be pursued (p. 3)."

The *infatuated* cyberstalker seeks intimate relationships with their victims. Here, communication was considerably more intimate than the ex-intimate cyberstalkers and when they were rebuffed, infatuates became increasingly more threatening. In other words, the infatuated cyberstalker's motivation shifts from attracting the victim to attacking the victim once the pursuer is rejected. McFarlane and Bocij noted that infatuates resemble what Mullen et al. (1999) called "rejected stalkers" (e.g., intimacy seekers who are unsuccessful suitors).

Last, McFarlane, and Bocij (2003) identified *collective cyberstalkers* as two or more individuals who engage in a coordinated effort to pursue the victim together. Corporate or organizational cyberstalking would fall into this category along with other cases where groups engage in a coordinated campaign of intrusion and pursuit of a victim.

Victim Characteristics

Data on victims' characteristics are important for explaining and understanding cyberstalking. Few studies have examined the characteristics of cyberstalking victims. As with the prevalence estimates and data on pursuers, inconsistent measures and definitions also make it difficult to summarize data on cyberstalking victims. Several studies suggest that women are more likely to report being victims of cyberstalking than are men (Dreßing et al., 2014; Holt & Bossler, 2008; Paullet, Rota,

& Swan, 2009; Reyns, 2012). In fact, Reyns (2012) observed that females had almost double the odds of being victims of online pursuit.

Victim Outcomes

The study of cyberstalking victimization is in the very early stages and data on victims' experiences are limited. Only a small number of empirical studies have examined victims' experiences (e.g., Alexy et al., 2005; Bocij, 2003; Dreßing et al., 2014; Jerin & Dolinsky, 2001; Reyns, 2012; Sheridan & Grant, 2007; Spitzberg & Hoobler, 2002). In one study that did examine victims' experiences, Dreßing et al. (2014) reported the most common consequences of cyberstalking were feelings of inner unrest (78.2% of victims), mistrust toward other people (68.2%), sleep disorders (64.2%), feelings of helplessness (55.4%), and anger/aggression (54.9%). Although less frequent, a quarter to a third of the victims reported more serious effects such as social withdrawal (34.6%), depression (34.6%), and panic attacks (23.1%). The results also suggested that "a victim's fear level was the best predictor of physical and psychological health consequences, mediating the relationship between victim gender and the consequences of stalking" (Dreßing et al., 2014, p. 6).

Despite many similarities, some scholars have argued that cyberstalking may affect victims more severely than traditional stalking. For example, Reyns (2012) speculated, "being physically followed and confronted (i.e., stalking) is probably more likely to generate fear of being harmed in the victim than receiving repeated, even threatening, messages electronically (i.e., cyberstalking)" (p. 11). Nobles et al. (2014) argued that cyberstalking "may be simultaneously more harmful to the victim's psychological well-being and reputation, thus more decisive in spurring quicker self-protective action" (p. 1007). To test this hypothesis, Nobles et al. (2014) examined data from the National Crime Victimization Survey, comparing stalking victims who had experienced cyberstalking with stalking victims who had not experienced cyberstalking. The results revealed that stalking victims who had experienced cyberstalking were significantly more likely to report fear at the onset of their victimization. However, the two groups did not differ on reported fear over time. The study also found that cyberstalking victims' self-protective behaviors were greater than physical stalking victims' were. "Perceived fear over time, the occurrence of a physical attack, and sex of the victim were all associated with a higher number of self-protective behaviors for cyberstalking victims compared to stalking victims, net of the effect of the control variables" (Nobles et al., 2014, p. 986).

In contrast to Nobles et al.'s (2014) results, other evidence suggests that cyberstalking and traditional stalking have similar effects. Short, Guppy, Hart, and Barnes (2015) found cyberstalking and physical stalking victims reported similarly high levels of anxiety and posttraumatic stress. Considering the sparse and inconsistent data, future research needs to examine whether there are unique, distinct, effects of cyberstalking.

Victim Responses to Cyberstalking

Other empirical research on cyberstalking victims has examined how they respond to cyberstalkers. Nobles et al. (2014) recognized that cyberstalking research "has not developed to the point where patterns in responses to victimization, including self-protective behaviors taken by the victim, have been clearly identified" (p. 8). According to Tokunaga and Aune (2015) "a well- developed a taxonomy of behaviors used to manage the risks involved with cyberstalking has not been constructed" (p. 2).

To advance the research on victim responses, Tokunaga and Aune (2015) proposed "creating a taxonomy of management tactics for cyberstalking" (2015, p. 3). The researchers conducted a thematic analysis of victims' written reflections to identify common stalking management tactics, distinguish between effective and ineffective strategies, and examine relationships between cyberstalking behaviors and risk management tactics. Tokunaga and Aune's (2015) study revealed that the most commonly reported victim response tactic was to ignore or avoid the cyberstalker. Victims reported they engaged in ignoring and avoiding with the hope it would stop the cyberstalking or because they did not know what else to do. Here, victims' efforts to avoid cyberstalkers resemble avoidant responses observed in research on physical stalking (e.g., Spitzberg & Cupach, 2003).

The next most frequent victim response tactic was for victims to use technology to end contact and prevent future interaction with the cyberstalker (Tokunaga & Aune, 2015). For example, victims changed privacy settings and blocked the pursuer on social networking sites. The third most common response was help-seeking. Here, victims sought assistance from outside third parties and sources. Often, victims reported contacting Internet service providers or law enforcement. Also, victims reported using negation and threats toward the cyberstalker. The least common victim response behaviors included directly confronting their pursuers to insult them (derogation) and falsely playing along with the pursuer.

Regarding effectiveness, victims reported that use of privacy protection strategies was the most effective approach for dealing with cyberstalking (Tokunaga & Aune, 2015). Active technological dissociation (blocking, unfriending) was the second most useful risk-management strategy. The study indicated that avoiding/ignoring and negating/threatening were less effective responses.

Tokunaga and Aune (2015) also found that victims' response behaviors varied according to the type of cyberstalking experienced. The ignore/avoid tactic was used disproportionately more than other tactics in response to hyperintimacy and threatening cyberstalking behaviors. However, as cyberstalking became more menacing, victims chose more confrontational and direct responses.

In existing relationships, cyberstalking may be part of a larger pattern of relational abuse. Researchers use different terms such as "digital dating abuse" or "cyberdating abuse" to describe "a pattern of behaviors that control, pressure, or threaten a dating partner using a cellphone or the Internet" (Reed, Tolman, & Ward, 2016, p. 1556). Similarly, other studies suggest cyberdating abuse is characterized by a pattern of jealousy, intrusion, surveillance, and control (Borrajo, Gámez-Guadix, Pereda & Calvete, 2015; Christofides, Muise, & Desmarias, 2009; Reed, et al., 2016; Zweig, Lachman, Yahner, & Dank, 2014). Recently, Wolford-Clevenger et al. (2015) created a measure of cyberdating abuse, the Partner Cyber Abuse Questionnaire, which includes items reflecting unwanted *pursuit*, *intrusion,* or *stalking.* The survey measures participants' agreement with statements such as, "My partner sent messages from my Facebook profile without my permission;" "My partner checked or read my e-mails or texts without my permission;" and "My partner sent me frequent e-mails or texts when he knew I didn't want them."

Overall, the research reviewed thus far offers few robust or consistent findings about cyberstalkers, their victims, or the prevalence of the problem. While the data do indicate that many people experience cyberstalking victimization, the published estimates vary dramatically. Compared to research on similar phenomena, such as cyberbullying, the cyberstalking literature offers relatively sparse information about the characteristics of victims and perpetrators. The available literature on cyberstalker characteristics suggests that often, the stalker is a former relational partner who likely struggles with interpersonal and psychological challenges. Although there are limited data, cyberstalking behavior may reflect broader problems with relational boundaries, emotion regulation, and insecurity. Future research should further examine the associations between relational deficits and engaging in computer-mediated relational intrusion and unwanted pursuit. As the next section explains, viewing cyberstalking as an interpersonal phenomenon can help organize the existing research and guide future work.

One reason that cyberstalking is challenging to define and measure is that research has not carefully differentiated it from related phenomena. For example, there are questions about how cyberstalking differs from traditional stalking. Similarly, the literature is unclear about how cyberstalking differs from other forms of online harassment, such as cyberbullying. The next section addresses both issues, using an interpersonal approach to distinguish cyberstalking from both traditional stalking and cyberbullying.

Addressing Conceptual Challenges in Cyberstalking Research

As the previous sections highlighted, cyberstalking research is hindered by conceptual ambiguity and a general lack of theory. Communication researchers have suggested we can best understand traditional stalking by considering it an interactive relational process (Spitzberg & Cupach, 1998). In a review of the stalking literature, Spitzberg and Cupach (2003) proposed, "Conceptualizing stalking as both relational and interactional represents a sea change in the paradigmatic underpinnings of stalking research" also noting, "even clinical approaches have defined stalking as a process of communication" (p. 350). Research on cyberstalking would benefit from examining fundamental communicative and relational processes such as message production, message reception, relational messages, power, and intimacy.

Distinguishing Cyberstalking and Traditional Stalking

One major conceptual debate involves disagreement about how to distinguish between cyberstalking and traditional stalking. Although cyberstalking is not entirely different from traditional stalking, the places they differ reveal areas for communication scholars to explore. Researchers disagree about whether cyberstalking and traditional stalking are distinct enough to merit separate attention or whether cyberstalking is a subset of a more general stalking phenomenon that also occurs offline. According to Reyns (2012), there is "little agreement regarding whether cyberstalking is different from physically proximal stalking, and this distinction becomes even more difficult to make when a stalker pursues his victim both online and in physical proximity" (p. 6). Nobles et al. (2014) observed, "It remains an open question, one deserving of further scientific scrutiny, whether cyberstalking is a variant of stalking that incorporates special circumstances (e.g., technology) or is an entirely separate and distinct criminal behavior" (p. 987).

Some scholars view cyberstalking as a new behavior. For example, in early research, Bocij (2004) argued, "the least helpful definitions of cyberstalking are those that consider it as nothing more than a variation on offline stalking" (p. 12). Instead, Bocij asserted that "cyberstalking should be regarded as an entirely new form of deviant behavior, albeit one that is related to offline stalking" (p. 4). It is important to recognize that Bocij's (2004) research was based on a world before smartphones and social networks.

Several years later, Sheridan and Grant (2007) proposed an "assumption of parallelism," explaining that "cyberstalking is a question of degree, rather than a distinct form of contact" (p. 636). Results from their study revealed that the harmful effects of cyberstalking were roughly equivalent to those associated with traditional stalking.

Today, most of the literature regards cyberstalking as an extension of offline stalking (for a review see Tokunaga & Aune, 2015). Nobles et al. (2014) argued that cyberstalking is most appropriately conceptualized as a subset of stalking noting, "Stalking offenders and victims may subsequently extend their interactions to the domain of cyberspace, making a conceptual differentiation between stalking and cyberstalking difficult or impossible" (p. 989). Earlier, Burgess and Baker (2002) asserted, "understanding cyberstalking is to understand stalking in general" (p. 202). In the future, as mediated communication becomes further embedded in our lives, we are more likely see unwanted pursuers who shift between modes or use them simultaneously.

Crossover and Co-Occurrence. Roberts (2008) argued that viewing cyberstalking as an extension of traditional stalking accounts for the "cross-over" between the use of both mediated and offline communication to pursue a victim (also see Spence-Giehl, 2003). Crossover is similar to the concept of "modality switching" (Caughlin & Sharabi, 2013; Caughlin, Basnyat, Sharabi, 2017; Sharabi & Caughlin, 2017; Ramirez & Zhang, 2007) where interactants switch between mediated and in-person channels. A detailed study of stalking crossover revealed crossover pursuit is the norm rather than the exception (Dreßing et al., 2014). The researchers observed that whereas 25.8% of cyberstalking cases were "purely cyberstalking" (i.e., did not involve any physical or in-person behaviors), three-quarters of the cases involved crossover. The most common pattern, observed in 42% of cases, was simultaneous onset of cyberstalking and offline stalking behaviors. Additionally, 16.5% reported cyberstalking that later moved to offline behaviors and 15.8% of cases began offline and then moved to mediated communication. Sheridan and Grant (2007) surveyed self-identified stalking victims and found that only 4% experienced purely online stalking (i.e., stalking that originated online and remained online) whereas 38.6% reported experiencing crossover pursuit including both offline stalking and computer-mediated harassment.

Crossover does not mean that online and in-person behaviors are experienced the same way. While acknowledging that in-person and mediated stalking usually happen together, the next section considers how mediated communication changes the experience of stalking for both pursuer and victim.

Although stalking includes a complex mix of in-person and mediated behaviors, there is theoretical value in examining how technology affects the interpersonal processes of unwanted pursuit. Communication researchers argue technology may change the communicative process of stalking. Tokunaga and Aune (2015) explained that online social technology "are enticing platforms for stalkers because they create unique opportunities for perpetration" (p. 3; also see Nobles et al., 2014; Reyns, Henson, & Fisher, 2011). Spitzberg and Cupach (2014) suggested that what makes cyberstalking worth studying is the way that technology affects the unwanted pursuit process. For example, cyberstalkers may be less inhibited because of the relative anonymity of reduced social presence online. Technology also affects how victims experience cyberstalking compared to traditional stalking. The following paragraphs highlight some of the most important communicative distinctions between cyberstalking and traditional stalking.

Proximity and Distance. Interpersonal technology eliminates constraints of physical distance. Early research by Burgess and Baker (2002) argued that cyberstalking does not require the physical, or even geographic, proximity necessary for most other types of stalking. Today, most people have personal relationships with their cyberstalkers (Cavezza & MacFarlane, 2014). As noted earlier, cyberstalkers may use location-based information available from social media to monitor their victim's location without needing to surveil them in person. For example, Chaulk and Jones (2011) contend that one reason people may use Facebook to engage in online obsessive relational intrusion is that many users reveal their location information in their profiles and posts.

Disinhibition and Reduced Social Presence. One hypothesis that researchers have explored is that reduced social presence in mediated contexts may lower inhibitions (Suler, 2004). The earliest research on computer-mediated communication noted that the text-based interactions of the time lacked social presence, or "the feeling that a medium is personal, warm, and sociable rather than impersonal, cold, and unsociable" (Hiltz, Johnson, & Turoff, 1986, p. 228; Short, Williams & Christie, 1976; Gunawardena, 1995, 1997). Gunawardena (1995) refined the concept to "the degree to which a person is perceived as a 'real person' in mediated communication" (p. 151).

Mediated communication may also help pursuers feel less guilty, furthering disinhibition. The diminished social presence online makes it harder for the stalker to see how the behavior is affecting the victim. A lack of sensory information and rich feedback cues from the victim may further disinhibit a stalker, making it less likely the stalker will experience guilt or reticence when confronting or harassing the victim (Meloy, 1996, 1998; Lapidot-Lefler & Barak, 2012; Suler, 2004). In a study of online obsessive relational intrusion, Chaulk and Jones (2011) claimed, "Facebook allows this behavior to occur in relative anonymity—i.e., it is near to impossible to determine who has been visiting one's space on Facebook and how often" (p. 250). Similarly, Bocij (2004) argued technology may motivate people who are otherwise law-abiding to take part in cyberstalking because of technological affordances that lower inhibitions.

Disinhibition might also help explain a finding by Alexy et al. (2005) where online stalkers were significantly more likely to threaten to hurt themselves than offline stalkers. Alexy et al. (2005) speculated that "cyberstalkers may behave in a more dramatic fashion because they are not in physical proximity of their victims and do not need to act on their threats" (p. 286). The question of whether cyberstalkers are more likely to display more dramatic emotions than traditional stalkers warrants further attention, especially considering that the premise here is that the lack of social presence either requires or allows more intense displays.

Victims may also be less inhibited online. Tokunaga and Aune (2015) identified several victim response tactics that were unique to cyberstalking. For example, some victims respond to cyberstalking by "playing along" or "feigning interest" because they perceive cyberstalking as less threatening. On the other hand, Tokunaga and Aune (2015) noted that "in offline stalking, victims rarely play along with the pursuit or make excuses for their inability to enter into a relationship because it could contribute to significant risk" (p. 20). The authors speculated that the reduced presence and increased distance from the cyberstalker might "embolden victims to behave in ways unintuitive to the cessation of cyberstalking" (p. 20).

Technology Weakens Boundaries. Technology makes it easier for stalkers to cross both physical and relational boundaries. Mobile devices enable a stalker to contact their victim at any time at any place with relative impunity. The stalker has access to a variety of modes of communication including voice, text, social media posts, video, and images. Technology also enables stalkers with greater opportunities to surveil their victims with GPS, hacking, streaming video, and web content.

As it stands, there are good arguments, and some evidence, supporting the view that cyberstalking differs from other modes of stalking in important ways that may alter the communication process. Studying the differences and similarities between online stalking and traditional stalking is especially tricky given that the two types of stalking usually co-occur. When referring to stalking and cyberstalking, it may be best for researchers to view them in a manner similar to how Spitzberg and Cupach (2014) refer to stalking and obsessive relational intrusion, as "roughly equivalent, except in such instances that their differences merit particular attention" (p. 20).

Distinguishing Cyberstalking and Cyberbullying

As noted in the cyberbullying chapter and throughout this chapter, research on various forms of online aggression and pursuit evade easy conceptual categorization. One important task for researchers is to disentangle and distinguish among different types of cyber aggression. When cyberbullying and cyberstalking are treated interchangeably in theory and measurement, results are difficult to summarize and understand. Research on cyberstalking and cyberbullying has not offered a detailed conceptual explanation of how cyberstalking and cyberbullying differ. This section proposes several ways to distinguish cyberstalking and cyberbullying that can help with building more detailed and more useful theories. As with other topics in this chapter, examining the communication processes reveals meaningful conceptual differences between cyberbullying and cyberstalking.

One reason cyberstalking and cyberbullying are challenging to differentiate is that cyberstalking is frequently included in operational definitions of cyberbullying. For example, Cassidy, Jackson, and Faucher (2016) used the word "stalk" in the definition of cyberbullying research participants received at the start of a survey. Cavezza and McEwan (2014) observed, "Cyberstalking overlaps considerably with similar behaviors such as cyberbullying" (p. 956), noting that both are unwanted and can evoke fear or distress in the victim. However, they did not differentiate the two. Spitzberg and Cupach (2014) argued there are blurred boundaries between cyberstalking and related phenomena such as cyberbullying and online aggression. They describe cyberstalking as "a fuzzy subset of behaviors along a broader spectrum of technological aggression" (p. 101).

Dempsey et al. (2010) argued that it is vital for researchers to distinguish cyberbullying from cyberstalking. Rather than suggesting that cyberstalking and cyberbullying are *entirely* distinct or similar, there is value in considering how mediation affects the interpersonal interaction. Such dissimilarities reveal where researchers can begin to demarcate the conceptual and empirical differences. To advance research in both cyberstalking and cyberbullying, the literature needs an analysis of how cyberbullying and stalking differ. The sections below represent an initial attempt at identifying the interpersonal differences between cyberbullying and cyberstalking.

Ages of Participants. Although there are not detailed theoretical explanations, most of the literature implies that a major difference between cyberstalking and bullying is age. Generally, researchers and the broader public think of children and adolescents when they talk about cyberbullying. Moreover, cyberstalking is usually framed as an experience among late-adolescents, college students, and other adults. For instance, Durkin and Patterson (2007) noted that although cyberstalking shares some traits with cyberbullying, stalking "normally involves adults rather than children and adolescents" (p. 452). However, there are distinct exceptions. Adults in abusive romantic relationships may engage in cyberbullying. Cyberbullying happens among adults in the workplace (Coyne, Farley, Axtell, Sprigg, Best, & Kwock, 2017; Vranjes, Baillien, Vandebosch, Erreygers, & De Witte, 2017). Therefore, although less common, cyberbullying does happen among adults and is not limited to children and teens.

Ambiguity about *how* or *why* age plays into the distinction between cyberbullying and cyberstalking contributes to the difficulty studying them. Articulating a conceptual difference would help advance both kinds of literature by bringing additional clarity to defining these phenomena. For example, many of the *motivations* involved in cyberstalking are uncommon among children. Cyberstalking often arises from adult relationship dynamics, including romantic infatuation, problematic ex-partners, and dysfunctional breakups. As adolescents approach young adulthood, these problems may begin to occur in their romantic relationships, but are unlikely to drive cyberstalking among younger children.

Behavior-Defined Versus Victim-Defined. Stalking researchers have argued that whereas cyberbullying is a behaviorally-defined phenomenon, stalking is victim-defined (Spitzberg & Cupach, 2014). Definitions of cyberbullying focus on behavior, or action. One widely cited definition defines cyberbullying as "an aggressive, intentional act carried out by a group or individual, using electronic forms of contact, repeatedly and over time against a victim who cannot easily define him or herself" (Smith, Mahdavi, Carvalho, Fisher, Russell, & Tippett, 2008, p. 376). With cyberbullying, intentional repeated online harassment is relatively easy to identify.

On the other hand, specific behaviors or intentions do not define stalking. The critical feature of cyberstalking is "the reactions of the recipient of the unwanted attention, who, in the act of experiencing themselves as victimized, create a stalking event" (Spitzberg &

Cupach, 2014, p. 9). In fact, "much of the behavior of relational stalking is indistinct from culturally sanctioned courtship behavior" (Spitzberg & Cupach, 2014, p. 16). Indeed, Finch (2001) asserted that early stages of intimate relationships might present "a range of potential situations in which normal dating behavior and stalking may overlap" (p. 66).

Additionally, Spitzberg (2016) pointed out that the threat or distress a stalking victims feels might not come from a single interaction. Instead, the distress results from the cumulative effect of many behaviors that are relatively benign but, when taken together, make the victim feel threatened. From this perspective, stalking only occurs if the victim deems it unwanted. The victim-defined nature of cyberstalking highlights the importance of research that examines victims' experiences and behaviors.

Researchers emphasize the victim's perspective when they stipulate that cyberstalking is unwanted pursuit (Dreßing et al., 2014). Although pursuit behaviors may resemble common expressions of romantic interest, they become stalking when they are unwanted by the victim. Cyberbullying, on the other hand, can be both "defined and operationalized in a purely behavioral manner" (Spitzberg & Cupach, 2014). Cyberbullying behaviors are not ambiguous in their meaning. When a cyberbully posts a hateful message on a social network, or when a cyberbully spreads rumors about the victim, there is little room for any interpretation other than the desire to harm.

Motivations. Cyberstalking and cyberbullying also differ in terms of the motivations that drive them. Bullying involves intentional, repeated aggression motivated by a *desire to cause to harm to the victim and to gain status* and *gain influence among peers* (Salmivalli, 2010; Zijlstra et al., 2008). Although cyberstalkers may engage in intentional aggression, it is not a necessary feature.

Cyberstalking motives are more varied than bullying. Perhaps most clearly, cyberstalking may start with benign motivations and later progress into purposeful harassment and pursuit. Unlike bullying, cyberstalking can occur unintentionally, or with well-intended motives (Westrup & Freemouw, 1998). The cyberstalker may be in love with the victim or trying to rekindle a former relationship. Additionally, online obsessive relational intrusion may be motivated by a desire to control the other partner or to reduce uncertainty (Alexy et al., 2005; Chaulk & Jones, 2011).

Obsession and Rumination. Cyberstalking and cyberbullying differ regarding the perpetrator's mindset. The concepts mentioned earlier, cyberobsessional pursuit and online obsessive relational intrusion, reflect a fundamental difference from cyberbullying regarding obsessiveness and the aggressor's mindset. Unlike bullying, cyberstalking involves obsessive thoughts and behavior. Here, the term obsessive does not refer to a psychiatric diagnosis, but rather to a pattern of preoccupied behavior and motivation (Meloy, 2001). The early stalking research described stalking as obsessional following (Meloy, 1999; Zona, Sharma, & Lane, 1993; Meloy & Gothard, 1995). Obsessive thoughts and behaviors are also common in descriptions of cyberstalking (e.g., Spitzberg & Cupach, 2014; Spitzberg & Hoobler, 2002). Lyndon, Bonds-Raacke, and Cratty (2011) describe "Facebook stalking" as obsessive. Similarly, scholars emphasize the role that fixation and rumination play in an unwanted relational pursuit (Spitzberg, Cupach, Hannawa, & Crowley, 2104).

On the other hand, the literature on cyberbullying does not characterize cyberbullies as obsessive or ruminative. Cyberstalkers' behaviors are more likely to be expressions of obsessive thinking whereas bullying is associated with anti-social characteristics. Indeed, the cyberbullying literature has noted bullying is correlated with diminished empathy, moral disengagement, and interpersonal problems (Ang & Goh, 2010; Brewer & Kerslake, 2015; Schultze-Krumbholz & Scheithauer, 2013).

Dyadic Versus Peer Group Involvement. Whereas cyberbullying is often conceptualized as a peer group activity, cyberstalking is dyadic and less public. Interpersonal communication researchers often employ Goffman's (1959, 1967) notion of "audience" to help describe the idea that interpersonal interaction is a social performance where actors attempt to influence others. Goffman's framework identifies the audience as people who witness or co-participate in the performance. Kernaghan and Elwood (2013) used Goffman's approach to study cyberbullying and suggested that cyberbullies are actors, performing to impress their audience of peers. The cyberbully seeks to demonstrate to an audience of peers that he is "better than" or more "powerful than" the victim. In bullying, the victim is a prop used to gain prestige and status from the bully's audience of peers (Salmivalli, 2010). With the Internet, the size and scope of the audience can increase rapidly as others share online material (Kernaghan & Elwood, 2013).

Further, some studies have examined bullying as a group process (e.g., Garandeau & Cillessen, 2006; Salmivalli, 2010; Salmivalli, & Peets, 2009) where participants play a variety of different of roles such as "Victim, Bully, Reinforcer of the Bully, Assistant of the Bully, Defender of the Victim, and Outsider" (Salmivalli, 2010; Salmivalli, Lagerspetz, Björkqvist, Österman, & Kaukiainen, 1996). Olweus (1991) described how group-related phenomena, such as diffusion of responsibility, play a role in bullying. Garandeau and Cillessen (2006) argued that bullying might function to create cohesiveness in a peer group and suggested, "in most cases, it results from the encounter between a skillful bully and a group that lacks true cohesiveness" (p. 612).

In contrast, cyberstalkers' pursuits are often hidden from public view and cyberstalking is a usually a one-on-one phenomenon. Spitzberg and Cupach (2007) describe the stalker-victim relationship as disjunctive, where one person wants interaction and the other desires the opposite. In cyberstalking, the victim, rather than peer group, is the audience. Victims of cyberstalking may be the only intended audience for the stalker. The disjunctive relationship between stalker and victim occurs because the victim (i.e., the audience) fails to accept the stalker's performance of potential romantic partner. The stalker derives satisfaction from the victim's responsiveness and attention but responds angrily to the victim's rejection. Hence, in Goffman's (1959, 1967) terms, when a romantic overture is rejected, the pursuer loses face and the performance fails. A stalker's emotional reaction to losing face may lead to further pursuit motivated by anger or desire for revenge. Taken together, the research above illustrates how examining the performer-audience dynamics in a communication situation can help distinguish cyberstalking and bullying.

Specific Versus Non-Specific Victims. Unlike stalkers, cyberbullies commonly have multiple victims. Bullies who harass multiple victims are known as "serial bullies" (Chan, 2006). In one study, Chan (2006) reported that 70% of the victims reported being harassed by a serial bully. Cyberbullies select targets based on opportunity and victims may be somewhat interchangeable. For instance, if a cyberbullying victim moved to a different school, the bully would probably seek out a new victim among the peer group (Chan, 2006). Bullies select victims who are submissive, insecure, physically weak, and in a low power, rejected position within the group (Salmivalli, 2010). On the other hand, in cases of cyberstalking, victims are not interchangeable. Cyberstalking involves a dyadic relationship between a pursuer who is interested a specific person (i.e., the ex-partner, a romantic crush, the object of revenge).

Power Dynamics. The cyberbullying relationship is defined by power imbalance and is often based on situational factors such as proximity, opportunity, and social network memberships (Salmivalli, 2010). The power imbalance between bully and victim is a necessary condition for identifying bullying (Olweus, 1993).

In contrast, a power imbalance is not a necessary condition for cyberstalking. Cyberstalking may be a response to a pursuer's sense of powerlessness or desire to control other (Burgess & Baker, 2008; Dreßing et al., 2014, Sheridan & Grant, 2007). As noted earlier in the chapter, cyberstalking often involves former relational partners (e.g., Cavezza & McEwan, 2014; Dardis, & Gidycz, 2016; Dreßing et al., 2014). In these cases, a stalker may view the victim as the one holding more significant power (i.e., the power to agree to accept the stalker's affections or the power to agree to reconcile a breakup). Of course, stalking victims may feel powerless when their boundaries and privacy are repeatedly intruded upon.

Roles of Aggressor and Victim. Cyberbullying often involves bully/victims, bullies who are also victims themselves (Salmivalli & Peets, 2009). Cyberstalking victims do not exhibit this pattern, they are not usually also stalkers. There is an interesting conceptual question here as to why bullying and stalking differ this way. Bullying, as noted earlier, is often an effort to assert one's power over another. Thus, bullying others may represent a type of compensation for those who are left feeling powerless by their own experiences of victimization.

Conclusion

Compared to the other types of problematic Internet use described in earlier chapters, there is relatively little empirical or conceptual scholarship on cyberstalking. Especially compared to the vast scholarship on cyberbullying, our understanding of cyberstalking is far behind. The few cyberstalking studies that are available reflect a lack of conceptual clarity and problems with inconsistent and invalid measures.

The small body of empirical data on cyberstalking is mostly atheoretical and studies are mostly descriptive, which is standard for a nascent line of research. As several reviews noted, the available prevalence estimates of cyberstalking are unreliable and inconclusive. Conceptual clarity about cyberstalking is necessary for valid and reliable measurement and operationalization. The ambiguity around the definition hampers theory development and results in disorganized empirical data that are difficult to compare.

This chapter sought to clarify two overarching questions that challenge researchers' efforts to define cyberstalking. First, the literature does not adequately distinguish cyberstalking from traditional forms of stalking. Second, cyberstalking research often blurs the line between cyberstalking and other forms of online aggression, such as cyberbullying. Focusing on the communicative context, as well as the characteristics and relationship of the people involved, offers useful ways to differentiate cyberstalking from these related phenomena. First, examining the distinctions between traditional stalking and cyberstalking helps illuminate how communicative differences between the two change the experience for stalker and victim. As the chapter argued, examining the places that cyberstalking diverges from cyberbullying also helps provide further conceptual clarity.

The twenty years of literature reviewed in this chapter indicate cyberstalking is fundamentally an interpersonal problem. It is a variant of traditional stalking and is distinct from cyberbullying. The chapter's focus on the communicative differences between cyberstalking and both traditional stalking and cyberbullying help explain how technology changes the traditional stalking experience for the pursuer and victim. Viewing cyberstalking as an interpersonal communication problem requires that researchers conceptualize the pursuit and response behaviors as interpersonal interaction. Spitzberg and Cupach's work on unwanted relational pursuit and obsessive relational intrusion provide a conceptual vocabulary for making sense of behavior that is most likely to occur among former relational partners. Moving forward, cyberstalking studies would benefit from more theory-driven research programs that seek to explain predictors and outcomes of unwanted online pursuit, obsessive online intrusion, and other types of cyberstalking.

References

Alexy, E. M., Burgess, A. W., Baker, T., & Smoyak, S. A. (2005). Perceptions of cyberstalking among college students. *Brief Treatment and Crisis Intervention, 5*(3), 279–289. doi:10.1093/brief-treatment/mhi020

Ang, R. P., & Goh, D. H. (2010). Cyberbullying among adolescents: The role of affective and cognitive empathy, and gender. *Child Psychiatry and Human Development, 41*(4), 387–397. doi:10.1007/s10578-010-0176-3

Barton, G. (1995). Taking a byte out of crime: E-mail harassment and the inefficacy of existing law. *Washington Law Review, 70*, 495–490.

Baum, K., Catalano, S., Rand, M., & Rose, K. (2009). *Stalking victimization in the United States.* U.S. Department of Justice (NCJ 224527). Washington, DC. Retrieved from: https://www.justice.gov/sites/default/files/ovw/legacy/2012/08/15/bjs-stalking-rpt.pdf

Bocij, P. (2004). *Cyberstalking: Harassment in the Internet age and how to protect your family.* Westport, CT: Praeger.

Borrajo, E., Gámez-Guadix, M., Pereda, N., & Calvete, E. (2015). The development and validation of the cyber dating abuse questionnaire among young couples. *Computers in Human Behavior, 48*, 358–365. doi:10.1016/j.chb.2015.01.063

Brewer, G., & Kerslake, J. (2015). Cyberbullying, self-esteem, empathy, and loneliness. *Computers in Human Behavior, 48*, 255–260. doi:10.1016/j.chb.2015.01.073

Burgess, A. W., & Baker, T. (2002). Cyberstalking. In J. Boon & L. Sheridan (Eds.), *Stalking and psychosexual obsession* (pp. 201–219). Hoboken, NJ: John Wiley & Sons. doi:10.1002/9780470713037.ch12

Cassidy, W., Jackson, M., & Faucher, C. (2016). Gender differences and cyberbullying towards faculty members in higher education. In R. Navarro, S. Yubero, & E. Larrañaga

(Eds.), *Cyberbullying across the globe: Gender, family, and mental health* (pp. 79–98). Switzerland: Springer International Publishing. doi:10.1007/978-3-319-25552-1_4

Caughlin, J. P., & Sharabi, L. L. (2013). A communicative interdependence perspective of close relationships: The connections between mediated and unmediated interactions matter. *Journal of Communication, 63*(5), 873–893. doi:10.1111/jcom.12046

Caughlin, J. P., Basnyat, I., & Sharabi, L. L. (2017). The connections between communication technologies and relational conflict: A multiple goals and communication interdependence perspective. In J. A. Samp (Ed.), *Communicating interpersonal conflict in close relationships: Contexts, challenges, and opportunities* (pp. 57–72). New York: Routledge.

Cavezza, C., & McEwan, T. E. (2014). Cyberstalking versus off-line stalking in a forensic sample. *Psychology, Crime & Law, 20*(10), 955–970. doi:10.1080/1068316X.2014.893334

Chan, J. H. F. (2006). Systemic patterns in bullying and victimization. *School Psychology International, 27*(3), 352–369. doi:10.1177/0143034306067289

Chaulk, K., & Jones, T. (2011). Online obsessive relational intrusion: Further concerns about Facebook. *Journal of Family Violence, 26*(4), 245–254. doi:10.1007/s10896-011-9360-x

Christofides, E., Muise, A., & Desmarias, S. (2009). Information disclosure and control on Facebook: Are they two sides of the same coin or two different processes? *CyberPsychology & Behavior, 12*(3), 341–345. doi:10.1089/cpb.2008.0226

Coyne, I., Farley, S., Axtell, C., Sprigg, C., Best, L., & Kwok, O. (2017). Understanding the relationship between experiencing workplace cyberbullying, employee mental strain and job satisfaction: A dysempowerment approach. *The International Journal of Human Resource Management, 28*(7), 945–972.

Cupach, W. R., & Spitzberg, B. H. (1998). Obsessive relational intrusion and stalking. In B. H. Spitzberg & W. R. Cupach (Eds.), *The dark side of close relationships* (pp. 233–263). Mahwah, NJ: Lawrence Erlbaum.

Dardis, C. M., & Gidycz, C. A. (2016). The frequency and perceived impact of engaging in in-person and cyber unwanted pursuit after relationship break-up among college men and women. *Sex Roles, 76*(1–2), 1–17. doi:10.1007/s11199-016-0667-1

De Smet, O., Loeys, T., & Buysse, A. (2012). Post-breakup unwanted pursuit: A refined analysis of the role of romantic relationship characteristics. *Journal of Family Violence, 27*(5), 437–452. doi:10.1007/s10896-012-9437-1

Dempsey, A. G., Sulkowski, M. L., Dempsey, J., & Storch, E. A. (2010). Has cyber technology produced a new group of peer aggressors? *Cyberpsychology, Behavior, and Social Networking, 14*(5), 297–302. doi:10.1089/cyber.2010.0108

Dreßing, H., Bailer, J., Anders, A., Wagner, H., & Gallas, C. (2014). Cyberstalking in a large sample of social network users: Prevalence, characteristics, and impact upon victims. *Cyberpsychology, Behavior, and Social Networking, 17*(2), 61–67. doi:10.1089/cyber.2012.0231

Finch, E. (2001). *The criminalisation of stalking: constructing the problem and evaluating the solution*. London: Cavendish Publishing.

Fox, K. A., Nobles, M. R., & Fisher, B. S. (2011). Method behind the madness: An examination of stalking measurements. *Aggression and Violent Behavior, 16*(1), 74–84. doi:10.1016/j.avb.2010.12.004

Garandeau, C. F., & Cillessen, A. H. N. (2006). From indirect aggression to invisible aggression: A conceptual view on bullying and peer group manipulation. *Aggression and Violent Behavior, 11*(6), 612–625. doi:10.1016/j.avb.2005.08.005

Goffman, E. (1959). *The presentation of self in everyday life*. New York: Doubleday Anchor Books.

Goffman, E. (1967). *Interaction ritual: essays on face-to-face interaction*. New York: Doubleday Anchor Books.

Gunawardena, C. N. (1995). Social presence theory and implications of interaction and collaborative learning in computer conferences. *International Journal of Educational Telecommunications, 1*(2–3), 147–166. doi:10.1111/j.1541-0420.2011.01694.x

Hiltz, S. R., Johnson, K., & Turoff, M. (1986). Experiments in group decision making communication process and outcome in face-to-face versus computerized conferences. *Human Communication Research, 13*(2), 225–252. doi:10.1111/j.1468-2958.1986.tb00104.x

Holt, T. J., & Bossler, A. M. (2008). Examining the applicability of lifestyle-routine activities theory for cybercrime victimization. *Deviant Behavior, 30*(1), 1–25.

Jerin, R., & Dolinsky, B. (2001). You've got mail! You don't want it: Cyber-victimization and on-line dating. *Journal of Criminal Justice and Popular Culture, 9*(1), 15–21.

Kernaghan, D., & Elwood, J. (2013). All the (cyber) world's a stage: Framing cyberbullying as a performance. *Cyberpsychology: Journal of Psychosocial Research on Cyberspace, 7*(1), Article 5. doi:10.5817/CP2013-1-5

Lapidot-Lefler, N., & Barak, A. (2012). Effects of anonymity, invisibility, and lack of eye-contact on toxic online disinhibition. *Computers in Human Behavior, 28*(2), 434–443. doi:10.1016/j.chb.2011.10.014

Lee, B. H., & O'Sullivan, L. F. (2014). The ex-factor: Characteristics of online and offline post relationship contact and tracking among Canadian emerging adults. *Canadian Journal of Human Sexuality, 23*(2), 96–105. doi:10.3138/cjhs.2415

Lyndon, A. E., Bonds-Raacke, J., & Cratty, A. D. (2011). College students' Facebook stalking of ex-partners. *Cyberpsychology, Behavior, and Social Networking, 14*(12), 711–716. doi:10.1089/cyber.2010.0588

McFarlane, L., & Bocij, P. (2003). An exploration of predatory behaviour in cyberspace: Towards a typology of cyberstalkers. *First Monday, 8*(9). Retrieved from https://firstmonday.org/issues/issue8_9/mcfarlane/index.html

Meloy, J. R. (1996). Stalking (obsessional following): A review of some preliminary studies. *Aggression and Violent Behavior, 1*(2), 147–162. doi:10.1016/1359-1789(95)00013-5

Meloy, J. R. (1998). The psychology of stalking. In J. R. Meloy (Ed.), *The psychology of stalking: Clinical and forensic perspectives* (pp. 2–21). San Diego, CA: Academic Press.

Meloy, J. R., & Gothard, S. (1995). Demographic and clinical comparison of obsessional followers and offenders with mental disorders. *American Journal of Psychiatry, 152*(2), 258–263.

Ménard, K. S., & Pincus, A. L. (2012). Predicting overt and cyber stalking perpetration by male and female college students. *Journal of Interpersonal Violence, 27*(11), 2183–2207. doi:10.1177/0886260511432144

Mullen, P. E., Pathço, M., Purcell, R., & Stuart, G. W. (1999). Study of stalkers. *American Journal of Psychiatry, 156*(8), 1244–1249. doi:10.1176/ajp.156.8.1244

Nobles, M., Reyns, B. W., Fox, K., & Fisher, B. S. (2014). Protection against pursuit: A conceptual and empirical comparison of cyberstalking and stalking victimization among a national sample. *Justice Quarterly, 31*(6), 986–1014. doi:10.1080/07418825.2012.723030

Olweus, D. (1991). Bully/victim problems among schoolchildren: Basic facts and effects of a school based intervention program. *The Development & Treatment of Childhood Aggression, 17*, 411–448.

Owens, J. G. (2016). Why definitions matter: Stalking victimization in the United States. *Journal of Interpersonal Violence, 31*(12), 2196–2226. doi:10.1177/0886260515573577

Parsons-Pollard, N., & Moriarty, L. J. (2009). Cyberstalking: Utilizing what we do know. *Victims & Offenders, 4*(4), 435–441. doi:/10.1080/15564880903227644

Paullet, K. L., Rota, D. R., & Swan, T. T. (2009). Cyberstalking: An exploratory study of students at a mid-Atlantic university. *Issues in Information Systems, 102*(2), 640–648.

Pereira, F., & Matos, M. (2015). Cyber-stalking victimization: What predicts fear among Portuguese adolescents? *European Journal of Criminal Policy and Research, 22*(2), 253–270. doi:10.1007/s10610-015-9285-7

Ramirez, A., & Zhang, S. (2007). When online meets offline: The effect of modality switching on relational communication. *Communication Monographs, 74*(3), 287–310. doi:10.1080/03637750701543493

Reed, L. A., Tolman, R. M., & Ward, L. M. (2016). Snooping and sexting. *Violence Against Women, 22*, 1556-1576. doi:10.1177/1077801216630143

Reno, J. (1999). Cyberstalking: A new challenge for law enforcement and industry: A report from the Attorney General to the Vice President (Vol. 1). Washington, DC. Retrieved from https://www.ncjrs.gov/App/publications/abstract.aspx?ID=179575

Reyns, B. W. (2012). *The anti-social network: Cyberstalking victimization among college students.* El Paso, TX: LFB Scholarly Publishing. doi:10.1515/zatw.1977.89.2.259

Reyns, B. W., Henson, B., & Fisher, B. S. (2012). Stalking in the twilight zone: Extent of cyberstalking victimization and offending among college students. *Deviant Behavior, 33*(1), 1–25. doi:10.1080/01639625.2010.538364

Roberts, L. (2008). Jurisdictional and definitional concerns with computer-mediated interpersonal crimes: An analysis on cyber stalking. *International Journal of Cyber Criminology, 2*(1), 271.

Rosenlind, S. (1994, April 1). Criminals lurk in the alleys of cyberspace. *The Baltimore Sun.* Retrieved from https://articles.baltimoresun.com/1994-04-01/features/1994091156_1_larry-greenberg-on-line-evelyn

Ross, E. (1995). Email stalking: Is adequate legal protection available? *John Marshall Journal of Computer and Information Law, 23*(3), 405–432.

Salmivalli, C. (2010). Bullying and the peer group: A review. *Aggression a Violent Behavior, 15*(2), 112–120. doi:10.1016/j.avb.2009.08.007

Salmivalli, C., & Peets, K. (2009). Bullies, victims, and bully-victim relationships in middle childhood and early adolescence. In K. H. Rubin, W. M. Bukoswki, & B. Laursen, *Handbook of peer interactions, relationships, and groups* (pp. 322–340). New York: Guilford Press.

Salmivalli, C., Lagerspetz, K., Björkqvist, K., Österman, K., & Kaukiainen, A. (1996). Bullying as a group process: Participant roles and their relations to social status within the group. *Aggressive Behavior, 22,* 1–15.

Schultze-Krumbholz, A., & Scheithauer, H. (2013). Is cyberbullying related to lack of empathy and social-emotional problems? *International Journal of Developmental Science, 7*(3–4), 161–166.

Sharabi, L. L., & Caughlin, J. P. (2017). What predicts first date success? A longitudinal study of modality switching in online dating. *Personal Relationships, 24*(2), 370–391. doi:10.1111/pere.12188

Sheridan, L. P., & Grant, T. (2007). Is cyberstalking different? *Psychology, Crime & Law, 13*(6), 627–640. doi:10.1080/10683160701340528

Short, E., Guppy, A., Hart, J. A., & Barnes, J. (2015). The impact of cyberstalking. *Studies in Media and Communication, 3*(2). doi:10.11114/smc.v3i2.970

Short, J. A., Williams, E., & Christie, B. (1976). *The social psychology of telecommunications.* New York: John Wiley & Sons.

Smith, P. K., Mahdavi, J., Carvalho, M., Fisher, S., Russell, S., & Tippett, N. (2008). Cyberbullying: Its nature and impact in secondary school pupils. *Journal of Child Psychology and Psychiatry, 49*(4), 376–85. doi:10.1111/j.1469-7610.2007.01846.x

Spitzberg, B. H. (2016). Stalking/obsessive relational intrusion. In C. Berger & M. Roloff (Eds.), *The international encyclopedia of interpersonal communication* (pp. 1–9). Hoboken, NJ: John Wiley & Sons. doi:10.1002/9781118540190.wbeic089

Spitzberg, B. H., & Cupach, W. R. (2003). What mad pursuit?: Obsessive relational intrusion and stalking related phenomena. *Aggression and Violent Behavior, 8*(4), 345–375. doi:10.1016/S1359-1789(02)00068-X

Spitzberg, B. H., & Cupach, W. R. (2007). The state of the art of stalking: Taking stock of the emerging literature. *Aggression and Violent Behavior, 12*(1), 64–86. doi:10.1016/j.avb.2006.05.001

Spitzberg, B. H., & Cupach, W. R. (2014). *The dark side of relationship pursuit: From attraction to obsession and stalking* (2nd ed.). Mahwah, NJ: Lawrence Erlbaum.

Spitzberg, B. H., & Hoobler, G. (2002). Cyberstalking and the technologies of interpersonal terrorism. *New Media & Society, 4*(1), 71–92. doi:10.1177/14614440222226271

Spitzberg, B. H., Cupach, W. R., Hannawa, A. F., & Crowley, J. P. (2014). A preliminary test of a relational goal pursuit theory of obsessive relational intrusion and stalking. *Studies in Communication Sciences, 14*(1), 29–36. doi:10.1016/j.scoms.2014.03.007

Strawhun, J., Adams, N., & Huss, M. T. (2013). The assessment of cyberstalking: An expanded examination including social networking, attachment, jealousy, and anger in relation to violence and abuse. *Violence and Victims, 28*(4), 715–730. doi:10.1891/0886-6708.11-00145

Suler, J. (2004). The online disinhibition effect. *CyberPsychology & Behavior, 7*(3), 321–326. doi:10.1089/1094931041291295

Tokunaga, R. S., & Aune, K. S. (2015). Cyber-defense: A taxonomy of tactics for managing cyberstalking. *Journal of Interpersonal Violence, 32*(10), 1451–1475. doi:10.1177/0886260515589564

Truman, J. L. (2010). Examining intimate partner stalking and use of technology in stalking victimization. Unpublished MA Thesis. University of Central Florida.

U.S. Justice Department (2016). Three family members receive life sentences for courthouse murder conspiracy. Retrieved from https://www.justice.gov/opa/pr/three-family-members-receive-life-sentences-courthouse-murder-conspiracy

Vranjes, I., Baillien, E., Vandebosch, H., Erreygers, S., & De Witte, H. (2017). The dark side of working online: Towards a definition and an emotion reaction model of workplace cyberbullying. *Computers in Human Behavior, 69*, 324–334.

Walker, L. (2016, February 26). Family receives life in prison for first-ever cyberstalking conviction. *Newsweek*. Retrieved from https://www.newsweek.com/family-receives-life-prison-first-ever-cyberstalking-conviction-430833

Westrup, D., & Fremouw, W. J. (1998). Stalking behavior: A literature review and suggested functional analytic assessment technology. *Aggression and Violent Behavior, 3*(3), 255–274. doi:10.1016/S1359-1789(97)00023-2

Wolford-Clevenger, C., Zapor, H., Brasfield, H., Febres, J., Elmquist, J., Brem, M., ... Stuart, G. L. (2015). An examination of the partner cyber abuse questionnaire in a college student sample. *Psychology of Violence, 6*(1), 156–162. doi:10.1037/a0039442

Zijlstra, B. J. H., Veenstra, R., & Duijn, M. A. J. (2008). A multilevel p2 model with covariates for the analysis of binary bully-victim network data in multiple classrooms. In N. A.Card, J. P. Selig, & T. D. Little (Eds.), *Modeling dyadic and interdependent data in the developmental and behavioral sciences* (pp. 369–386). New York: Routledge.

Zona, M. A., Sharma, K. K., & Lane, J. C. (1993). A comparative study of erotomanic and obsessional subjects in a forensic sample. *Journal of Forensic Sciences, 38*(4), 894–903.

Zweig, J. M., Lachman, P., Yahner, J., & Dank, M. (2014). Correlates of cyber dating abuse among teens. *Journal of Youth and Adolescence, 43*(8), 1306–1321.

Chapter Six

Copresent Device Use

Using Mobile Devices During In-Person Interaction

People's use of smartphones in face-to-face interactions has quickly emerged as a new interpersonal problem. One student Turkle (2015) interviewed explained, "Our texts are fine, it's what texting is doing to in-person conversation that's a problem" (Turkle, 2015, p. 21). Popular media and press reports describe concerns about the way mobile devices interfere with face-to-face interactions and close relationships (Brody, 2017). For example, recent headlines have included, "Just look me in the eyes already" (Shellenbarger, 2016) and "Ignoring people for phones is the new normal" (Beck, 2016). Recent books addressing the issue include *The Big Disconnect* (Steiner-Adair, 2013), *Alone Together* (Turkle, 2011) and *Reclaiming Conversation* (Turkle, 2015). Researchers have proposed a variety of terms to describe this phenomenon, including "copresent phone use" (Halpern & Katz, 2017), "technoference" (McDaniel & Coyne, 2016a), "mobile relational interference" (Baym, Hall, & Miltner, 2014), "multicommunicating" (Seo, Kim, & David, 2015), "parallel communication" (Kneidinger-Müller, 2017), and "phubbing" (phone snubbing; Chotpitayasunondh & Douglas, 2016), all of which refer to using mobile devices during a face-to-face interaction.

For consistency and clarity, this chapter uses the term *copresent device use* to describe checking or using a mobile device during an in-person interaction. The chapter reviews research indicating copresent device use is common in everyday interaction, that it can interfere with in-person conversation, and may have adverse effects on close relationships among romantic partners and between parents and children. Currently, the literature lacks theories explaining how and why copresent device use results in negative outcomes. This chapter identifies a number of established communication and psychology theories that can explain interpersonal problems arising from copresent device use. The chapter argues that interpersonal and relational communication research can help inform and advance the emerging study of copresent device use.

Conversational Effects

A small number of recent studies have found a consistent pattern of results: copresent device use leads to negative conversational outcomes. Here, studies have employed both experimental and naturalistic observation. A clear pattern emerges from the data suggesting that *the use, or even the mere presence, of a smartphone leads to lower evaluations of both impression of partner and the quality of conversation.*

Device Use Effects

In a study of college-aged friends, Brown et al. (2016) hypothesized that "friends who spend greater proportions of their time together distracted by their mobile phones may experience poorly coordinated conversations" (p. 441). In this study, two same-sex friends were instructed to wait together in a room for five minutes. Researchers recorded the amount of time that participants spent engaged in mobile phone use. Later, participants completed self-report measures about the quality of the interaction. The results revealed that 76% of the dyads used their phones during the five-minute interaction. The data revealed that amount of time spent using their phones was associated with lower interaction quality. Dyads that had no copresent device use reported higher levels of empathetic concern for their conversation partners and greater connectedness with one another than dyads that used phones. This study reveals that it is common for college-aged students to use their phones even during a short five-minute interaction with a friend. Second, the study also shows that copresent device use correlates with diminished interaction quality. Further, the absence of mobile devices resulted in the highest levels of emotional connection between the friends.

Another set of studies sought to determine what variables might moderate the effects described above. Two studies reported by Van den Abeele et al. (2016) investigated the impact of texting during an in-person conversation on impression formation, perceived conversational quality, and social attraction. In these studies, researchers manipulated whether the phone use appeared to be *self-initiated* (participants would pick up the phone and use it when given a hidden cue by the researcher) or *other-initiated* (participants would check the phone after receiving a text message sent by the researcher). The manipulation allowed the researchers to examine whether *attributions of intent* are involved in reactions to copresent device use.

Perceived conversation quality and impressions of partners were both negatively affected by copresent device use (Van den Abeele et al., 2016). People who used their phone during the conversation were perceived by their partners as less polite and less attentive. Results supported the researchers' hypotheses that, *self-initiated device use* was likely be attributed to internal qualities of the partner (i.e., she is rude, he is impolite) whereas *other-initiated device use* was attributed to the situation (i.e., it was not her fault, the phone beeped). The data supported the hypothesis that self-initiated use would be perceived more negatively that other-initiated use because of differences in the non-device users' attributions of intent. Overall, Van den Abeele et al.'s (2016) studies revealed that receivers' attributions of intent play a role in their reactions to copresent device use; when the non-device using partner places blame on the device user, evaluations are more negative.

Sprecher, Hampton, Heinzel, and Felmlee (2016) used a novel procedure to determine if conversational partners could pick up on cues that the other person was distracted by incoming text messages. To carefully control available cues, participants interacted with a partner via Skype (to simulate face-to-face interaction). Although their partners could not see it, some of the participants were instructed to read text messages that appeared on their screen during the conversation. These messages were supposed to simulate the type of media multitasking and distraction that might occur during copresent device use. Since the other person could not tell messages were being received and read, researchers observed whether participants would be able to pick up on any nonverbal cues indicating their partner was multitasking that would negatively influence the interaction. In other words, the study asked whether people reading messages are distracted enough that their partner can notice it. Here, the researchers sought to disentangle effects on the speaker (i.e., distraction from multitasking leads to poor performance) or from their partner's attitudes about texting during in-person conversations. The results suggested that multitasking (reading incoming messages during conversation), in and of itself, did not have any noticeable effect on the other partner's evaluations of the interaction. In other words, if the sender was distracted by multitasking, the receiver did not notice it.

Sprecher et al.'s (2016) study is important because it demonstrates that *distraction may not be the only factor influencing conversational outcomes*. When receivers were unaware that their partner was messaging, the behavior had no effect on perceptions of the conversation; suggesting that negative effects of copresent device use is not entirely due to the effects of distraction from multitasking. The findings indicate that negative outcomes may arise from the non-device using partner's interpretation of what the copresent device use means, as a nonverbal relational message. Such results are consistent with research on how people respond when expectations are violated; the consequence depends largely on what the behavior means to the receiver in that context (Burgoon, 1993; Burgoon & Hale, 1984; Burgoon, Newton, Walther, & Baesler, 1989)

"Mere Presence" Effects

The previous section reviewed evidence indicating that the effects of copresent device use are not explained entirely by multitasking distraction. A related line of research has demonstrated similar effects, *even if the phone is never actually used*. Several studies have found what is known as the *mere presence effect*, in which the mere presence of a phone that is never used appears to diminish conversation quality. These studies lend further support to the idea that distracted speakers are not as much of a problem as the perception of the receiver. In the first mere presence study, participant dyads were instructed to have a short conversation and researchers manipulated whether a phone was in view or not (Przybylski & Weinstein, 2012). Surprisingly, the study found that conversations where the phone was in view resulted in lower evaluations of interaction quality and closeness, even though the phone was never touched.

In a second study, Przybylski and Weinstein (2012) manipulated both (a) the presence of a mobile phone and (b) the salience of in-person conversation (casual versus important). Researchers hypothesized that important conversations would probably be more negatively influenced by phone presence than casual conversations. Consistent with their prediction, results revealed the mere presence effect was more pronounced when the discussion was important rather than casual. In the important conversations, "the mere presence of mobile phones inhibited the development of interpersonal closeness and trust, reduced felt empathy and reduced understanding for the partner" (p. 244). These results were more pronounced if the conversation involved a personally meaningful topic.

An intriguing set of studies by Thornton, Faires, Robbins, and Rollins (2014) showed evidence that the mere presence of a phone can increase distraction and diminish cognitive functioning. In the first study, participant dyads were given a task to work on (manipulated as either simple or difficult). In the experimental condition, the experimenter left a cellphone on the table and in the control condition the researcher left a notebook. Consistent with previous mere presence studies, the results revealed that task performance was impaired by the presence of the phone. The researchers speculated that cognitive functioning might be hindered by the presence of the phone, arguing the "mere presence of a cellphone may be sufficiently distracting to produce diminished attention and deficits in task-performance, especially for tasks with greater attentional and cognitive demands" (Thornton et al., 2014, p. 479).

In a second study, Thornton et al. (2014) replicated the first study but this time had participants use their own devices as the experimental stimuli. In the experimental condition, participants were instructed to put their phones in view on the table (control subjects did not get this instruction). This study also found reduced performance in the presence of the phone, but only for difficult tasks. The results also indicated that perceptions of conversational quality were diminished by the presence of the phone.

A study using naturalistic observation investigated how the mere presence of a mobile device might affect the quality of real conversations (Misra, Cheng, Genevie, & Yuan, 2014). Researchers observed people having ten-minute conversations in "naturalistic settings" and noted whether a mobile device was out in plain view. After the conversation, participants were asked about the closeness of their relationship with their partner and researchers measured perceptions of partners' empathic concern and connectedness. When mobile devices were present, participants evaluated their partners as less empathically concerned. The effect was moderated by relational closeness; the adverse outcomes were stronger in interactions between close partners (i.e., friends) compared to less familiar partners.

In another mere presence experiment, Allred and Crowley (2016) identified an additional moderator of the mere presence effect on conversation satisfaction, *the non-device user's recall*. In the experimental condition, one partner's phone was visible and in the control no phone was visible. Results supported the hypothesized mere presence effect, *but only when participants recalled the phone's presence*. This suggests that it was not just distraction, but something about the phone that resonated with some participants enough for them to recall it. Those participants who remembered a cell phone being present reported lower conversational satisfaction from pre-test to post-test compared to those who did not remember seeing a phone (about 78% of the sample recalled the phone's presence correctly). Here, the data suggested that it is the receiver that is generating the effect, since it only occurred when the perceiver remembered it. Moreover, it is worth asking: Did the negative reactions cause the event to be stored in memory or did the memory stoke the negative reaction?

Conceptual Explanations for Conversational Effects

Most of the literature on copresent device use has speculated that the negative conversational effects are due to distractions caused by either the use or presence of the devices. Researchers have hypothesized that distraction leads to impaired interpersonal performance by the device user which impedes the flow of the conversation. Humphreys (2005) reported that mobile phones frequently distract people in face-to-face interactions. Using a device is physically distracting in that it requires at least one hand (but usually two), mental multitasking, and looking at a screen. Other studies on media multitasking indicated that people who multitask with media exhibit poorer cognitive task performance (Ophir, Nass, & Wagner, 2009) and problems with attention and concentration (Ralph, Thomson, Cheyne, & Smilek, 2014). Regarding copresent device use, Cumiskey and Ling (2015) explain "negotiating the demands of actors in the field of social interaction becomes more complicated with the additional actors made 'present' through the use and presence of mobile devices. This negotiation can lead to perceptual errors and increase tension between copresent others and the user of the mobile device" (p. 233). Thus far, the explanations offered for the negative effects of copresent device use have argued that multitasking distracts the device user from the in-person interaction (Aagaard, 2016). Misra et al. (2014) also speculated that the presence of the phone creates an urge to use it that partners may pick up on.

The literature suggests that even if a phone is not used, it's very presence may disrupt conversation. Misra et al.'s (2014) task study showed that the presence of the phone is distracting even when it is not being used—it resulted in poorer task performance. The researchers suggested that, in our perpetually connected lives, "we are in a constant state of poly-consciousness in which multiple relationships and settings can be the focus of one's attention at any given time regardless of location or context" resulting in a diminished quality of the "here and now" interactions with copresent others (p. 17). Further, they argued, the presence of mobile devices "has the potential to divide consciousness between proximate and immediate setting and the physically distant and invisible networks and contexts" (p. 17). Misra et al. (2014) proposed that distraction occurred because phones hold "symbolic meaning even when they are not in use," representing "people's wider social network and a portal to immense compendium of information" (p. 5). Consequently, Misra et al. (2014) argued, and demonstrated, distraction from the mere presence of a device hinders verbal and nonverbal indicators of interpersonal connection.

Summary of Conversational Effects

The studies reviewed above support the argument that copresent device use, and even a device's mere presence, both have negative interpersonal effects. Although there are currently few studies on copresent device use, the available data indicate that the effects may be due to both distraction on the part of the device user and also negative perceptions of the device user by the partner. Although individual results vary depending on method and measures, the studies reported above reveal a consistent pattern in which the use or presence of a mobile device appears to hinder or impede interpersonal interaction. However, these effects are dependent upon context and interpretation of the non-device using partner.

    To progress, research in this area needs a conceptual framework for explaining how people assign meaning to nonverbal behaviors that accompany copresent device use. In addition to distraction-based explanations, research on interpersonal communication suggests that it is equally important to consider how the non-device user experiences the situation and applies meaning to it. Communication literature can also help explain how to understand contextual variables that might influence this process (i.e., topic, situation, relationship to other person, attributions of intent, whether it is recalled). The next section identifies specific interpersonal theories that can inform research on the conversational effects of copresent device use.

Explaining Copresent Use With Interpersonal Communication Theory

Research on interpersonal communication and nonverbal behavior offers a rich conceptual foundation for explaining the conversational effects of copresent device use. The literature on nonverbal communication has developed theoretical accounts that can help explain why device use and presence produce negative interpersonal outcomes. Copresent device use usually involves nonverbal cues that may interfere with conversations and how people view one another. Aaggard (2016) identified several nonverbal cues that accompany copresent device use such as divided attention, mechanical intonation, delayed responses, and reduced eye contact, together creating a sense of "absent presence" or interpersonal disconnection. Aaggard (2016) argued that "combined, these dynamics lead to an awkward interpersonal rhythm" (p. 230). Specifically, a copresent device user's in-person behaviors mismatch the vitality of their conversational partner regarding both rhythmic timing (i.e., delayed responses) and emotional intensity (i.e., mechanical intonation). Several lines of interpersonal communication research can help explain how the non-device-using partner might interpret the nonverbal cues associated with copresent device use.

Involvement and Immediacy Cues

The relational, or pragmatic, approach to studying interpersonal communication argues that, beyond the surface-level conversation topic, nonverbal behaviors often convey *relational-level messages* indicating how one feels about the situation (Burgoon et al., 1984; Watzlawick, Bavelas, & Jackson, 1967). The nonverbal cues common during copresent device use may hinder interpersonal interaction because they signal low involvement and are generally disconfirming.

People use conversational involvement cues to indicate they are engaged in the interaction. A person's forward leaning posture and focused eye contact might send the relational message: "I am engaged with this conversation," "I am interested in what you have to say," "what you have to say is worth listening to," and most importantly, "you are worth listening to." Regardless of the situation, relational messages signaling high involvement enhance interpersonal interactions and impression formation (Cegala et al., 1982; Coker & Burgoon, 1987; Spitzberg & Hecht, 1984). Communication research has consistently observed that cues indicating involvement are "central to accomplishing the goal of conversational management" (Burgoon & Bacue, 2003, p. 194). Other studies have found results suggesting that conversational involvement is a key component to supportive communication (Bodie & Jones, 2012; Jones & Guerrero, 2001). Using involvement cues is an important social skill or type of interpersonal competence (Cegala et al., 1982; Coker & Burgoon, 1987; Spitzberg & Hecht, 1984). Conceptually, the relational approach explains that involvement cues are beneficial because they *confirm* the receiver's sense of self. Thus, involvement sends confirming relational messages, facilitates effective conversations, makes others feel valued, and implies an acceptance of others' self-definition (Cissna & Sieburg, 1981).

When nonverbal cues indicate low involvement, the relational approach suggests that those behaviors send disconfirming relational messages that may cause receivers to feel slighted or less valued. The effects of copresent device use may occur because the receiver interprets the device user's low involvement cues as signs of disinterest, preoccupation, and disconfirmation. In Aagaard's (2016) interviews, participants mentioned the "choppy and unfocused vitality of a person periodically looking at their phone during a conversation" (p. 227) and described the pattern of their partner's engagement as "on/off." Here, the participants' descriptions are good examples of low involvement cues. Rather than having frequent eye contact, device users avert gaze and instead look at their screen. Similarly, rather than having expressive gestures, their hands are on the device. Participants in Aagaard's (2016) study also identified a flat, uninterested tone of voice as a characteristic of absent presence. Aaggard suggests that this mechanical tone, when used duirng regular in-person conversations, is often a regulating cue signaling "a closing out, a suggestion that the narrator move on" (p. 227). Thus, the nonverbal relational message in the tone of voice could be interpreted as uninterested and attempting to end the conversation. Consistent with the relational approach, Aaggard (2016) explains the averted gaze characteristic of copresent device use "means you immediately sense the lack of attentiveness in your conversational partner" (p. 228).

From this perspective, one reason that copresent device use resulted in negative conversational outcomes is that the nonverbal behaviors are *disconfirming relational messages* that upset the other partner. The nonverbal cues of copresent device use suggest the device user places a greater value on the device than on the other person (Nakamura, 2015). Gergen (2002) argued that when we are in a situation with another person who is using a mobile device, "we are present but simultaneously rendered absent; we have been erased by absent presence" (p. 227). Becoming invisible, absent, or irrelevant is the ultimate disconfirming message.

Thus, the relational approach and research on nonverbal immediacy provide plausible explanations for how and why copresent device use may negatively affect interpersonal outcomes. They suggest that the receiver's interpretation of the nonverbal cues plays a central role in determining the effects of copresent device use.

Expectancy Violation Theory

Expectation violation theory (EVT) helps explain how individuals ascribe meaning to their partner's unexpected behaviors (Burgoon, 1993; Burgoon & Hale, 1988). The central assumption of EVT is that relational partners develop expectations about the other's communicative behavior, and their nonverbal behaviors, in particular. EVT argues that meaning is ascribed to unexpected behavior based on how individuals appraise the norm violation. EVT predicts that unexpected behavior activates a cognitive-affective appraisal process in the receiver, leading to an assessment of whether the violation is positive (rewarding) or negative (undesirable). These appraisals mediate our reaction to others' copresent device use. In the case of copresent device use, when it occurs unexpectedly, or as a norm violation, the theory suggests that the non-device using partner's reactions will be based on her expectations and appraisals of any violations.

Studies examining how people react to unexpected nonverbal behaviors can inform research on copresent device use. EVT researchers have examined reactions a partner's unexpected changes in gaze (Burgoon, Coker, & Coker, 1986), touch (Burgoon, 1991), and conversational involvement. For example, Burgoon et al. (1989) examined people's appraisals of unexpected changes in conversational involvement and found that an unexpected decrease in conversational involvement predicted less attraction, credibility, and persuasiveness. Given that nonverbal cues are subject to multiple interpretations, communication researchers have tried to explain how behavioral expectations may play into how people act when those expectations are violated.

One hypothesis EVT suggests is that when copresent device use is viewed as a negative expectancy violation, it is more likely to result in negative relational outcomes. On the other hand, not engaging in copresent device use when it is normal or acceptable to do so might lead to positive expectancy violation, resulting in more positive outcomes. Not using the device when it is expected that you will could be a way reaffirm the in-person relationship. At other times, device use is expected and, consequently, not a problem. For example, college students recognize the importance of their friends answering a message from a parent and are unlikely to view that as slight (Miller-Ott & Kelly, 2015). Warning an in-person partner that you may need to check the phone minimizes the expectancy violation.

Facework and Politeness Theory

Facework and politeness theories are useful conceptual approaches for explaining people's reactions to copresent device use. According to politeness theory, face threats occur when our desired self-image is called into question or invalidated (Brown & Levinson, 1987; Goffman, 1967). Copresent device use presents a face threat to both the device user (it may be embarrassing to have the phone beep during an interview and need to check it) and to the non-device using receiver (who may view the device use as disconfirming).

During interpersonal interactions, people are generally motivated to help maintain one another's face (Goffman, 1967). Effective facework during conversations is a foundation of interpersonal competence (Cegala, 1981; Ting-Toomey & Kurogi, 1998). As Cegala explained, "Goffman's view of competence is found in the social actor's efficacy or face-work" (1981, p. 110). Goffman suggested that if we anticipate a face threat, we engage in facework to minimize injuring our partner's face. Drawing from Goffman's (1959, 1967) work on face and self-presentation, Brown and Levinson's politeness theory (1987) argued that people employ politeness strategies to reduce face threat. Politeness strategies are verbal and nonverbal facework behaviors that attempt to maintain face and to correct face loss. As Goldsmith (2007) explained, "politeness refers to all the verbal and nonverbal resources available in a language for making a face threatening act less face threatening" (p. 224).

Kneidinger-Müller (2017) observed that copresent device use is similar to Goffman's (1971/2010) concept of "cross-talk." Cross talk occurs when an interaction partner starts communicating with another person and excludes the primary conversation partner. Goffman (1971/2010) defined cross talk as "a conversation or conversation-like activity maintained by persons who differentially have other interaction capacities" (p. 25).

Politeness theory suggests that people are likely to respond less negatively if device users employ verbal politeness strategies that apologize for the face threat and give an explanation indicating why it is necessary or important (Cody & Dunn, 2007; Goldsmith, 2007). Thus, the hypothesis here is that the way the receiver interprets the copresent device use may vary depending upon how well the device user employs facework and politeness strategies. Whereas involvement helped explain ways people might nonverbally reduce the negative effects of copresent device use, politeness theory suggests that verbal politeness strategies can serve a similar function.

There is little empirical data on the effects of politeness during copresent device use. In an unpublished dissertation, Maginnis (2011) observed that politeness strategies mitigated negative effects of texting during in-person conversations. Consistent with politeness theory, when a conversation was interrupted by an incoming text, the person receiving the text was viewed more positively (appropriate or polite) when they mitigated face threat by mentioning who they were texting or why they were texting. Maginnis (2011) speculated that these verbal efforts to redress the interruption and face threat also served to make the "left out" partner feel more included. Thus, confirming relational level messages may counteract the invalidating effects of copresent device use. As predicted, Maginnis found that although the texting did have a negative impact on perceptions, the negative impact was mitigated by verbal politeness efforts.

Future research should continue to examine and elaborate on politeness during copresent device use. One important area to examine is how device users attempt to minimize face threats with verbal politeness and whether those efforts successfully mitigate the adverse effects. The ability to use politeness strategies is central to effective interpersonal communication (Lim & Bowers, 1991). Thus, the ability to minimize the disconfirming effects of copresent device use is likely to be a feature of skilled communicators.

Summary of Conversational Effects

Although the literature on how people react to copresent device use is sparse, empirical studies have consistently documented negative interpersonal effects of copresent device use on in-person conversation. The data also indicate that the negative effects are due to more than just a distracted device user struggling to multitask. Rather, they suggest that how the receiver interprets the behaviors mediates the behavior's effects.

Theory and research on interpersonal communication offer a resource for building conceptual models to understand the effects of copresent device use in conversation. Research on the relational perspective suggests that copresent device use conveys nonverbal indicators of noninvolvement that are disconfirming. In the language of politeness theory, these behaviors may constitute a face threat to the person not using the device. Expectancy violation theory further explains how people may react differently to unexpected copresent device use. Here, the theory suggests that the face threat (device use) is going to be interpreted as a positive or negative expectancy violation and that the receiver's appraisal will influence how the message is evaluated. Politeness theory proposes that the negative effects of copresent device use may also be minimized by verbal politeness strategies. At least one study indicates that politeness strategies can mitigate the potential harms of copresent device use in conversations. As copresent device use increases, the ability to manage in-person partners' face needs may become an increasingly relevant interpersonal skill. Additionally, face theory suggests other potential moderators of copresent device use effects, such as the power dynamic between the two people (e.g., a subordinate doing it is more offensive than if a superior does it) and the importance of the conversation (casual versus serious). Taken together, the literature on copresent device use and earlier research on interpersonal communication both suggest that copresent device use does not have homogenous effects; its effects are based in part on the symbolic meaning interactants assign the behavior and how they manage the face and relational needs of the in-person partner while also using their devices.

According to Vanden Abeele, Antheunis, and Schouten (2016), "empirical research on the relational impact of copresent phone use remains scarce" (p. 562). Thus far, the chapter has examined the impacts of copresent device use on conversations. Beyond the problems copresent device use presents in conversations, it is also important to consider how recurring patterns of copresent device use might affect intimate relationships, including both romantic and parent-child relationships. The following sections address copresent device use in both types of close relationships.

Copresent Device Use Problems in Romantic Relationships

Just as copresent device use creates problems in conversations, it is also likely to create challenges for romantic relationships (X. Wang, Xie, Y. Wang, P. Wang, & Lei, 2017). The adverse conversational effects of copresent device use may be worsened when people are in a romantic relationship. The few available studies suggest copresent device use in couples leads to device-related conflict, erodes intimacy, and negatively affects relational satisfaction (Halpern & Katz, 2017; McDaniel and Coyne, 2016a).

McDaniel and Coyne (2016a) studied the negative outcomes of copresent device use among married couples. The results revealed that 62% of wives reported that their husband frequently used a mobile device during couple leisure time. Additionally, 33% of the women stated that their husbands frequently used devices during mealtime. Another third (35%) said that their husbands frequently checked the phone when it sounded during a couple conversation. Finally, 25% noted that their husbands frequently texted or emailed during the couple's face-to-face conversations. Interestingly, copresent device use reportedly occurs more often during leisure time (and it is more allowed then; see discussion of "hanging out" below).

Additionally, copresent device use did not have a simple direct effect on relational outcomes. Rather, conflict about technology use mediated the association between copresent device use and relational outcomes. In other words, conflict, rather than the device use itself, accounted for diminished relational satisfaction. Consistent with the points made earlier about relational meaning and facework, the copresent device use was perceived as a greater violation during "couple time," where in-person expectations were higher. As copresent device use becomes more habituated and normalized, couples' ability to manage its effects is an increasingly important relationship maintenance skill.

Roberts and David's (2016) study of "partner phubbing" made a similar mediation argument, hypothesizing that the relationship between copresent device use and relational satisfaction was mediated by conflict about the device use. Consistent with their hypothesis, Roberts and David's results revealed that conflict mediated the impact of copresent device use on satisfaction. The study also found a moderating effect due to attachment insecurity. Attachment insecurity amplified the conflict; couples who were both anxiously attached and high copresent device users had the most conflict. Among low copresent device using couples, attachment insecurity had no effect. This suggests that the effects of copresent device use on couples are not homogenous. Rather, device use may be problematic or lead to conflict for some couples but not others, depending on a variety of variables including attachment insecurity, conflict skills, and degree of online habit strength. This is another area ripe for future research consideration. The attachment security effects reported in this study illustrate how interpersonal and relational theory can help explain the effects of copresent device use in couples.

In another study of mediated effects, Halpern and Katz (2017) proposed that the association between copresent use and relationship quality was mediated by both conflict about device use and diminished intimacy. A longitudinal study followed 275 participants in romantic relationships for a year and tracked copresent device use frequency (texting in partners' presence), conflict about device use, emotional closeness, and romantic satisfaction. The results supported Halpern and Katz's claim that that "texting is what leads to lower levels of quality in romantic relationships and not vice-versa" (p. 15). Halpern and Katz (2017) determined that copresent texting indirectly lowered relationship quality in two distinct ways. First, device use predicted relational conflict that, in turn, led to lower relational quality. The data also revealed a smaller indirect effect in which copresent texting use weakened intimacy and closeness.

The studies reviewed above suggest that the problems that couples experience with copresent device use may be due to conflict about the behaviors. Attributions, expectations, norms, and rules all influence how partners perceive copresent device use and whether it leads to conflict. The data from these studies (Halpern & Katz, 2017; McDaniel & Coyne, 2016a; Roberts & David, 2016) raise three important questions for future research. First, what determines whether device use leads to conflict, or the quality of the conflict? Second, how does copresent device use weaken intimacy? Third, why are some couples more susceptible than others to the effect?

Halpern and Katz (2017) argued that copresent texting creates conflict because the "person's attention is not in line with the expectations that his/her significant other has of him/her, which in turn, elicits negative arousal" (p. 388). McDaniel and Coyne concluded that, "When individuals place their technology above their partner, even if only for a brief moment, they can sow conflict in their romantic relationship, which may then lead to negative outcomes" (2016a, p. 94). They wrote, "It is quite possible that the devices are intruding or interrupting their couple interactions and communication, which in turn, leads to increased conflict about technology, which in turn predicts lower satisfaction, depression, and lower life satisfaction" (p. 85). Future research might examine possible bi-directional, or cyclical, processes between copresent device use, increased conflict, and reduced intimacy.

Interpersonal and relational communication research offers several guiding conceptual models to explain copresent device use in relationships. For example, the paragraphs below demonstrate how theories of copresent device use can draw upon attribution theory, expectancy violation theory, and relational dialectics theory as guiding conceptual models.

Attribution Theory and Romantic Conflict

Attribution theory (Heider, 1958) can help explain how people perceive a partner's copresent device use. According to attribution theory, people judge others' behaviors based on appraisals about the other person's intentions and personality. The theory predicts that these attributions are sometimes biased and erroneous. In terms of copresent device use, attribution theory predicts that conflict about device use arises based on the non-device using partner's attributions about the behavior, and people appraise it differently. These appraisals determine how the people respond to a partner's copresent device use and how device use and conflict about it affect relationship quality.

Research on marital conflict indicates that conflict destructiveness varies depending on the attributions a person makes about their spouse's behavior (Bradbury & Fincham, 1990; Fincham & O'Leary, 1986; Gottman, 1993; Holtzworth-Munroe & Jacobson, 1985; McDonald, Follette, & Berley, 1985; Miller & Rempel, 2004). These studies have generally found *distress-maintaining* attributions among unhappily married people, in which attributions about their partner's negative behaviors intensified anger and dissatisfaction (e.g., they believed that the upsetting behavior was done intentionally or due to a flaw in the spouse's character). In contrast, people in healthier couples formed more *relationship-enhancing* attributions about partners' behaviors (e.g., the behavior was due to unintentional external circumstances and not a result of malice or carelessness). The literature here demonstrates that the way that partners appraise each other's behaviors contributes to how they respond, both emotionally and behaviorally, to copresent device use.

One way to determine how copresent device use affects conflict and relational well-being is to examine attributions that one partner makes about the other's copresent device use. Recently, work by Amichai-Hamburger and Etgar (2016) examined people's attitudes and attributions about self and partner copresent device use and the effects of both on intimacy. The study found that negative relationship outcomes resulted from an attribution bias (actor-observer bias) whereby each viewed their partner's device use as caused by internal states and intentional factors but attributed their own device use to situational factors. Thus, the way people think about their partner's copresent device use may play a role in whether or not that use threatens relational well-being. Attribution theory provides a useful conceptual foundation for developing models that explain how and why device use affects relational outcomes, suggesting that attributions are an important mediator between behavior and relational outcomes.

Expectancy Violation Theory

Expectancy violation theory offers a conceptual explanation for people's different reactions to copresent device use. As with conversations, romantic relationships are based on partners' norms and expectations. Studies of copresent device use in romantic relationships have noted the role that *expectations*, and their violations, play in how people interpret their partner's device use (Miller-Ott & Kelly, 2015). Hall et al. (2014) argued, "The path to a deeper understanding of how mobile use colors relational quality starts by rejecting the common presumption that there is only one behavioral standard and that violations of that standard affect everyone the same way ... If we are going to unravel the threads connecting mobile use to relational quality, we will need to understand mobile norms of behavior as ever shifting and dynamically constructed in specific contexts of social identities and contexts" (p. 148).

Long term committed couples participating in the research developed rules regarding device use and used directness to discuss them. Consistent with EVT's claim, Miller-Ott and Kelly (2015) noted that conflict around copresent device use often involved violated relational rules. The study also revealed that relational device-use rules had special exceptions to help meet external obligations. Among the college-aged sample, copresent device use was expected and acceptable when a parent called or texted. Expectations also change as relationships develop. In early relationship stages, participants were less willing to discuss these rules or expectations. Instead, in new relationships participants relied on indirect responses, or not responding, (i.e., avoiding the issue). Participants in more established relationships discussed negotiating and enacting rules about device use during formal dating times.

The study found that more established couples also expected that some situations were rule-free (Miller-Ott & Kelly, 2015). For example, for participants in established relationships, copresent device use while "hanging out" was both expected and acceptable. For these participants, the meaning of the device use was entirely different when "hanging out" compared to a romantic dinner. "Hanging out" was described as a type of dating behavior in which partners did not expect the same level of undivided attention they might expect during a meal together. Miller-Ott and Kelly reported, "hanging out often included more fluid expectations about cell phone usage" (2015, p. 2). When hanging out, participants expected their partners to use their cell phones, expected to be able to use their own phones, and were okay with cell phone usage, so long as it was not excessive.

Similarly, research by Hall et al. (2014), looking at how mobile phone norm adherence was related to relationship satisfaction, sheds light on how people react to expectancy violations. The results revealed a partner's device use becomes a problem (interference) when it is perceived as violating one's internal standards or expectations. The context also matters; in public, participants thought it most important to behave normatively. "The more their partners followed internalized norms in public, the less they felt mobiles interfered with their relationship" (Hall et al., 2014, p. 146). Thus, one important skill or task for healthy couples is managing expectations and norms around copresent device use.

Relational Dialectics Theory

The research on romantic conflict around device use suggests that part of maintaining healthy relationships is learning to manage the tensions that create these conflicts. Relationship dialectics theory proposes that relationship well-being is based on how well couples manage a series of tensions between competing demands (i.e., the tension between seeing friends and spending time together as a couple; Baxter & Simon, 1993). While we know copresent device use creates tension and conflict, we know little about the nature the tensions or how couples manage them. The extensive literature on relationship dialectics theory (Baxter, 1990) provides useful guide for examining how couples manage these tensions.

Research on device-related conflict in couples has identified two types of dialectical tensions involving copresent device use. Miller-Ott and Kelly (2015, 2016) conducted focus groups in which participants talked about mobile device use in their relationships. The researchers used relational dialectics theory to examine the nature of the mobile-related tensions that couples struggle over. The data revealed two primary tensions related to copresent device use: a tension between community versus romance and a tension between control versus freedom.

Community Versus Romance Dialectic. The community versus romance dialectic describes the ongoing tension between the competing demands of being available and responsive to outside family and friends, while at the same time managing the romantic partner's demands for attention. Some participants felt a pressure to be available to friends regardless of being physically present with their romantic partner. One participant remarked, "You have a world outside of this relationship and your phone is that gateway" (Miller-Ott & Kelly, 2016, p. 64). Another participant explained, "talking to your friends is part of your daily life. Like, you shouldn't stop talking to your friends just because you are out with someone" (p. 64). On the other hand, within a romantic interaction, they expected partners to be completely available to them. One participant voicing the need for in-person involvement of romantic partners said, "You should have mutual respect for each other ... you shouldn't have to be begging for their attention" (pp. 64–65).

The extreme end of the romance expectation involved first dates or early stages of relationships. During these formative interactions, participants viewed texting as especially "rude" and "annoying." The researchers noted, "Their remarks about rudeness and other comments implied an expectation that cellphones were off limits during dates" (Miller-Ott & Kelly, 2016, p. 65). However, one exception to this rule involved responding to messages from parents. Participants indicated that it was more acceptable to use the device on a date if was to communicate with a parent. One participant even said, "I think it's sweet if a guy says 'Oh, I have to text my mom real quick.' I hope they're not lying but it shows that they care about texting their mom back" (Miller-Ott & Kelly, 2016, p. 66).

Control Versus Freedom Dialectic. A second tension that emerged reflected the struggle between control and freedom, or between individuality and availability. Miller-Ott and Kelly (2015) stated that "Participants have expectations for undivided attention on formal dates and when spending intimate time together and divided attention when informally 'hanging out' with one another" (p. 253). Aagaard (2016) explains that "due to its relatively small screen size, a mobile device like a smartphone constitutes a private perspective that is not necessarily shared with copresent others and thus transforms me into a 'windowless monad' closed around my own personal projects (e.g., my work)" (p. 224). Unlike television, where people can view it together, smartphone screens constitute a private non-shared experience that excludes the other physically present partner.

The research on copresent device use in romantic relationships has just begun. The few published studies indicate that copresent device use is an issue that can create conflict and weaken intimacy in couples. These studies also suggest that people's reactions to copresent device use were variable and contingent upon how they interpreted the behavior. Theories of interpersonal and relational communication can guide future research on copresent device use in romantic relationships. The next section explores how copresent device use may affect parent-child relationships.

Copresent Device Use in Parent-Child Relationships

"To be sure, the family may all be physically present in the same dwelling. However, psychologically speaking, they are living separately" (Gergen, 2010, p. 16). To date, there is little empirical research on parents' use of devices during child care. A recent review of literature on parent device use found, "Little research has investigated the role of parents' mobile device distractions on child development and parent-child interactions" (Kildare & Middlemiss, 2017, p. 580). However, the few available studies reveal that parents struggle with their own device use during family time. Children report that they dislike their parents' copresent device use (McDaniel & Coyne, 2016b). This section presents the emerging research on copresent device use during parent-child interaction and identifies several established theories to explain how copresent device use might interfere with important parent-child communicative processes. The first subsection below presents empirical findings currently available from studies on parental device use during meals and childcare.

Parental Absorption During Child Care

Several different studies have demonstrated that parents engage in copresent device use when caring for their children in a variety of contexts including playgrounds (Hinicker et al., 2014), restaurants (Radesky et al., 2014) and in structured laboratory task interactions

(Radesky et al., 2015). Together, these studies indicate that parents frequently engage in device use and exhibit indications of absent presence (or absorption) while caregiving. The results also suggest that a child notices a parent's absorption and may exhibit signs of distress through resisting, limit testing, and making bids for connection.

One study unobtrusively observed caregivers and their children in a fast food restaurant and used the observations to develop a categorization scheme of parental device use and absorption (Radesky et al., 2014). Absorption was defined as "the extent to which the primary focus of the caregiver's attention and engagement was with the device rather than the child" (Radesky et al., 2014, p. e845). The study also examined how children responded to parental absorption and what patterns of interaction took place between the child and caregiver. Radesky et al.'s (2014) study "documented the behavior of many caregivers whose attention was highly absorbed in their mobile devices, with varying child reactions to this absorption" (p. e843). Among the interactions observed in the restaurants, absorption "consistently arose as most salient to the caregiver-child relationship" (p. e845). Further, the researchers identified three aspects of characteristics of caregiver absorption: caregiver device use (frequency, duration, modality of use), children's bids for attention, and caregiver responses.

In the study, caregiver absorption was defined as how frequently and continuously caregivers used their devices. The researchers noted "many caregivers used the device almost continuously throughout the meal, eating and talking while looking at the device or only putting it down briefly to engage in other activities" (Radesky et al., 2014, p. e846). The modality of device use also indicated absorption—the highest degrees of absorption occurred when device use consisted mainly of continuous typing and swiping, rather than phone calls. Whereas caregivers can watch a child while talking on phone, the caregiver cannot maintain eye contact on the child when typing, reading, and swiping. In other words, absorption seemed to be greatest when eye contact was infrequent and fleeting. Lack of gaze seems to be a particularly salient characteristic of absorption and one that the child is likely to be highly reactive to. Here, the concepts of absorption and absent presence clearly overlap—*both describe diminished visual cues and infrequent gaze.*

On the other hand, caregivers who exhibited lower levels of absorption used their phones sporadically. For example, these parents picked up the phone when bored, when children were still eating, or when they received calls. Additionally, during phone calls, these less absorbed caregivers made nonverbal bids to stay connected to their child. For example, they "usually maintained eye contact with children during these calls, which did not last through the entire meal as texting or swiping would" (Radesky et al., 2014, p. e846). This is an important finding in that it suggests that parents can moderate the effects of absorption by making efforts to stay nonverbally connected with the child during device use. It may also suggest that among adults, there are remedial or preventive facework strategies that might mitigate the problems arising from copresent device use.

Less absorbed parents used their devices intermittently, rather than continuously, to quickly check or send messages before putting the device back down. The less absorbed caregivers "appeared to balance their attention between device and child by using it quickly when children were otherwise engaged, and then returning to conversation" (Radesky et al., 2014, p. e846). Overall, the greatest levels of parental absorption occurred when parents were continually typing and swiping and it occurred the least when caregivers could balance attention between the device and their child.

Caregivers' absorption also related to how children responded to the device use. Radesky et al. (2014) observed that when caregivers were continuously absorbed in device use, some children did not make any bids for caregiver attention; the children were already engaged in other activities and did not seem to notice. Other children were observed, "exhibiting limit testing or provocative behaviors during adult device absorption" (p. e847).

When responding to their children, highly absorbed caregivers demonstrated a longer latency to respond to bids and some did not respond at all. Highly absorbed caregivers frequently ignored the child's behavior for a while and then reacted with a scolding tone of voice and gave repeated instructions with mechanical intonation. High caregiver absorption was also related to caregivers' physical responses to childrens' bids, including kicking a child's foot under the table and pushing a child's hands away when the child was attempting to lift the caregiver's face from the phone screen.

The study's findings suggest that highly absorbed parents reacted to their children's bids for attention with disconfirming verbal and nonverbal messages. Radesky et al. (2014) also characterized the ways that highly absorbed caregivers responded to their children's bids. In subsequent study, Radesky et al. (2015) speculated that children are doubly disconfirmed—once by the absorption and then later by their caregiver's negative reaction to the child's bids.

Research also highlights the salience of gaze and the role of lack of gaze in parental absorption. Radesky et al. (2014) reported that "the highest degree of caregiver absorption was evidenced by responses such as gaze being directed primarily at the device, keeping the gaze on the device while answering questions or giving instructions to others" (p. e847). The article emphasized that the greatest absorption occurred when parents' gaze was directed at their devices, rather than at their children, most of the time.

In addition, parents' device use was assessed during a structured parent–child interaction task (Radesky et al., 2015). Researchers coded conversation behaviors to measure mobile device use, along with verbal and nonverbal interaction behaviors signaling engagement. Results from the study revealed that when parents spontaneously used a mobile device during the task, they produced fewer verbal and nonverbal engagement cues toward the child.

The studies reported above have made important contributions to our understanding of how children respond to parental absorption. Thus far, the studies involved caregivers with children old enough to play on a playground or go to a fast food restaurant. To date, there is no research about how caregiver absorption might influence infants and their development. However, extensive research on the importance of caregiver gaze and reciprocity are well documented in child psychology.

Attunement and Attachment Processes

Radesky et al. (2014) hypothesized out that "mobile devices can also distract parents from face to face interactions with their children, which are crucial for cognitive, language, and emotional development" (p. e844). Although there are no studies of how caregiver device use might affect infant development, established research on infant-caregiver communication offers a conceptual model and suggests hypotheses that research can explore. Specifically, this section employs Stern's (1985) concept of *affect attunement* and infant attachment theory (Ainsworth, 1979; Ainsworth & Bell, 1970; Bowlby, 1969) to build a conceptual model for how some of the nonverbal characteristics of copresent device use might hinder infants' development.

For decades, researchers have documented the importance of nonverbal coordination, reciprocity, and attunement between a caregiver and an infant (Cappella, 1981; Siegel, 1999; Tronick, 1989). Research on maternal distraction during infant feeding found that infants respond in negative ways to mothers' distraction (Golen & Ventura, 2015a). The research also shows that mothers use mobile devices as a type of distraction during feeding. According to Golen and Ventura (2015a), "Distraction in the form of using a mobile device is a frequent practice among caregivers during child-feeding interactions" (p. 789). Golen and Ventura (2015a) observed that about 52% of mothers reported engaging in distractions while feeding. They noted that almost one third of these feedings involved technological distractors. By far, television accounted for the most common distraction (29%), whereas copresent device use only occurred in 2% of the cases (Golen & Ventura, 2015b). In their recent study, Ventura and Teitelbaum (2017) concluded that 26% of mothers reported using technological distractions during feeding. Again, the most common distraction was watching television (reported by 20% of mothers). Only 6% of mothers reported mobile device use such as smartphones, tablets, and computers. However, it is reasonable to expect that the effects of device use during feeding are like those of watching television.

In a study presented earlier, Aaggard (2016) suggested that nonverbal characteristics of copresent device use resembled what Stern (1985) described as "misattunement." Affective misattunement occurs when the infant and caregiver are "out of sync" with one another. Extensive literature on infant development emphasizes the importance of caregiver-infant attunement (Siegel, 1999). This research can help inform conceptual models explaining how device use may impact infant-caregiver interactions.

According to attachment theory, infants seek to form a secure relationship with a caregiver who can keep them safe and meet their needs. Researchers have noted that nonverbal interactions between infant and caregiver play a crucial role in helping a child develop healthy attachment. Stern's concept of attunement describes a back-and-forth, coordinated, reciprocal pattern of nonverbal interaction between a caregiver and infant. According to Siegel (1999), exposure to co-regulation and attunement (what he calls alignment and emotional resonance) is important for children's brain development.

The nonverbal elements of a parent's device use (e.g., averted gaze, motionless face) may interfere with attunement. Attachment theory explains why misattunement can hinder attachment and other developmental tasks. In addition to facilitating secure attachment, infant-caregiver attunement teaches infants the basic dynamics of back-and-forth interaction and provides practice reading facial cues. Caregivers absorbed in device use may provide the infant less opportunities to experience and develop these interpersonal skills (Siegel, 1999).

Diminished eye contact can also interfere with parents' sensitivity to infants' cues and signals. According to Siegel (1999), a parent's sensitivity to an infant's signals (i.e., ability to notice an infant's efforts to communicate, especially at lower levels of intensity) "is the essence of secure attachment" (p. 70). The infant feeding studies mentioned earlier found distracted mothers showed lower sensitivity to infant cues compared to undistracted mothers. Radesky et al.'s (2014) study suggested that lack of eye contact is one of the most prominent and salient characteristics of high caregiver absorption.

Nonverbal Reciprocity and the Still Face Effect

Another line of research, known as the "still face experiments," documented the distress that infants experience when caregivers disrupt the nonverbal attunement and become still-faced, or facially unresponsive. Tronick et al. (1978) explained that a facially unresponsive parent distorts the feedback that infants normally receive during contingent interaction. The study reported that when parents displayed a still face, infants became agitated and upset. According to Tronick et al. (1978), a caregiver's still face is a "violation of reciprocity" (i.e., attunement) that the infant expects and needs from the parent. Tronick et al. (1978) noted "if the system is violated, the infant will respond appropriately" (p. 10). According to Tronick et al., if caregivers are consistently non-responsive, a demand-withdraw pattern can be established as early as four weeks of age. In these cases, when the infant repeatedly tries and fails to engage in facial reciprocity, the infant eventually withdraws, tries to calm down, and then tries again to reconnect with the caregiver. Taken together, the literature on attunement, attachment, and facial responsiveness may help researchers understand how device use during caregiving might influence infants.

Copresent Device Use and Co-Parenting

Co-parenting refers to the quality of interaction and relationship between parents, regarding child rearing (Feinberg, 2003; McHale & Cowan, 1996). Research on family communication indicates that, in two-parent families, the level of cooperation between the parents influences important outcomes for the child, the marriage, and the family system. The co-parenting relationship refers to the way partners work together in child rearing. According to Feinberg (2003), co-parenting describes the ways that parents negotiate responsibilities and roles involving childcare.

Feinberg describes co-parenting as "a central element to family life that influences parental adjustment, parenting, and child outcomes" (p. 95). The quality of co-parenting promotes children's sense of family and co-parenting problems can undermine that. The importance of healthy co-parental relationship persists into adolescence (e.g., Schrodt & Shimkowski, 2017; Shimkowski & Schrodt, 2012). A meta-analysis on co-parenting and family outcomes uncovered that "co-parenting is a relevant factor in child development from toddlerhood to late adolescence" (Teubert & Pinquart, 2010, p. 288). Shimkowski and Schrodt (2012) associated co-parenting quality with adolescents' mental health. Other studies have found that co-parenting is associated with greater parent-parent relationship quality, fewer parent depressive symptoms, and fewer child behavior problems (e.g., Feinberg, Brown, & Ken, 2012; McDaniel & Teti, 2012; Murphy et al., 2016; Schoppe, Mangelsdorf, & Frosch, 2001; Schoppe-Sullivan Mangelsfdorf, Frosch, & McHale, 2004).

Recent research by McDaniel and Coyne (2016) provided evidence that copresent device use may undermine co-parenting relationship quality. The study found that 96% of parents reported "interference by at least one device in their co-parenting relationship and cellphones were rated as interfering most often" (McDaniel & Coyne, p. 438). The mothers indicated that device use during co-parenting happens most frequently during playtime but also occurs while spending time with the child, having conversations about parenting, during educational activities, with bed time activities, and at meals. According to McDaniel and Coyne (2016b), "Since technology is pervasive and potentially intrusive, interactions with technology have the power to interrupt or interfere with parenting in small ways at times" (p. 436) and "technology likely decreases coordination between parents (p. 435).

Family Rules for Copresent Device Use

Other research has examined how parents and adolescents communicate about device use and the rules constraining it. Although there is a broader literature about families and technology, in a general sense, few studies have examined how families negotiate boundaries around copresent device use. Hiniker, Schoenebeck, and Kientz (2016) examined parents' and their teenagers' rules about technology use during meal times. Overall, they learned that children struggled to follow rules based on context or situation. In other words, rules such as "no phones during dinner" were more difficult for children to adhere to than universal rules such as "no phone use at all." Obviously, this creates a challenge for parents who want to help their children learn how to use devices skillfully. One of the themes running throughout this chapter has been that knowing how to engage in copresent device use is emerging as a type of interpersonal skill. The skill is based on understanding context and considering what the device use means to other people.

Given the relatively sparse literature on copresent device use in families, this section attempted to frame the few empirical studies within theoretical models from family communication and child development. Although the research on how copresent device use may affect family relationships is only just beginning, the sections above offer some ways to link this work with established theories of family communication and infant development. The research on attachment and attunement during infant caregiving provides a conceptual base for studying copresent device use during these interactions. Research on co-parenting and communication in family systems identifies another way that copresent device use might create problems in families with older children and teenagers.

Summary of Copresent Device Use in Close Relationships

Copresent device use creates a host of challenges for everyday conversations as well as management of ongoing close relationships. Although the device use itself may not be a problem, the research presented above indicates that copresent device use is a source of relational conflict that results in lower relational quality. Moreover, copresent device use also weakens relationship quality by lessening intimacy and contributing to a psychological disconnection within the couple.

One major task for copresent device use research is to articulate a detailed conceptual narrative explaining how and why device use creates the problems noted throughout the chapter. Although there are few studies on copresent device use in couples, the chapter demonstrated how expectancy violation theory, attribution theory, and research on marital communication and dialectical tensions could help inform a theoretical explanation of how copresent device use impacts romantic relationships.

The final section suggested that copresent device use might also interfere with family and parent-child communication processes. As the research above demonstrated, parents do engage in device use during meals and childcare and exhibit nonverbal behaviors indicating absorption. Attachment theory and research on caregiver/infant attunement help explain how copresent device use might impact the important nonverbal dance that promotes healthy development. The research suggests that the nonverbal characteristics of parental absorption are similar to the misattunement that hinders healthy attachment and impedes learning important socio-emotional skills such as turn taking, nonverbal expression, and reading nonverbal cues. These types of hypotheses, rooted in attachment theory, are examples of how research on copresent device use could build theories about parent-child effects.

Conclusion

This chapter sought to explore how copresent device use may be a common feature of in-person interaction and a potential hindrance to effective communication. The few studies about the conversational effects of copresent device indicate that, during in-person interactions, both device use and even the mere presence of the device have negative effects on interpersonal outcomes. To advance research on copresent device use, it is important to begin developing theory-driven hypotheses that can explain the negative interpersonal effects. Thus far, the most common explanations for effects are that copresent device use is a type of media multitasking that distracts the user from the other partner.

Research on interpersonal communication and nonverbal cues can help guide theory and help organize research on copresent device use. The relational perspective of communication emphasizes the importance of relational messages that signal how involved and interested one is. From this perspective, the low involvement that characterizes device use is likely to send disconfirming messages to the other partner indicating disinterest, and perhaps even complete unawareness of the physically present partner. Many of the nonverbal cues that accompany copresent device use are similar to those indicating a lack of conversational involvement, or disengagement and disinterest. Gergen's concept of "absent presence" suggests that copresent device use can symbolically render the non-device-using partner invisible.

Expectancy violation theory explains why people react differently to partners' copresent device use in different circumstances. The theory emphasizes the importance of considering how the receiver interprets the other's copresent device use. Thus, expectancy violation theory helps explain contextual factors that might determine how someone responds to a partner's copresent device use.

The chapter also noted that politeness theory could help explain the effects of copresent device use. Here, copresent device use may be interpreted as a potential face threat. Facework and politeness theory also suggest that people can engage in politeness strategies to offset or repair potential face loss during copresent device use. Future studies might consider the ways that device users employ politeness strategies to minimize the face threat. In fact, this may become an important social skill as copresent device use becomes more common.

The literature reveals that copresent device use can have an impact on romantic relationships and parent-child interactions. Research on communication in romantic relationships helps explain why copresent device use can impair relational well-being. Overall, the studies reviewed above suggested that copresent device use creates problems for couples in two ways. First, conflict about copresent device use can weaken the relationship. Second, the nonverbal disconnection that occurs during copresent device use diminishes intimacy and emotional connection. Couples who manage to negotiate norms and expectations around copresent device use are less likely to experience fewer problems from it. The romantic relationship research can further inform research on copresent device use among couples. Relational dialectics theory explains that successful relations involve learning to manage or balance, rather than eliminate, dialectic tensions between two opposing demands. The research reviewed here suggests that couples experience dialectical tensions around being available to their friends and family while also be being present and being available for the partner. Another tension exists between control (conforming to norms) and freedom (not wanting to have to restrict device use). Couples that learn to manage these tensions develop rules and norms that help them avoid some of the problems that copresent device use might create.

The section on parent-child relationships explained that parental copresent device use does occur, and may lead to a state of parental absorption, or distraction. Studies reviewed here suggested that parents' absorption upsets children and leads them to limit-testing and demand-withdraw patterns. The chapter proposed that attachment theory and research on affective attunement could help explain how device use during infant care might affect the child's development and the parent-child relationship. Research on infant development and parental communication indicates that infants form crucial secure attachment bonds when parents engage in attuned and contingent patterns of nonverbal interaction. Using attachment theory and the research on attunement, researchers can begin to develop hypotheses about how copresent device use might impair the crucial nonverbal interplay between the infant and caregiver. Finally, the research on co-parenting suggests that device use may also be a problem between parents that affects the broader family system. Studies reviewed above indicate that parents do get upset about their partner using devices during co-parenting situations. Here, research could begin to examine how copresent device use interferes with co-parenting relationships.

In sum, copresent device use represents a type of interpersonal nonverbal behavior that is becoming increasingly common, and at the same time generally disliked. This chapter suggests that established areas of theory and research on interpersonal and relational communication can help guide and inform the burgeoning study of copresent device use. The research presented in this chapter also suggests that interpersonal and relational researchers need to begin to consider device use in more general studies of communication.

Perhaps more than any of the others in the book, this chapter demonstrated the importance of the intersection between interpersonal and mediated communication. The two are no longer distinct. Future research on interpersonal communication will need to begin to consider and explain how technology facilitates and hinders face-to-face interaction. Tying back to this book's first chapter, the literature on copresent device use suggests that problematic habits play a substantial role in driving people's copresent device use; people do it despite its physical dangers and its social costs. According to a Pew study (Rainee & Zickhur, 2015), 89% of people surveyed reported copresent device use in their last social interaction. Thus, copresent device use is a mundane habit, but it is also one that may contribute to problems in relationships. These types of mundane habits that also cause problems are an excellent example of the point Chapter One tried to make, that we need to stop focusing on the small percentage of pathological cases and instead look at how problematic online habits can interfere with everyday conversations and interpersonal relationships.

References

Aagaard, J. (2016). Mobile devices, interaction, and distraction: A qualitative exploration of absent presence. *AI & Society, 31*(2), 223–231. doi:10.1007/s00146-015-0638-z

Ainsworth, M. S. (1979). Infant-mother attachment. *American Psychologist, 34*(10), 932–937.

Ainsworth, M., & Bell, S. (1970). Attachment, exploration, and separation: Illustrated by the behavior of one-year-olds in a strange situation. *Child Development, 41*(1), 49–67.

Allred, R. J., & Crowley, J. P. (2017). The "mere presence" hypothesis: Investigating the nonverbal effects of cell-phone presence on conversation satisfaction. *Communication Studies, 68*(1), 22–36.

Amichai-Hamburger, Y., & Etgar, S. (2016). Intimacy and smartphone multitasking—A new oxymoron? *Psychological Reports, 119*(3), 826–838. doi:10.1177/0033294116662658

Baxter, L. (1990). Dialectical contradictions in relationship development. *Journal of Social & Personal Relationships, 7,* 69–88. doi:10.1177/0265407590071004

Baxter, L., & Simon, E. (1993). Relationship maintenance strategies and dialectical contradictions in personal relationships. *Journal of Social & Personal Relationships, 10,* 225–242. doi:10.1177/026540759301000204

Beck, J. (2016, June). Ignoring people for phones is the new normal. *The Atlantic.* Retrieved from https://www.theatlantic.com/technology/archive/2016/06/ignoring-people-for-phones-is-the-new-normal-phubbing-study/486845/

Bodie, G. D., & Jones, S. M. (2012). The nature of supportive listening II: The role of verbal person centeredness and nonverbal immediacy. *Western Journal of Communication, 76*(3), 250–269.

Bowlby, J. (1969). *Attachment and loss.* New York: Basic Books.

Bradbury, T. N., & Fincham, F. D. (1990). Attributions in marriage: Review and critique. *Psychological Bulletin, 7*(1), 3–33. doi:10.1037/0033-2909.107.1.3

Brody, J. E. (2017, January 9). Hooked on our smartphones. *New York Times.* Retrieved from https://nyti.ms/2jAlqFBpre

Brown, G., Manago, A. M., & Trimble, J. E. (2016). Tempted to text: College students' mobile phone use during a face-to-face interaction with a close friend. *Emerging Adulthood*, 4(6), 440–443.

Brown, P., & Levinson, S. C. (1987). *Politeness: Some universals in language usage.* Cambridge: Cambridge University Press.

Burgoon, J. K. (1991). Relational message interpretations of touch, conversational distance, and posture. *Journal of Nonverbal Behavior*, 15(4), 233–259. doi:10.1007/BF00986924

Burgoon, J. K. (1993). Interpersonal expectations, expectancy violations, and emotional communication. *Journal of Language & Social Psychology*, 12(1–2), 30–48. doi:10.1177/0261927X93121003

Burgoon, J. K., & Bacue, A. (2003). Nonverbal communication skills. In J. O. Greene & B. R. Burleson (Eds.), *Handbook of communication and social interaction skills* (pp. 179–220). Mahwah, NJ: Lawrence Erlbaum.

Burgoon, J. K., & Hale, J. L. (1984). The fundamental topoi of relational communication. *Communication Monographs*, 51(3), 193–214.

Burgoon, J. K., Buller, D. B., Hale, J. L., & de Turk, M. A. (1984). Relational messages associated with nonverbal behaviors. *Human Communication Research*, 10(3), 351–378. doi:10.1111/j.1468-2958.1984.tb00023.x

Burgoon, J. K., Coker, D. A., & Coker, R. A. (1986). Communicative effects of gaze behavior: A test of two contrasting explanations. *Human Communication Research*, 12(4), 495–524.

Burgoon, J. K., Newton, D. A., Walther, J. B., & Baesler, E. J. (1989). Nonverbal expectancy violations and conversational involvement. *Journal of Nonverbal Behavior*, 13(2), 97–119. doi:10.1007/BF00990793

Cappella, J. N. (1981). Mutual influence in expressive behavior: Adult–adult and infant–adult dyadic interaction. *Psychological Bulletin*, 89(1), 101–132. doi:10.1037/0033-2909.89.1.101

Cegala, D. (1981). Interaction involvement: A cognitive dimension of communicative competence. *Communication Education*, 30(2), 109–121.

Cegala, D., Savage, G., Brunner, C., & Conrad, A. (1982). An elaboration of the meaning of interaction involvement: Toward the development of a theoretical concept. *Communication Monographs*, 49, 229–248. doi:10.1080/03637758209376087

Chotpitayasunondh, V., & Douglas, K. M. (2016). How "phubbing" becomes the norm: The antecedents and consequences of snubbing via smartphone. *Computers in Human Behavior*, 63, 9–18. doi:10.1016/j.chb.2016.05.018

Cissna, K. N. L., & Sieburg, E. (1981). Patterns of confirmation and disconfirmation. In C. Wilder-Mott & J. H. Weakland (Eds.) *Rigor and imagination: Essays from the legacy of Gregory Bateson,* (pp. 253–282). New York: Praeger.

Cody, M. J., & Dunn, D. (2007). Accounts. In B. Whaley & W. Samter (Eds.), *Explaining communication: Contemporary theories* (pp. 263–282). Mahwah, NJ: Lawrence Erlbaum.

Coker, D. A., & Burgoon, J. (1987). The nature of conversational involvement and nonverbal encoding patterns. *Human Communication Research*, 13(4), 463–494.

Cumiskey, K. M., & Ling, R. (2015). The social psychology of mobile communication. In S. Sundar (Ed.), *The handbook of the psychology of communication technology* (pp. 228–246). Malden, MA: Wiley-Blackwell. doi:10.1002/9781118426456.ch10

Epstein, N. (1982). Cognitive therapy with couples. *The American Journal of Family Therapy, 10,* 5–16.

Feinberg, M. E. (2003). The internal structure and ecological context of co-parenting: A framework for research and intervention. *Parenting: Science and Practice, 3*(2), 95–131. doi:10.1207/S15327922PAR0302_01

Feinberg, M. E., Brown, L. D., & Kan, M. L. (2012). A multi-domain self-report measure of co-parenting. *Parenting, 12*(1), 1–21.

Gergen, K. (2002). Cellphone technology and the challenge of the absent present. In J. Katz & M. Aakhus (Eds.), *Perpetual contact: Mobile communication, private talk, and public performances* (pp. 227–241). New York: Cambridge University Press.

Gergen, K. (2010). Mobile communication and the new insularity. *QWERTY: Journal of Education, Culture, and Technology, 5*(1), 14–28.

Goffman, E. (1959). *The presentation of self in everyday life.* New York: Doubleday Anchor Books.

Goffman, E. (1967). *Interaction ritual: Essays on face-to-face interaction.* New York: Doubleday Anchor Books.

Goffman, E. (1971/2010). *Relations in public.* New Brunswick: Transaction Publishers

Goldsmith, D. J. (2007). Brown and Levinson's politeness theory. In B. Whaley & W. Samter (Eds.), *Explaining communication: Contemporary theories* (pp. 243–262). Mahwah, NJ: Lawrence Erlbaum.

Golen, R. B., & Ventura, A. K. (2015a). What are mothers doing while bottle-feeding their infants? Exploring the prevalence of maternal distraction during bottle-feeding interactions. *Early Human Development, 91*(12), 787–791. doi:10.1016/j.earlhumdev.2015.09.006

Golen, R. B., & Ventura, A. K. (2015b). Mindless feeding. Is maternal distraction during bottle-feeding associated with overfeeding? *Appetite, 91,* 385–392. doi:10.1016/j.appet.2015.04.078

Gottman, J. M. (1993). A theory of marital dissolution and stability. *Journal of Family Psychology, 7*(1), 57–75. doi:10.1037/0893-3200.7.1.57

Hall, J. A., Baym, N. K., & Miltner, K. M. (2014). Put down that phone and talk to me: Understanding the roles of mobile phone norm adherence and similarity in relationships. *Mobile Media & Communication, 2*(2), 134–153. doi:10.1177/2050157913517684

Halpern, D., & Katz, J. E. (2017). Texting's consequences for romantic relationships: A cross-lagged analysis highlights its risks. *Computers in Human Behavior, 71,* 386–394. doi:10.1016/j.chb.2017.01.051

Heider, F. (1958). *The psychology of interpersonal relations.* New York: Wiley.

Hiniker, A., Schoenebeck, S. Y., & Kientz, J. A. (2016). Not at the dinner table: Parents' and children's perspectives on family technology rules. *Proceedings of the 19th ACM Conference on Computer-Supported Cooperative Work & Social Computing,* 1376–1389.

Hiniker, A., Sobel, K., Suh, H., Sung, Y. C., Lee, C. P., & Kientz, J. A. (2015). Texting while parenting: How adults use mobile phones while caring for children at the playground. *Proceedings of the 33rd Annual ACM Conference on Human Factors in Computing Systems, 727–736*. doi:10.1145/2702123.2702199

Holtzworth-Munroe, A., & Jacobson, N. S. (1985). Causal attributions of married couples: When do they search for causes? What do they conclude when they do? *Journal of Personality and Social Psychology, 48*(6), 1398–1412. doi:10.1037/0022-3514.48.6.1398

Humphreys, L. (2005). Cellphones in public: Social interactions in a wireless era. *New Media & Society, 7*(6), 810–833.

Jacobson, N. S., McDonald, D. W., Follette, W. C., & Berley, R. A. (1985). Attributional processes in distressed and nondistressed married couples. *Cognitive Therapy & Research, 9*(1), 35–50.

Jones, S. M., & Guerrero, L. K. (2001). The effects of nonverbal immediacy and verbal person centeredness in the emotional support process. *Human Communication Research, 27*(4), 567–596.

Kildare, C. A., & Middlemiss, W. (2017). Impact of parents' mobile device use on parent-child interaction: A literature review. *Computers in Human Behavior, 75*, 579–593. doi:10.1016/j.chb.2017.06.003

Kneidinger-Müller, B. (2017). Mobile communication as invader in face-to-face interactions: An analysis of predictors for parallel communication habits. *Computers in Human Behavior, 73*, 328–335. doi:10.1016/j.chb.2017.03.055

Lim, T., & Bowers, J. (1991). Facework solidarity, approbation, and tact. *Human Communication Research, 17*(3), 415–450. doi:10.1111/j.1468-2958.1991.tb00239.x

Maginnis, J. A. (2011). *Texting in the presence of others: the use of politeness strategies in conversation.* Unpublished Dissertation. University of Kentucky.

McDaniel, B. T., & Coyne, S. M. (2016a). "Technoference": The interference of technology in couple relationships and implications for women's personal and relational well-being. *Psychology of Popular Media Culture, 5*(1), 85–98. doi:10.1037/ppm0000065

McDaniel, B. T., & Coyne, S. M. (2016b). Technology interference in the parenting of young children: Implications for mothers' perceptions of co-parenting. *The Social Science Journal, 53*(4), 435–443.

McDaniel, B. T., & Teti, D. M. (2012). Coparenting quality during the first three months after birth: The role of infant sleep quality. *Journal of Family Psychology, 26*(6), 886–895.

Miller, P. J., & Rempel, J. K. (2004). Trust and partner-enhancing attributions in close relationships. *Personality & Social Psychology Bulletin, 30*(6), 695–70.

Miller-Ott, A. E., & Kelly, L. (2015). The presence of cell phones in romantic partner face-to-face interactions: An expectancy violation theory approach. *Southern Communication Journal, 80*(4), 253–270. doi:10.1080/1041794X.2015.1055371

Miller-Ott, A. E., & Kelly, L. (2016). Competing discourses and meaning making in talk about romantic partners' cell-phone contact with non-present others. *Communication Studies, 67*(1), 58–76. doi:10.1080/10510974.2015.1088876

Miller-Ott, A. E., & Kelly, L. (2017). A politeness theory analysis of cell-phone usage in the presence of friends. *Communication Studies, 68*(2), 190–207. doi:10.1080/10510 974.2017.1299024

Misra, S., Cheng, L., Genevie, J., & Yuan, M. (2014). The iPhone Effect: The quality of in-person social interactions in the presence of mobile devices. *Environment & Behavior, 48*(2), 1–24. doi:10.1177/0013916514539755

Murphy, S. E., Jacobvitz, D. B., & Hazen, N. L. (2016). What's so bad about competitive co-parenting? Family-level predictors of children's externalizing symptoms. *Journal of Child & Family Studies, 25*(5), 1684–1690. doi:10.1007/ s10826-015-0321-5

Nakamura, T. (2015). The action of looking at a mobile phone display as nonverbal behavior/communication: A theoretical perspective. *Computers in Human Behavior, 43*(0), 68–75. doi:10.1016/j.chb.2014.10.042

Ophir, E., Nass, C., & Wagner, A. D. (2009). Cognitive control in media multitaskers. *Proceedings of the National Academy of Sciences, 106*(37), 15583–15587. doi:10.1073/ pnas.0903620106

Przybylski, A. K., & Weinstein, N. (2012). Can you connect with me now? How the presence of mobile communication technology influences face-to-face conversation quality. *Journal of Social & Personal Relationships, 30*(3), 237–246. doi:10.1177/0265407512453827

Radesky, J. S., Kistin, C. J., Zuckerman, B., Nitzberg, K., Gross, J., Kaplan-Sanoff, M., … Silverstein, M. (2014). Patterns of mobile device use by caregivers and children during meals in fast food restaurants. *Pediatrics, 133*(4), e843–e849. doi:10.1542/ peds.2013-3703

Radesky, J. S., Miller, A. L., Rosenblum, K. L., Appugliese, D., Kaciroti, N., & Lumeng, J. C. (2015). Maternal mobile device use during a structured parent-child interaction task. *Academic Pediatrics, 15*(2), 238–244. doi:10.1016/j.acap.2014.10.001

Rainie, L., & Zickuhr, K. (2015). Americans' views of mobile etiquette. Pew Research Center. Retrieved from http://www.pewinternet.org/2015/08/26/americans-views-on-mobile-etiquette/

Ralph, B. C. W., Thomson, D. R., Cheyne, J. A., & Smilek, D. (2014). Media multitasking and failures of attention in everyday life. *Psychological Research, 78*(5), 661–669. doi:10.1007/s00426-013-0523-7

Rempel, J. K., Ross, M., & Holmes, J. G. (2001). Trust and communicated attributions in close relationships. *Journal of Personality & Social Psychology, 81*(1), 57–64. doi:10.1037/0022-3514.81.1.57

Roberts, J. A., & David, M. E. (2016). My life has become a major distraction from my cell phone: Partner phubbing and relationship satisfaction among romantic partners. *Computers in Human Behavior, 54*, 134–141. doi:10.1016/j.chb.2015.07.058

Schoppe-Sullivan, S. J., Mangelsdorf, S. C., Frosch, C. A., & McHale, J. L. (2004). Associations between co-parenting and marital behavior from infancy to the preschool years. *Journal of Family Psychology, 18*(1), 194–207. doi:10.1037/ 0893-3200.18.1.194

Schoppe, S. J., Mangelsdorf, S. C., & Frosch, C. A. (2001). Coparenting, family process, and family structure: Implications for preschoolers' externalizing behavior problems. *Journal of Family Psychology, 15*(3), 526–545. doi:10.1037/0893-3200.15.3.526

Schrodt, P., & Shimkowski, J. R. (2017). Family communication patterns and perceptions of coparental communication. *Communication Reports, 30*(1), 39–50. doi:10.1080/08934215.2015.1111400

Seo, M., Kim, J. H., & David, P. (2015). Always connected or always distracted? ADHD symptoms and social assurance explain problematic use of mobile phone and multicommunicating. *Journal of Computer-Mediated Communication, 20*(6), 667–681.

Shellenbarger, S. (2016, May 28). Just look me in the eye already. *Wall Street Journal*, 1–7. Retrieved from https://www.wsj.com/articles/SB10001424127887324809804578511290822228174

Shimkowski, J. R., & Schrodt, P. (2012). Coparental communication as a mediator of interparental conflict and young adult children's mental well-being. *Communication Monographs, 79*(1), 48–71. doi:10.1080/03637751.2011.646492

Siegel, D. J. (1999). *The developing mind: How relationships and the brain interact to shape who we are*. New York: Guilford Press.

Siegel, D. J. (2001). Toward an interpersonal neurobiology of the developing mind: Attachment relationships, "mindsight," and neural integration. *Infant Mental Health Journal, 22*(1–2), 67–94. doi:10.1002/1097-0355(200101/04)22:1<67::AID-IMHJ3>3.0.CO;2-G

Spitzberg, B. H., & Hecht, M. L. (1984). A component model of relational competence. *Human Communication Research, 10*(4), 575–599. doi:10.1111/j.1468-2958.1984.tb00033.x

Sprecher, S., Hampton, A. J., Heinzel, H. J., & Felmlee, D. (2016). Can I connect with both you and my social network? Access to network-salient communication technology and get-acquainted interactions. *Computers in Human Behavior, 62*, 423–432. doi:10.1016/j.chb.2016.03.090

Stern, D. N. (1985). *The interpersonal world of the infant: A view from psychoanalysis and developmental psychology*. New York: Basic Books.

Teubert, D., & Pinquart, M. (2010). The association between co-parenting and child adjustment: A meta-analysis. *Parenting: Science and Practice, 10*(4), 286–307. doi:10.1080/15295192.2010.492040

Thornton, B., Faires, A., Robbins, M., & Rollins, E. (2014). The mere presence of a cell phone may be distracting. *Social Psychology, 45*(6), 479–488. doi:10.1027/1864-9335/a000216

Ting-Toomey, S., & Kurogi, A. (1998). Facework competence in intercultural conflict: An updated face-negotiation theory. *International Journal of Intercultural Relations, 22*(2), 187–225. doi:10.1016/S0147-1767(98)00004-2

Tronick, E. Z. (1989). Emotions and emotional communication in infants. *American Psychologist, 44*(2), 112–119.

Tronick, E., Als, H., Adamson, L., Wise, S., & Brazelton, T. B. (1978). The infant's response to entrapment between contradictory messages in face-to-face interaction.

Journal of the American Academy of Child Psychiatry, 17(1), 1–13. doi:10.1016/S0002-7138(09)62273-1

Turkle, S. (2012). *Alone together: Why we expect more from technology and less from each other.* Cambridge, MA: Basic Books.

Turkle, S. (2015). *Reclaiming conversation: The power of talk in a digital age.* New York: Penguin Press.

Vanden Abeele, M., Antheunis, M. L., & Schouten, A. P. (2016). The effect of mobile messaging during a conversation on impression formation and interaction quality. *Computers in Human Behavior, 62,* 562–569.

Ventura, A. K., & Teitelbaum, S. (2017). Maternal distraction during breast- and bottle feeding among WIC and non-WIC Mothers. *Journal of Nutrition Education and Behavior, 49*(7), S169–S176.e1. doi:10.1016/j.jneb.2017.04.004

Wang, X., Xie, X., Wang, Y., Wang, P., & Lei, L. (2017). Partner phubbing and depression among married Chinese adults: The roles of relationship satisfaction and relationship length. *Personality and Individual Differences, 110,* 12–17. doi:10.1016/j.paid.2017.01.014

Watzlawick, P., Bavelas, J., & Jackson, D. (1967). *Pragmatics of Human Communication.* New York: Norton & Co.

Chapter Seven

Moving Forward

An Agenda for Future Research

Interpersonal technology changes faster than research can examine it. Early theories of problematic Internet use and the term computer-mediated communication described technology that bore little resemblance to modern online interaction. Initial Internet research described a world in which only half of Americans used the Internet and smart phones and social networking were over a decade away.

The term problematic Internet use can no longer be limited to compulsive use and so-called "addictions." As the book demonstrated, changes in technology and culture have created a variety of new interpersonal problems involving online social behavior. Over the years, Internet technology has become increasingly more mobile and social, and our personal lives have become increasingly mediated. With these changes, new types of problematic Internet use have emerged. Beyond compulsive online behavior, modern problematic Internet use now entails aggression, harassment, unwanted pursuit, relationship transgressions, and device use that interferes with in-person interactions. Cyberbullying, cyberstalking, conflict about social networking, and growing concerns about copresent device use are all examples of relatively newer forms of problematic Internet use. Despite the changing landscape of social technology, the book illustrated the importance of using theories of basic interpersonal processes to ground and guide emerging studies of technology-mediated communication.

Whereas the other chapters looked back on two decades of research, this chapter focuses on the future. The chapter identifies three general research questions that emerged repeatedly throughout the book. These provide an agenda for future scholarship on problematic online social interaction and personal relationships. The last part of the chapter restates the book's main thesis that theories of interpersonal and relational dynamics are useful conceptual starting points for theory-driven research on various forms of problematic Internet use.

Three Questions to Guide Future Research

Moving forward, there are three general questions that can help organize and guide research into problematic online social behavior:

1. How does technology-mediated communication affect interpersonal and relational processes?
2. How do interpersonal and relational resource deficits contribute to problematic online behavior?
3. How do mediated interpersonal behaviors threaten in-person conversational and relational outcomes.

How Does Technology Affect Interpersonal and Relational Processes?

Each chapter in the book described ways that mediated-communication changes fundamental interpersonal processes. These technological changes represent affordances, or benefits, in terms of interpersonal interaction. For instance, researchers have long noted that mediated communication can be either synchronous or asynchronous. The ability to respond at a later time on asynchronous media allows people to delay or avoid interaction.

Other communicative differences in mediated communication are reduced nonverbal cues. As the hyperpersonal theory (Walther, 1996) noted almost 20 years ago, mediated communication offers people greater ability to edit and plan messages. People can use text-based interactions to hide nonverbal cues of emotion. On the other hand, the diminished nonverbal cues also can inhibit one's ability to empathize, indicate conversational involvement, and send or receive regulative cues. The lack of cues has also been identified as a key reason that people feel less inhibited when engaging in problematic online social behavior.

Compared to face-to-face behavior, online communication can quickly spread among a wide audience. Embarrassing images or posts can go viral as other people retweet, share, and forward the content. Social networking, texting, and other mediated communication technologies are semi-permanent, they leave records and the messages are easily available in perpetuity, whereas in-person behaviors are generally fleeting and leave no record. For victims of online harassment, the relative permanence of online images and videos may mean that the assault never really ends. As long as the harmful material is still online, the victimization continues.

Mobile technologies afford people the ability to contact anyone, anywhere, at any time. In a culture that some researchers describe as "permanently online and permanently connected" (Vorderer & Kohring, 2013), cheating spouses can be with their affair partner anytime. The affordances of mobility are attractive to people who fear missing out as they can keep tabs on what their friends are doing (Przybylski, Murayama, DeHaan, & Gladwell, 2013).

Additionally, the ways that various technologies alter the communication process are useful for understanding what makes cyberbullying and its effects distinct from in-person equivalents. The affordances of the mediated communication increase the types of power the cyberbully has over the victim. A cyberbully has more power to reach a victim online at any time and at any place. And, for the victim, the features of online bullying may result in more devastating effects than traditional bullying (Sticca & Perren, 2013). Being embarrassed by a bully front of a small group is different from the entire school viewing something online and talking about it through mediated backchannels. The distinction between bullying and cyberbullying is most relevant when considering how technology alters interpersonal contexts.

The question for future cyberbullying research is not whether it is more harmful or easier to commit than traditional bullying. Rather, the question is: How do the differences in the communicative context change the meaning of the interaction for the people involved? Similarly, the cyberstalking research must theoretically explain how computer-mediation changes the experience of unwanted pursuit for the stalker and the victim.

How Do Interpersonal and Relational Resource Deficits Contribute to Problematic Online Behavior?

Navigating the potential interpersonal perils of online behavior requires many of the same skills that predict success in face-to-face communication. Those with lower social skills appear to be drawn to mediated modes to compensate for their deficits (Caplan, 2005). Studies supporting the poor get poorer hypothesis indicate people with offline problems experience difficulty online as well. In other words, the affordances of the technology do not functionally compensate for skill or resource deficits (Clerkin, Smith, & Hames, 2013).

Research on social skill and relational competence can explain why some people are more likely than others to develop strong habits, engage in online harassment, and use mobile devices in ways that in-person partners consider rude. Research on problematic online habits has revealed links between online habit strength and a number of relational and social deficits including low self-presentational skill, high social anxiety, low emotional intelligence, and attachment insecurity. The chapter emphasized the importance that preference for online social interaction plays in explaining and predicting problematic online habits.

Relational transgressions occur when relational rules are broken. Online transgressions may be associated with impaired interpersonal skill and relationship abilities. Knowing the rules, and being able to follow them, are both critical relational skills. Similarly, social skills may help explain why some people are better able to mitigate the damage of online transgressions. Thus, being able to use mediated communication in ways that honor rules of different relationships and effectively repair damage has become an increasingly important type of interpersonal competence.

Social skills are also central to the literature on cyberbullying and cyberstalking. Interpersonal problems are correlated with being a bully and being a victim, and with being involved in the dual role of "bully/victim" (Gámez-Guadix & Calvete, 2015; Gradinger, Strohmeier, & Spiel, 2012). Research indicates that bullies have difficulty with empathy, emotion regulation, and antisocial behavior (Baroncelli & Ciucci, 2014; Schulze-Krumbholz & Scheithauer, 2013). Managing aggression and need for approval in ways that do not victimize others is an essential social skill that eludes many bullies. Cyberbullies' victims also exhibit interpersonal deficits such as lower social skills (Dooley, Shaw, & Cross, 2012), lower empathy (Wong, Chang, & Cheng, 2014), and higher social anxiety (Dempsey et al., 2011; Pabian & Vandebosch, 2015).

In cases of cyberstalking, people who deal with rejection and insecurity by engaging in unwanted pursuit may lack critical skills for initiating, maintaining, and ending relationships. Theories of uncertainty reduction help explain why anxious, insecure, and jealous partners may be motivated to engage in online intrusion or surveillance (Fox & Anderegg, 2014; Stewart & Dainton, 2014; Tokunaga, 2015). Diminished interpersonal skills do not excuse online abuse or harassment, but they may explain why it occurs.

The chapter on copresent device use explored one of the newest online interpersonal problems to emerge in recent years. Managing competing demands of in-person interaction and online activity is an increasingly important social skill. Moreover, copresent device use may correlate with broader sets of interpersonal skill deficits. In particular, skillful copresent device use will require an ability to minimize negative effects of device use with politeness, facework, and nonverbal relational messages.

One hypothesis for future research on copresent device use research is that social skill is likely to predict efforts to mitigate potential face threats to the in-person partner. Knowing when and how to check a device requires the ability to read regulative nonverbal signals and to understand the dynamics of nonverbal behavior, immediacy cues, and conversational involvement. As our lives have become more intertwined with technology, future research should focus on how people manage the competing demands of in-person and online relational expectations.

How Do Online Interpersonal Behaviors Threaten Face-to-Face Conversational and Relational Goal Outcomes?

A third area for future research involves the ways that problematic online behaviors can impact in-person interactions and relationships. A major argument throughout the book was that modern interpersonal and relational communication research should begin to consider mediated communication, in its many forms, as a basic feature in most interpersonal relationships. Technology has created new ways to break relational rules and upset friends and romantic partners. Jealous people can use technology for surveillance, intrusion, and control over their partner. Mobile devices and constant connection can weaken boundaries between work and home life. Social networking technology can also erode the boundaries that keep out potential threats (e.g., ex-partners, attractive coworkers and other potential affair partners).

Chapter One examined how people's online habits are affecting their close personal relationships. The literature indicated that online habits are associated with problems in romantic relationships (Musses, Finkenauer, Kerkhof, & Righetti, 2015). The research also suggested that interpersonal conflict often mediates the association between online habit strength and problems in personal relationships (Clayton, 2014). In other words, online habits become an interpersonal relationship problem when they create conflict or when couples cannot functionally manage the conflict.

Each year, copresent device use has become a more common nonverbal behavior during in-person situations. Copresent device use, device habits, and perpetual connectivity present challenges in conversations as well as in close relationships. The research indicates copresent device use, and even the mere presence of a smartphone, negatively influence conversational outcomes and create problems for families and romantic couples (Vanden Abeele, Antheunis, & Schouten, 2016). Copresent device use can signal disinterest and be interpreted as rude. During conversations, copresent device use results in poor impression formation and negative evaluations by interaction partners. In romantic relationships, copresent device use during together time at home can erode intimacy and hinder relational maintenance (X. Wang, Xie, Y. Wang, P. Wang, & Lei, 2017). For parents who use devices during childcare, absorption might adversely affect child development and the parent-child relationship (Radesky et al. 2014).

Cyberstalking and online obsessive relational intrusion are types of relationship dysfunction since most cases involve current or former relational partners. Jealous partners use technology to control, surveil, and invade the privacy of their mate. Recently, cyberdating abuse has emerged as another type of problematic Internet use that damages relationships (e.g., Borrajo, Gámez-Guadix, Pereda, & Calvete, 2015; Reed, Tolman, & Ward, 2016; Wolford-Clevenger et al., 2015). Cyberdating abuse is an example of an interpersonal technology problem that did exist a decade ago but is likely to become increasingly more common in the future.

Using Interpersonal and Relational Theories to Advance Literature on Problematic Internet Use

Throughout the book, I have argued that research on problematic Internet use can benefit from theories of social interaction and personal relationships. Many of the research areas discussed in this book suffer from conceptual ambiguity and inconsistent measurement. One of the problems with defining phenomena such as cyberbullying, problematic online habits, copresent device use, and cyberstalking is that the technologies and their roles in our lives are constantly changing. Unlike technology, the fundamental aspects of interpersonal interaction and close relationships do not vary. Thus, research explaining basic interpersonal processes can inform theory-driven inquiry into problematic online social behavior.

For example, regardless of the context, Goffman's (1959, 1967) concepts of performance, audience, and face are especially helpful for explaining how online mediation changes aspects of bullying. The concepts of facework and politeness are invaluable for developing a theoretical narrative explaining the adverse effects of copresent device use. Further, politeness and facework theories provide conceptually-grounded hypotheses about how people can mitigate or repair the negative effects of copresent device use.

Theories of emotional intelligence, social anxiety, self-presentation, and social skill lend conceptual frameworks explaining why some people prefer online social interaction and develop strong online habits. Chapter Two argued that people who lack interpersonal and relational competencies view the affordances of mediated communication as a means of overcoming such challenges. Attachment insecurity may lead people to develop strong habits around checking their messages and using social networking to keep track of what others are doing. People who have trouble regulating emotions are likely to be especially prone to developing online habits to manage moods.

Theories of uncertainty reduction identify an essential interpersonal goal that people pursue, regardless of context (Gudykunst, 1995; Gibbs & Ellison, 2011). No matter the situation, people are motivated to reduce uncertainty about relational partners. Technology is interesting because it changes *how* people engage in uncertainty reduction online, not *that* they do it.

Attribution theory can help explain message reception processes. The appraisals and attributions people make about their partner's behaviors influence responses and relational outcomes. Aside from the technologies, or how people use them, the meaning-making processes described in attribution and appraisal theories offer conceptual foundations to study how people react to copresent device use, unwanted online relational pursuit, or a partner's online gaming habit.

Theories of nonverbal behavior can help shed light on copresent-device use. Nonverbal research indicates that during a conversation people use a variety of immediacy cues to indicate involvement and attention. Copresent device use interferes with one's ability to encode and decode nonverbal cues. Thus, the literature on conversational involvement, relational-level meaning, and disconfirmation are promising foundations for developing theories of copresent device use. Additionally, the literatures on attachment theory and affective attunement provide a conceptual and empirical basis for explaining how parental absorption during copresent device use might hinder infant development.

Conclusion

The next generation of interpersonal theory needs to approach mediated interaction as a common way relational partners communicate. The distinction between face-to-face and computer-mediated communication becomes less useful each year. Today, almost all of our close relationships take place across both in-person and mediated messaging. Flirting and romantic interactions involve a complex interplay of mediated and in-person communication. Couples and families use technology during conflicts and have conflicts about technology use.

Recently, scholars have begun to capture the interplay of online and mediated interaction between relational partners. Media multiplexity theory seeks to explain why our closest relationships are also the ones in which we use the widest variety of mediated-channels (Haythornthwaite, 2005; Ledbetter, 2015). Similarly, research on modality switching and communicative interdependence examines how people shift between mediated and in-person interactions with their relational partners (Ramirez & Zhang, 2007; Ramirez, Sumner, Fleuriet, & Cole, 2015; Sharabi & Caughlin, 2017). One interesting and promising idea behind the modality switching research is that the *interpersonal process* is more salient than any specific technology (which will continue to evolve).

In sum, interpersonal research can help bring more organization and conceptual depth to future research on technology-mediated communication. Insight into fundamental dynamics of interpersonal and relational communication can help advance researchers' understanding of each of the problems described in this book. These fundamental dynamics will continue to prove useful even as technology changes. Regardless of what types of technologies are involved, people value signs of conversational involvement, want to be validated by others, try to avoid embarrassment, seek affection and attention, attempt to reduce uncertainty, and try to minimize anxiety. As the face of problematic Internet use continues to change, researchers can draw upon theories of interpersonal communication and social interaction for conceptual narratives and theory-driven hypotheses to guide future work.

References

Caplan, S. E. (2005). A social skill account of problematic Internet use. *Journal of Communication, 55*(4), 721–736. doi:10.1093/joc/55.4.721

Clerkin, E. M., Smith, A. R., & Hames, J. L. (2013). The interpersonal effects of Facebook reassurance seeking. *Journal of Affective Disorders, 151*(2), 525–530. doi:10.1016/j.jad.2013.06.038

Clayton, R. B. (2014). The third wheel: The impact of Twitter use on relationship infidelity and divorce. *Cyberpsychology, Behavior, and Social Networking, 17*(7), 425–430. doi:10.1089/cyber.2013.0570

Baroncelli, A., & Ciucci, E. (2014). Unique effects of different components of trait emotional intelligence in traditional bullying and cyberbullying. *Journal of Adolescence, 37*(6), 807–815. doi:10.1016/j.adolescence.2014.05.009

Borrajo, E., Gámez-Guadix, M., Pereda, N., & Calvete, E. (2015). The development and validation of the cyber dating abuse questionnaire among young couples. *Computers in Human Behavior, 48*, 358–365. doi:10.1016/j.chb.2015.01.063

Dempsey, A. G., Sulkowski, M. L., Dempsey, J., & Storch, E. A. (2011). Has cyber technology produced a new group of peer aggressors? *Cyberpsychology, Behavior, and Social Networking, 14*(5), 297–302. doi:10.1089/cyber.2010.0108

Dooley, J. J., Shaw, T., & Cross, D. (2012). The association between the mental health and behavioural problems of students and their reactions to cyber-victimization. *European Journal of Developmental Psychology, 9*(2), 275–289. doi:10.1080/17405629.2011.648425

Fox, J., & Anderegg, C. (2014). Romantic relationship stages and social networking sites: Uncertainty reduction strategies and perceived relational norms on Facebook. *Cyberpsychology, Behavior, and Social Networking, 17*(11), 685–691. doi:10.1089/cyber.2014.0232

Gámez-Guadix, M., Gini, G., & Calvete, E. (2015). Stability of cyberbullying victimization among adolescents: Prevalence and association with bully–victim status and psychosocial adjustment. *Computers in Human Behavior, 53*, 140–148. doi:10.1016/j.chb.2015.07.007

Gibbs, J. L., Ellison, N. B., & Lai, C. H. (2011). First comes love, then comes Google: An investigation of uncertainty reduction strategies and self-disclosure in online dating. *Communication Research, 38*(1), 70–100. doi:10.1177/0093650210377091

Goffman, E. (1959). *The presentation of self in everyday life.* New York: Doubleday Anchor Books.

Goffman, E. (1967). *Interaction ritual: Essays on face-to-face interaction.* New York: Doubleday Anchor Books.

Gradinger, P., Strohmeier, D., & Spiel, C. (2012). Motives for bullying others in cyberspace: A study on bullies and bully-victims in Austria. In Q. Li, D. Cross, & P. K. Smith (Eds.), *Cyberbullying in the global playground: Research from international perspectives.* (pp. 263–284). Malden, MA: Wiley-Blackwell. doi:10.1002/9781119954484.ch13

Gudykunst, W. B. (1995). The uncertainty reduction and anxiety-uncertainty reduction theories of Berger, Gudykunst, and associates. In D. P. Cushman & B. Kovačić (Eds.), *Watershed research traditions in human communication theory* (pp. 67–100). Albany, NY: SUNY Press.

Haythornthwaite, C. (2005). Social networks and Internet connectivity effects. *Information, Communication & Society, 8*(2), 125–147. doi:10.1080/13691180500146185

Ledbetter, A. M. (2015). Media multiplexity theory: Technology use and interpersonal tie strength. In D. O. Braithwaite & P. Schrodt (Eds.), *Engaging theories in interpersonal communication: Multiple perspectives* (2nd ed., pp. 363–376). Thousand Oaks, CA: Sage.

Muussess, L. D., Finkenauer, C., Kerkhof, P., & Righetti, F. (2015). Partner effects of compulsive Internet use: A self-control account. *Communication Research, 42*(3), 365–386. doi:10.1177/0093650212469545

Pabian, S., & Vandebosch, H. (2016). An investigation of short-term longitudinal associations between social anxiety and victimization and perpetration of traditional bullying and cyberbullying. *Journal of Youth & Adolescence, 45*(2), 328–339. doi:10.1007/s10964-015-0259-3

Przybylski, A. K., Murayama, K., DeHaan, C. R., & Gladwell, V. (2013). Motivational, emotional, and behavioral correlates of fear of missing out. *Computers in Human Behavior, 29*(4), 1841–1848. doi:10.1016/j.chb.2013.02.014

Radesky, J. S., Kistin, C. J., Zuckerman, B., Nitzberg, K., Gross, J., Kaplan-Sanoff, M., … Silverstein, M. (2014). Patterns of mobile device use by caregivers and children during meals in fast food restaurants. *Pediatrics, 133*(4), e843–e849. doi:10.1542/peds.2013-3703

Ramirez, A., & Zhang, S. (2007). When online meets offline: The effect of modality switching on relational communication. *Communication Monographs, 74*(3), 287–310. doi:10.1080/03637750701543493

Ramirez, A., Sumner E. M., J., Fleuriet, C., & Cole, M. (2015). When online dating partners meet offline: The effect of modality switching on relational communication between online daters. *Journal of Computer-Mediated Communication, 20*(1), 99–114. doi:10.1111/jcc4.12101

Reed, L. A., Tolman, R. M., Ward, L. M., & Safyer, P. (2016). Keeping tabs: Attachment anxiety and electronic intrusion in high school dating relationships. *Computers in Human Behavior, 58*, 259–268. doi:10.1016/j.chb.2015.12.019

Schultze-Krumbholz, A., & Scheithauer, H. (2013). Is cyberbullying related to lack of empathy and social-emotional problems? *International Journal of Developmental Science, 7*(3–4), 161–166.

Sharabi, L. L., & Caughlin, J. P. (2017). What predicts first date success? A longitudinal study of modality switching in online dating. *Personal Relationships, 24*(2), 370–391. doi:10.1111/pere.12188

Sticca, F., & Perren, S. (2013). Is cyberbullying worse than traditional bullying? Examining the differential roles of medium, publicity, and anonymity for the perceived severity of bullying. *Journal of Youth & Adolescence, 42*(5), 739–750. doi:10.1007/s10964-012-9867-3

Stewart, M. C., Dainton, M., & Goodboy, A. K. (2014). Maintaining relationships on Facebook: Associations with uncertainty, jealousy, and satisfaction. *Communication Reports, 27*(1), 13–26. doi:10.1080/08934215.2013.845675

Tokunaga, R. S. (2015). Interpersonal surveillance over social network sites: Applying a theory of negative relational maintenance and the investment model. *Journal of Social and Personal Relationships, 33*(2), 171–190. doi:10.1177/0265407514568749

Vanden Abeele, M., Antheunis, M. L., & Schouten, A. P. (2016). The effect of mobile messaging during a conversation on impression formation and interaction quality. *Computers in Human Behavior, 62*, 562–569.

Vorderer, P., & Kohring, M. (2013). Permanently online: A challenge for media and communication research. *International Journal of Communication, 7*(1), 188–196. doi:1932-8086/2013FEA0002

Wolford-Clevenger, C., Zapor, H., Brasfield, H., Febres, J., Elmquist, J., Brem, M., ... Stuart, G. L. (2015). An examination of the partner cyber abuse questionnaire in a college student sample. *Psychology of Violence, 6*(1), 156–162. doi:10.1037/a0039442

Wang, X., Xie, X., Wang, Y., Wang, P., & Lei, L. (2017). Partner phubbing and depression among married Chinese adults: The roles of relationship satisfaction and relationship length. *Personality & Individual Differences, 110*, 12–17. doi:10.1016/j.paid.2017.01.014

Wong, D. S. W., Chan, H. C. & Cheng, C. H. K. (2014). Cyberbullying perpetration and victimization among adolescents in Hong Kong. *Children and Youth Services Review, 36*, 133–140. doi:10.1016/j.childyouth.2013.11.006

Author Index

A

Aagaard, J., 191–93, 204, 209
Aboujaoude, E., 48
Adams, N., 158–59
Agatston, P. W., 107
Alexy, E. M., 158, 168
Allred, R. J., 188
Amichai-Hamburger, Y., 201
Anderegg, C., 81
Anders, A., 157, 159, 161
Ang, P. C., 84
Ang, R. P., 133–34
Antheunis, M. L., 185, 197
Argyle, M., 65
Atfab, P., 107
Aune, K. S., 151–52, 156, 160, 162–63, 167–69

B

Baesler, E. J., 194
Bailer, J., 157, 159, 161
Baker, T., 158, 166–68
Barak, A., 112
Barlett, C. P., 112, 119
Barnes, J., 162
Barrows, J. R., 33
Bauman, S., 114, 130
Baxter, L. A., 81–82
Baym, N. K., 9, 201–2, 203
Beard, K. W., 1
Betts, L. R., 41, 44
Bevan, J. L., 84
Binder, J. F., 41, 44
Birnholtz, J., 85
Birtchnell, J., 39
Bocij, P. 159–60
Boyd, D. M., 107, 115, 121
Bradshaw, C. P., 118, 120, 128
Brody, N., 88, 94
Brown, P., 65, 88, 195
Bryant, E. M., 86, 88–89, 92–93
Buglass, S. L., 41, 44
Burgess, A. W., 158, 166–67
Burgoon, J. K., 194

C

Calussi, P., 128–29
Calvete, E., 116, 125, 127
Caplan, S. E., 37
Cappadocia, M. C., 110, 115, 117, 136
Cartun, M. A., 71, 89, 90–91
Carvalho, M., 117, 119, 129
Casale, S., 37
Cassidy, W., 120, 170
Caughlin, J. P., 10
Cavezza, C., 157–59, 170
Cayemberg, C., 82
Cegala, D., 195
Chang, J., 123
Chaulk, K. 154, 167, 168
Cheng, L., 189–90
Chester, A., 36
Chung-do, J., 123
Cillessen, A. H. N., 174
Clerkin, E. M., 49
Cohen, R., 122
Connor, J. P., 106, 121
Cook, C., 116–17
Coulter, R. W. S., 118
Coyne, S. M., 119, 198–99, 211
Craig, W. M., 110, 115, 117, 136
Cravens, J. D., 71–72, 75, 78
Cross, D., 107–109, 114, 128
Crowley, J. P., 188
Cumiskey, K. M., 189
Cupach, W. R., 153, 157, 165, 167, 177

D

Daciuk, J., 115, 116–117
Danielwicz, J., 82
David, M. E., 198
Davis, R. A., 26
Deiss, D. M., 117, 132
Delfabbro, P. H., 34
De la Piedad Garcia, X., 129
Demetrious, A., 136
Demetrovics, Z., 25–26

Dempsey, A. G., 110, 170
Dempsey, J., 110, 170
DePalo, V., 40
Diener-West, M., 118, 124
Dinakar, A., 5
Docan, C. A., 67–69, 71
Docan-Morgan, T., 67–69, 71
Dooley, J. J., 107–09, 114, 128
Dredge, R., 129
Dreßing, H., 157, 159, 161
Drouin, M., 75
Durkin, K., 171

E

Eastin, M. S., 27, 28
Eden, J., 117, 132
Elphinstone, R. A., 80
Else, I., 123
Elwood, J., 173
Emmers-Sommer, T. M., 65, 69
Etgar, S., 201

F

Faires, A., 187–88
Famá, F. I., 40
Fanti, K., 136
Farrington, D. P., 126
Faucher, C., 120, 170
Fearns, J. B., 84
Feinberg, M. E., 211
Felmlee, D., 186
Finch, E., 172
Finkenauer, C., 43–44
Fioravanti, G., 37
Fisher, B. S., 156–57, 161–62, 165–66
Fisher, S., 117, 119, 129
Fox, J., 62, 81–82, 84
Fox, K., 157, 161–62, 165–66
Fremouw, W. J., 135, 151
Fricker, J., 70
Frisén, A., 134

G

Gadalla, T., 115–16
Gallas, C., 157, 159, 161
Gámez-Guadix, M., 116, 125, 127
Garandeau, C. F., 174
Genevie, J., 189–90
Gergen, K., 193, 214
Gerson, M. J., 74
Gervaisi, A. M., 40
Gini, G., 116, 125, 127
Giumetti, G., W., 120–121, 136
Gleeson, J. F. M., 129
Goebert, D., 123
Goffman, E., 3, 64–65, 88, 114, 173–74, 195, 232
Goh, D. H., 134
Goldsmith, D. J., 195
Golen, R. B., 209
Goodboy, A. K., 134
Gradinger, P., 117
Grant, T., 166–67
Greenfield, D., 76
Gregg, J., 27–28
Griffiths, M. D., 40
Gross, J., 206, 207–10
Grohol, J. 24
Guadagno, R. E., 82
Guerra, N. G., 115, 117, 120, 126
Gunawardena, C. N., 168
Guppy, J. A., 162

H

Hall, J. A., 201–2, 203
Halpern, D., 78–79
Hames, J. K., 49
Hampton, A. J., 186
Hancock, J. T., 85
Harbaugh, A. G., 117, 126
Harte, J. A., 162
Hawa, V., 136
Heinzel, H. J., 186
Heirman, W., 112

Helsper, E. J., 69, 71
Henderson, M., 65
Henson, B., 156, 158
Hertlein, K. M., 71
Hesper, E. J., 69, 71
Hinduja, S., 103–4
Hiniker, A., 212
Ho, S. S., 25
Hodges, E. V. E., 117, 127
Hoobler, G., 154–55
Hormes, J. M., 37
Huss, M. T., 158–59

J

Jackson, C. L., 122
Jackson, M., 120, 170
Jones, K. E., 71
Jones, L. M., 104, 128, 130
Jones, T., 167–68

K

Kalaitzaki, A. E., 39
Kaplan-Sanoff, M., 206, 207–10
Katz, J. E., 78–79
Kearns, B., 37
Keelan, C. M., 135
Kelly, L., 202–04
Kerkhof, P., 43–44
Kernaghan, D., 173
Khoury-Kassabri, M., 115
Kientz, J. A., 212
Kim, J. E., 5
King, D. L., 34
Király, O., 25–26
Kistin, C. J., 206, 207–10
Kline, S. L., 65
Kneidinger-Müller, 195
Korchmaros, J. D., 115
Kowalski, R. M., 107, 120–21, 136
Kowert, R., 39
Kraut, R., 6, 7
Kubey, R. W., 33

L

Lapidot-Lefler, N., 112
LaRose, R., 27–28, 25
Lattanner, M. R., 120–121, 136
Lavin, M. J., 33
Leaf, P. J., 118, 124
Leckie, K. R., 71
Lee, B. H., 157
Lee, E. W. J., 25
Lemmens, J. S., 36
Levinson, S. C., 65, 88, 195
Limber, S. P., 107
Lin, C. A., 89
Ling, R., 189
Litt, E., 89, 90–91
Loeber, R., 126
Lösel, F., 126
Luo, S., 71
Lwin, M. O., 25
Lynch, M., 128

M

Maginnis, J. A., 195–96
Mahdavi, J., 117, 119, 129
Mansor, A. T., 133
Manzella, S., 40
Maraz, A., 25–26
Marmo, J., 86, 88–89, 92–93
Martin, M. M., 134
Matos, M., 153
Matsu, C., 123
McDaniel, 75, 19–99, 212
McEwan, T. E., 157–59, 170
McFarlane, L., 159–60
Ménard, K. S., 158
Menesini, E., 128–29
Metts, S., 64
Miller-Ott, A. E., 202–04
Miltner, K. M., 201–2, 203
Minchin, J., 117, 126
Mishna, F., 115–17

Misra, S., 189–90
Mitchell, K. J., 104, 111, 128, 130, 132–33
Modecki, K. L., 117, 126
Monacis, L., 40
Moore, S., 70
Morahan-Martin, J., 33
Mullen, P. E., 160
Murphy, S., 82
Muscanell, N. L., 82
Muusses, L. D., 43–44

N

Nelson, T., 73
Newman, M. L., 114, 130
Newton, D. A., 194
Nie, N. H., 7
Nitzberg, K., 206, 207–10
Nobles, M., 157, 161–62, 165–66
Nocentini, A., 128–29
Noller, P., 80
Northrup, J. S., 47

O

O'Donnell, L., 118
Oeldorf-Hirsch, A., 85
Oldmeadow, J. A., 39
Oppenheim, J. K., 107, 115, 121
Osborn, J. L., 62, 81–82, 84
O'Sullivan, L. F., 157
Owens, J. G., 156

P

Pabian, S., 136
Papp, L. M., 82
Parcell, R., 160
Passanisi, A., 40
Patchin, J. W., 103–4

Pathço, M., 160
Patterson, M., 171
Peña, J., 88, 94
Peplar, D., 110, 115, 117, 136
Pereira, F., 153
Perren, S., 111, 130
Peter, J., 36
Piercy, F. P., 73
Pincus, A. L., 158
Przyblski, A. K., 187
Purcell, R., 160
Pyzalski, J., 107–09, 114

Q

Quinn, S., 39

R

Radesky, J. S., 206, 207–10
Rains, S. A., 36
Ramirez, A., 9
Ramos-Salazar, L., 117, 132
Raskauskas, J., 117
Reece, J., 36
Reyns, B. W., 152–53, 156–58, 161–62, 165–66
Rice, L., 82
Riggio, R. E., 35
Robbins, M., 187–188
Roberto, A. J., 117, 132
Roberts, J. A., 198
Roberts, L., 166
Rollins, E., 187–188
Runions, K. C., 117, 126
Russell, S., 117, 119, 129
Ryan, T., 36

S

Sabella, R. A., 103–4
Sainio, M., 117, 127

Salmivalli, C., 117, 127
Samenow, C., 68, 75
Savage, M. W., 117, 132
Scheithauer, H., 136
Schenk, A. M., 135
Scherer, K., 33
Schimmenti, A., 40
Schneider, J. P., 68, 74
Schneider, S. K., 118
Schoenebeck, S. Y., 212
Scholte, R., 125
Schouten, A. P., 185, 197
Schrodt, P., 211
Schroeder, A. N., 120–121, 136
Schultze-Krumbholz, A., 136
Schumacher, P., 33
Scott, J. G., 106, 121
Selman, R. L., 4, 5
Sharabi, L. L., 10
Shattuck, A., 130
Shaw, T., 128
Sheridan, L. P., 166–67
Shimkowski, J. R., 211
Short, E., 162
Shumway, S., 47
Siegel, D. J., 210
Silverstein, M., 206–10
Sinatra, M., 40
Slojne, R., 129, 134
Smith, A. R., 49
Smith, P. K., 108, 112, 117, 119, 129, 134
Smoyak, S. A., 158, 168
Snider, A. G., 71, 89–91
Solomon, S., 116–117
Spiel, C., 117
Spitzberg, B. H., 153, 154–55, 157, 165, 167, 177
Sprecher, S., 186
Sprenkle, D. H., 73
Stafford, L., 65
Starcevic, V., 48
Stern, D. N., 209
Sticca, F., 111, 130
Stoltz, A. D., 117

Storch, E. A., 110, 170
Strawhun, J., 158–59
Strohmeier, D., 117
Stuart, G. W., 160
Stueve, A., 118
Sulkowski, M. L., 110, 170

T

Tan, K. A., 133
Tanilon, J., 130
Teitelbaum, S., 208
Thomas, H. J., 106, 121
Thomas, S., 5
Thornton, B., 187–88
Timko, C. A., 37
Tippet, N., 117, 119, 129
Tokunaga, R. S., 151–52, 156, 160, 162–63, 167–69
Tronick, E. Z., 210–11
Ttofi, M. M., 126
Turner, H. A., 130

U

Underwood, J., 41, 44

V

Valenzuela, S., 78–79
Valkenburg, P. M., 36
Van Debosch, H., 136
Vanden Abeele, M., 185, 197
Van den Eijnden, R., 125
Vanden Mheen, D., 125
Van Geel, M., 130
Van Rooij, A. J., 125
Veader, P., 130
Ventura, A. K., 209
Vermulst, A., 125

W

Waasdorp, T. E., 118, 120, 128
Wagner, H., 157, 159, 161
Walrave, M., 112
Walther, J. B., 9, 35, 77, 194
Warber, K. M., 62, 81–82, 84
Weinstein, E. C., 4, 5
Weinstein, N., 187
Weiss, R., 68, 75
Westrup, D., 151
White, A. E., 5
Whiting, J. B., 71, 78
Whitty, M. T., 67–71, 75–76
Wigderson, S., 128
Williams, K. R., 115, 120
Wilmot, W. W., 81–82
Wolack, J., 130
Wolf, E. M., 1
Wolford-Clevenger, C., 163

X

Xenos, S., 36

Y

Ybarra, M. L., 107, 111, 115, 118, 121, 124, 132–33
Young, K. S., 23, 33, 71
Yuan, M., 189–90

Z

Zuckerman, B., 206, 207–10
Zimmerman, J., 35

Subject Index

A

"Ace Model," 76
addiction
   approaches to
      addiction paradigm, 23–26
      cognitive approach, 26–31
   and displacement, 6–7
   and on-line habits and compulsion, 11–12, 21–48
   Internet, 48, 225
   perspective, 48
adolescent(s)
   and coparenting quality, 211
   gamers, 44
   and rules for device use, 212
   find security online, 10
   digital stressors for, 4–5
   See also bullying; children; cyberbullying
American Psychological Association (APA), 23, 26

anonymity, 8–9, 29, 75–76, 110–13, 130, 167
association effect, 89
attachment theory, 38, 208–10, 214, 216, 233
attribution theory, 70, 200–1, 232
attunement, 208–11, 213–14, 216, 233

B

BBS (Bulletin Board Systems), 76
bullying, traditional, 13, 104–18, 126–37, 227–28. *See also* cyberbullying

C

changing conceptualizations (of social behavior), 5–11
channel differences, 8–9
children
   and attachment theory, 38, 210

and family rules, 212–13
and parental online relational
 transgression, 62, 74
and parental/caregiver copresent
 device use, 205–8, 212, 216
See also adolescents; cyberbullying;
 infants
cockpit effect, 112
cognitive behavioral model, 26, 28–31
communication processes, 170, 213
conversational effects (of copresent
 device), 184–91, 196–98, 214
coparenting, 211–13, 216
copresent device use, 14–15, 184–87,
 196, 197, 231. *See also* conversational
 effects (of copresent device)
crossover and co-occurrence, 166–67
cyberbullies, characteristics of, 131–32
 behavioral characteristics of, 135
 predictors and consequences of,
  135–36
 emotional problems among, 133–35
 interpersonal problems among,
  132–33
 See also cyberbullying
cyberbullying
 and adolescents
  among different age groups,
   119–20, 170–71
  girls engaged in, 117
  perceptions of, 129
  estimates of victimization, 115–16
  vulnerability to, 125
 and online interpersonal aggression,
  103–38
 and anonymity, 110–13
 audience for and dispersal of, 113–14
 and cyberstalking, 156, 169–76
 defined, 105
 literature on, 13, 103–4
 myths, 103
 power imbalance in, 209–10
 estimating prevalence of, 114–22

 gender, 118–19
 limitations of, 121–22
 perpetration, 116–17
 alongside traditional, 117–18
 by proxy, 106–7
 and repetition vs. persistence, 108–9
 research on, 111–37
 and time and space boundaries, 110
 and traditional bullying
  differences, 107–8, 228
  comparing effects of, 128–31
  similarities, 105–7
 correlates of victimization, 122–31
  causes and consequences of,
   125–31
  behavioral problems, 124–25
  emotional problems, 123–24
  interpersonal problems, 122–123,
   229
 See also cyberbullies
cyberdating abuse, 163, 231
cyberobsessional pursuit, 154–55, 173
cybersex, 45, 67, 69–70, 74–75
cyberspace, 2, 166
cyberstalkers
 characteristics, 158–60, 164, 167
 collective, 160
 composed, 159
 and crossover and co-occurrence,
  166–67
 versus cyberbullying, 172–74
 and disinhibition, 168–69
 infatuated, 160
 and proximity and distance, 167–68
 technology weakens boundaries for,
  169
 versus traditional stalkers, 168
 vindictive, 159
 See also cyberstalking
cyberstalking
 collective, 160
 composed, 159
 initial concerns raised, 151–52

easily confused with other online harassment, 14, 120, 156
and crossover and co-occurrence, 166–67
and cyberbullying, 169–76
defining, 151, 153, 156–58, 164, 171
and disinhibition, 168–69
empirical findings in research on, 156–64
infatuated, 160
as interpersonal and relational process, 153
intimate, 160
and the Justice Department, 152
motivation for, 159
prevalence of, 157–58
and proximity and distance, 167–68
rejected, 160
relational approach to, 154
  hyperintimacy, 154–55
  invasion, 155
  sabotage, 155
  threats, 155
research and conceptual challenges, 152–53, 164–76
future research on, 228, 231
technology weakens boundaries for, 169
and traditional stalking, 165–69
victim
  characteristics, 160–61
  outcomes, 161–62
  response to, 162–64
vindictive, 159
See also cyberstalkers; obsessive relational intrusion (ORI); stalking, traditional

D

"dark side," viii, ix, 4
deception. *See* secrecy

deficit hypothesis, 35–37
deficient self regulation (DSR), 27
dichotomy, on-line vs. offline, 2
digital dating abuse, 163
digital stressors, 4
dimensions
  conceptual, 159
  functional-normative, 8
  moral-immoral/functional-dysfunctional, 4
disinhibition, 76, 110–13, 134, 137
displacement, social, 2
  and addiction, 6–7
  hypothesis, 42–43
Dunbar conjecture, vii

E

effect hypothesis, 125
emotional intelligence, 12, 36–38, 134, 228, 232
empathy, 112–13, 123, 134–35, 136, 137, 173, 229
EVT (expectancy violation theory), 193–94, 202
expectancy violation theory (EVT), 193–94, 202
extradyadic behavior, 67, 70–71, 76, 79, 83
eye contact, 112, 191–92, 206–7, 210

F

face
  needs, 197
  maintaining the other's, 64–65
  and politeness theory, 63
  still, effect, 210–11
  theory, 197
  threat, 3, 9, 85, 87–91, 94, 114, 196, 215
  work, 88–91, 194–96
  See also face-to-face interactions

Facebook
    and attachment needs, 39–40
    and relational intrusive behavior, 154, 167
    and friendships, 84, 85–96
    "official," 82
    and the poor-get-poorer hypothesis, 43–44
    and relational health, 45–46, 79–80
        and divorce, 61
        and infidelity, 77–78
        and relational transgressions, 62, 65–66, 72
    and past relationship partners, 78–79
    use of separation tests, 81
    and the social skills deficit hypothesis, 36–37
    "stalking," 156, 173
face-to-face interactions
    and the displacement theory, 7
    mediated, 8
facework, 88–91, 194–96
flaming, 103
FOMO (Fear of Missing Out), x, 40–42, 44
friendship rules, 83–84, 86–87, 91–94

G

gambling, 23, 29
"gamer widows," 46–47
gaming, online
    adolescent, 44
    and social anxiety, 36–37
    early concern about, 6
    and attachment disorder, 39
    disorder, 23–26
    and habit strength, 33
    and online social interaction, 22
    multiplayer, 30, 34
    and relational problems, 46–47

H

habit framework, 31–32
habit strength, online
    associated with deficits, 12, 22–23, 34–48, 228, 230
    and maladaptive cognitions, 30–32
    and problematic online habits, 32–34
    ranges from mundane to extreme, 27
habituation
    as a cognitive process, 27
    as a concept can help define terms, 22–23
    and deficits in core social abilities, 42–43
    model, 43
    driven by reward-learning results, 28–29, 31, 41
hyperintimacy, 154, 163
hyperpersonal communication, 8–9, 35, 38, 77, 227

I

idealized self-presentation, 89
infants, 38, 208–11, 216. See also children; adolescents
infidelity, online, 40, 63, 66–79, 83, 95. See also transgressions, online
information processing theory, 8
in-person interpersonal processes, 4
Internet
    addiction, 10–11, 21
    spatial metaphor for, 2
    use, problematic
        conceptual approaches to, 22–31
        and interpersonal and relational communication processes, 3–4, 15
        inconsistent definitions of, 21
        early to contemporary research on, 5–11, 67, 76, 225

future research on, 226–31
   organizing twenty years of research on, 31–48
   See also cyberbullying; cyberstalking; Facebook; problematic online habits; transgressions, online
"Internet paradox," 6–7
interpersonal approach, ix–x, 62, 164
interpersonal communication theory
   and copresent use, 191–97
   and expectation violation theory, 193–94
   and facework and politeness theory, 194–96
   and involvement and immediacy cues, 191–93
interpersonal deficits, 8–9, 43, 123, 229
interpersonal theory research, 233
involvement and immediacy cues, 191–93

M

Machiavellianism, 134
management, 3, 4, 42, 162, 213
Massively Multiplayer Online Games (MMOG), 36
media multiplexity theory, 9–10, 95, 233
mediated channels, 2, 30, 233
mediated communication
   changes caused by, 1–2
   and extradyadic affairs, 67, 70
   and friendship transgressions, 84
   and interpersonal affordances, 33, 35, 76–77, 216
   and interpersonal aggression, 103
   early research on, 8–9, 111
   and resource deficits, 47–48
   emerging studies of, 226–27
   See also cyberbullying; cyberstalking
mediated interaction, 8, 10, 12, 29, 37, 233
MMOG (Massively Multiplayer Online Games), 36

"mobile relationship interference," 183
MOOS (Multi-user Dimensions Object Oriented), 76
"multicommunicating," 183

N

narcissism, 133–34, 136
National Crime Victimization Survey, 157, 161
nonverbal reciprocity, 210–11

O

obsessive relational intrusion, 153–54, 159, 167–69, 172–73, 177, 231
online habituation, 23, 41–44
online transgressions. *See* transgressions, online

P

"parallel communication," 183
parental absorption, 206–8, 214, 216, 233
Partner Cyber Abuse Questionnaire, 163–64
phubbing, 183, 198
PIU (Problematic Internet Use), 27, 19
politeness theory, 63, 65, 88, 94, 194–97
pornography, 70
"problematic," term explained, 4–5
Preference for online social interaction, 30
problematic behaviors
   moral-immoral and functional-dysfunctional, 4
problematic Internet use, defined, 1–2
   generalized and specific, 29–30
"problematic online habits," term explained, 21–22
psychopathy, 127, 134, 158

R

reduced social presence, 87, 110–13, 138, 168–69
relational dialects theory, 200, 203–5, 215
relational maintenance, 3, 45, 48, 93, 231
relational norms and rule violations, 68–69
relational partners
   and cyberstalking, 152, 158, 160, 175, 177, 231
   and displacement hypothesis, 42
   and exceptional violation theory, 193
   and mediated interaction, 233
   rules for, 3
   and switching among media types, 9
   and uncertainty, 81
   See also relationships
relationship(s)
   adolescent, 5, 10, 12, 125
   and attachment theory, 38–39
   and copresent device use, 97–217
   and emotional intelligence, 37
   infringement, ix
   and insecurity, 38
   intimate, 3, 10–12, 40, 44–47, 66–83
   online intrusion of, 13–14, 32, 183
   online/offline distinction, 9
   optimal number of, viii
   parent-child, 123
   and problematic online habits, 42–47
   rules, 3–4, 12, 64–66
   and third party, 69–70, 79–80
   withdrawal from, 7
   See also attachment theory; cyberbullying; cyberstalking; deficit hypothesis; transgressions, online
research
   on cyberbullying, 111–37
   on cyberstalking, 152–77
   and need for common conceptual definitions/uniform measures, 21
   future, 226–34
   on "Internet Addiction"/problematic Internet use, 22–31
   and interpersonal communication theory research, 184–216
   organizing/summarizing last twenty years of, 31–48
   and online relational transgressions, 63–96
resource deficit framework, 34–38, 41–42, 47, 226, 228

S

secrecy, 68, 71–72, 74, 93–94, 96
"Seven A's," 76
SIDE Theory, 77
smartphone(s)
   addiction, 23
   and online affairs, 72–73, 75
   interfere with face-to-face interaction, 183–84, 204
   and nursing mothers, 208–9
   and habit strength, 37
   and users permanently online, 10–11
   and social networking, 9–10
social information processing theory, 8
social networking
   addiction, 23, 25
   and habit strength, 33–34, 41
   and relational health, 45–47
   and smartphones, 9–10
   and social skill deficits, 36–37, 39–40, 44
   and social interaction, 22
   See also cyberbullying; cyberstalking; Facebook; Internet; transgressions, online

social skill deficit model, 36
sociocognitive model, 26–28
socio-digital stress, 4, 5
spatial metaphor, 2
stalking, traditional, x, 159, 161–62, 164,
 165–77. *See also* cyberstalking
still-face effect, 210–11

T

"technoference," 183
telepressure, x
television, 6, 7, 204, 209
transgressions, online
 and online infidelity, 66–79
  harmful effects of, 73–75
  explaining, 75–79
  online infidelity defined, 67–68
  leads to jealousy and stress, 40
  and research on, 63–96
  involving secrecy, 71–73
  involving a third party, 70–71
 online friendship, 83–85
  and social networking, 85–94
 and other romantic conflicts, 79–83
 future research on, 95–96
 and relational rules, 12–13, 64–66,
  68–70
Twitter, 3, 66, 105

V

violence, 64, 106, 159
vulnerability hypothesis, 125

www.ingramcontent.com/pod-product-compliance
Ingram Content Group UK Ltd.
Pitfield, Milton Keynes, MK11 3LW, UK
UKHW021844140426

5217IPUK00022B/1586